Kanha Tiger Reserve

Portrait of an Indian National Park

Second Edition

KANHA TIGER RESERVE

PORTRAIT OF AN INDIAN NATIONAL PARK

Second Edition

Carroll Moulton and **Ernie J. Hulsey**

VAKILS, FEFFER AND SIMONS PVT. LTD.
Hague Building, 9, Sprott Road,
Ballard Estate, Mumbai 400 001.

First edition 1999
Second edition 2002

Price in India Rs. 250/-

Published by Bimal A. Mehta for
Vakils, Feffer and Simons Pvt. Ltd.,
Hague Building, 9, Sprott Road,
Ballard Estate, Mumbai 400 001.

Printed by Arun K. Mehta at
Vakil & Sons Pvt. Ltd., Industry Manor,
Appasaheb Marathe Marg, Worli,
Mumbai 400 025.

ISBN 81-87111-17-8

And so the knowledge you absorb today will be added to the knowledge you will absorb tomorrow, and on your capacity for absorption, not on any fixed standard, will depend the amount of knowledge you will ultimately accumulate. And at the end of the accumulating period — be that period one year or fifty — you will find that you are only at the beginning, and that the whole field of nature lies before you waiting to be explored and to be absorbed. But be assured that if you are not interested, or if you have no desire to acquire knowledge, you will learn nothing from nature.

—Jim Corbett, *Jungle Lore*

To Annie Ruth Hammock and

Frances Vera DeLoaché

and to the memory of

Sister Anita Horsey

Table of Contents

List of Illustrations

[Colour plates follow pages 76, 92 and 108]

Foreword

IN 1963, I TRAVELLED WIDELY through India in search of a suitable place to study wildlife. Hidden deep in the forests in the centre of the country, I came upon a small national park named Kanha and was entranced by it. My wife, two small sons, and I lived there for fourteen months among deer and tigers, seeing an India as if from the century past. I remember the eerie bugles of barasingha stags, the raucous calls of peacocks, morning mist on the meadow with bulky gaur moving like ghost galleons through it, and the stately *sal* trees unfurling their leaves into a canopy of fresh green just when everything else is listless in the brutal heat before the monsoon. And, above all, I remember the tigers striding on velvet paws through golden grass, powerful, self-assured, elegant.

Fortunately India realized that Kanha is a treasure, a part of its heritage that must be protected for the future. When I visited Kanha in 1991 after an absence of a quarter century with tiger biologist Ullas Karanth, I was impressed with the changes. Park size had been increased from 308 km² to 940 km², villagers had been resettled outside the borders, and, better protected, wildlife had increased greatly. Instead of a trickle of visitors, over 40,000 a year now came to enjoy the wilderness; there was a visitor centre, and hotels catered to tourists at the park's periphery.

Carroll Moulton and Ernie Hulsey have become so devoted to Kanha that they spend months there each year. In this book they share their knowledge with insight and enthusiasm. It is a combination of park guide, natural history, and personal reminiscence. As such the authors help create an awareness of Kanha's splendour, and they provide valuable and intriguing information. But, I hope that the book will also inspire visitors to cherish and protect these forests and meadows so that the tiger and other creatures will continue to roam there in security and freedom.

George B. Schaller
Wildlife Conservation Society

Preface

KANHA IS TRULY the land of the tiger. We first fell in love with Kanha National Park over ten years ago, in February 1990. Not coincidentally, it was a tiger on Sandukhol Road, first glimpsed in silhouette against the golden rays of a winter setting sun, that hooked us. Long after that visit, we learned from one of our regular park guides, Ashok Kumar, that the name "Sandukhol" refers to the opening of a box.

How appropriate! After close to 300 tiger sightings in Kanha, we will never forget the animal that opened the marvelous world of this national park to us. Although there are other Indian parks with more spectacular scenery—Corbett, Periyar, Ranthambhore, and Simlipal come to mind—there is no better place in India, and probably in the entire world, to see the tiger than in Kanha.

How did this park come to be what it is today? How has it managed to deal with the problems that beset protected areas everywhere throughout the Indian Union? Specifically, what factors have enabled Kanha to achieve its current pre-eminence as the flagship of the Indian system of national parks? How has Kanha acquired the best infrastructure of any park, as well as the most credible record in the protection of highly endangered species? What are the attitudes of the park's employees, and how do Kanha's neighbors feel about its mission?

These are some of the questions we have set out to answer in this book. The chapters that follow aim not only at introducing Kanha to the first-time visitor, but also at giving a portrait of an Indian national park in a fashion that, we believe, has not yet been attempted. According to the ecosystem principle, a physical environment must be considered in its totality. Expanding this premise one step further, we would like to examine the idea that an institution such as a national park comprises both an ecosystem and the human organization involved in administering it. The remarkable dedication that the people of Kanha continue to extend in order to make this place possible is a major part of the story that follows.

Since our first visit to Kanha, we have spent over 2,000 hours in the field. We have maintained tape-recorded field notes for every game drive. These notes include the route taken, the name of the driver and the guide, the exact time and location of animals and birds sighted, the details that we observed about their behaviour, the temperature and other weather conditions, and comments about relevant features of the terrain and flora within the park. Highlights of these notes were transcribed each season in a diary, which also contains a detailed summary of every sighting of tigers, leopards, and wild dogs. The resulting record supplements extensive photographic and video documentation of each visit we have made to the park.

Although we have not seen every mammal or bird that occurs in Kanha or met every park employee, we have endeavoured through many hours of research and interviews to fill in the gaps in our knowledge about this very special place in the Central Indian Highlands. In this regard, our debts are many and various: see the list of acknowledgements below.

Most books published to date on Indian wildlife have focused, understandably, on the animals themselves. The spectacular diversity of the Indian subcontinent's fauna and flora is in itself a story that needs highlighting. Few people are aware, for example, that India is home to nearly 15% of the world's bird species, even though the country occupies only about 3% of the world's land area. The importance of India in the worldwide effort to save such charismatic mammals as the tiger, the Asian elephant, and the great one-horned rhinoceros cannot be overestimated.

Current approaches to conservation, however, have insisted with ever-increasing coherence that no effort to save an ecosystem and its wildlife can ultimately succeed in isolation from human parameters. If India offers a showcase for wildlife second only to East Africa, the subcontinent's population density makes it a veritable laboratory for the study of conservation vs. development conflicts. At the same time, it is important for us to realize that this challenge is not unique to India: many of the same tensions are common to quite different regions, including eastern and southern Africa, Australia, Latin America, and the United States.

Specific forerunners of this study have been very helpful. Foremost among these are the overview given of Kanha in H. S. Panwar's *Kanha National Park: A Handbook* (1991) and Hashim Tyabji's guide to Bandhavgarh National Park (1994). Sadly, at the time of writing, the English edition of Panwar's work has been out of print for several years.

A few words follow about the organization of this book. In Chapter 1 we present a basic introduction to Kanha. Here you will find practical information concerning travel arrangements, climate conditions, accommodation choices, opening hours, fees, vehicle hire, and guides. We also discuss the history of Kanha and offer an overview of its importance to wildlife conservation generally, and in particular to the current embattled effort to save the tiger. We include a detailed section on the "tiger show" at Kanha, which offers many tourists to this park their best chance for a tiger sighting.

We begin Chapter 2 by describing Kanha as an ecosystem, in which each of the parts of a landscape, with all its diverse flora and fauna, has an important role to play. After giving an overview of the habitat and the food chain, as well as the grasses and trees of Kanha, we proceed to species descriptions of 15 major mammals in the park, including the tiger. Each description ends with notes on photography. This section concludes with briefer accounts of 15 mammals that are more rarely seen. In the section on birds, we have been forced to be selective, singling out for brief description a group of 40 "top birds of Kanha." These have been chosen for their intrinsic interest on the basis of appearance, calls, behaviour, and habitat. We conclude this chapter with brief notes on the snakes and the other reptiles found in the park.

In Chapter 3, the emphasis shifts to Kanha's people. In Section 1, we describe the park's administrative structure, focusing especially on the forest guards and their vital contribution to Kanha's security. Section 2 offers a series of vignettes and anecdotes about the wonderfully diverse collection of people whose dedication and knowledge make visiting this park such a fascinating experience.

Finally, in Chapter 4 we turn to Kanha's future. Clearly, the destiny of the park is intertwined to a great extent with the future of the tiger, and we devote considerable discussion to the current poaching crisis. We also consider the impact of ecotourism, both negative and positive, on Kanha. In an attempt to widen the focus, we include some comparative material touching on problems that India's protected areas share with national parks in East Africa, the United States, and elsewhere. In the twenty-first century it will be increasingly valuable, we believe, for Indian wildlife policy-makers to consider the problems of conservation in the subcontinent in an international perspective. Chapter 4 concludes with a detailed list of recommendations for future planning and improvement at Kanha.

The illustrations in this book, which are the work of Ernie J. Hulsey, have been planned to reflect the holistic emphasis of the text. Recognizing that most visitors to Kanha have the tiger as their #1 priority, we have included a number of tiger photographs from the last nine years of sightings in the park. We have also aimed to present a cross-section of the other mammals, as well as to show some of the faces of Kanha's people. Our special thanks are due to Deepika Singh for her illustrations of four of the park's most beautiful birds.

This book has benefited greatly from international collaboration, and we have accumulated many debts that it is a pleasure to acknowledge here. In Kanha, we are grateful to the Field Director and Conservator of Forests, Dr. Rajesh Gopal, as well as to Deputy Director J. S. Chauhan, Park Interpretation Officer H. S. Negi, and Assistant Director R. K. Sharma. The following current or former employees of Kanha provided helpful information and insights: Jagdish Chandra, Bastaram Nagpure, Ravishanker Kanoje, B. S. Maravi, N. S. Maravi, I. Katre, B. K. Sen, N. K. Bisen, Munglu Baiga, Mohan Baiga, and Nandu Das Sharve. Kanha's mahouts have been most helpful: our special thanks to Ahmet Sabir, Lakhan Singh, Bir Singh, and Dharam Singh.

Every visitor to Kanha benefits from the knowledge and alertness of the park guides, and over the years we have learned a great deal from these dedicated young men. Compared to the guides in the other parks we have visited in India, the Kanha crew is far and away the best. It is therefore a pleasure to acknowledge here the assistance of the following guides from Kisli: Ashok Kumar Jhariya, Harishchandra Rajurkar, A. P. Singh, Sanjay Kumar Paserker, T. S. Tomer, Deviprasad Patel, Anand Lakhera, Gulab Singh, Jivan Singh Vikui, Phagan Singh Maravi, Murari Patel, Nain Singh Sayan, Sukhlal Kherwar, Madan Choubey, Suresh Das Sharve, Ramsunder Pandey, Arvind Vaishnavi, Prem Singh Markam, Ramesh Badre, Pratap Singh Yadav, and Devendra Tiwari. We thank the following guides from Mukki: Tirath, Guruprasad, Shravan, Pritam, and

Mahavir. We are also greatly indebted to drivers Rehman Khan, Balram Yadav, Bafati Khan, and Biru.

Captain Navneet Singh and his wife Deepika Singh have accorded us gracious hospitality at Royal Tiger Resort in Mukki, and we have benefited greatly from their knowledge of the history and operations of Kanha.

In Mumbai we are grateful first and foremost to Jane Swamy and her family and to Ashok and Saroj Kumar. Sister Anita Horsey has been a continuing inspiration ever since we first travelled to India. Other friends who have extended valued help include Ravi and Asha Sandilya, Jyotsna Parulekar, Pesi Hathiram, and Arun Mehta and Katey Cooper of Vakils, Feffer and Simons Ltd., who took a chance on this project and encouraged us to finish our "tiger book."

Also in India, we would like to thank Bob and Anne Wright in Calcutta, Belinda Wright in Delhi, Garima and Sudhanshu Varma in Bangalore, Neelesh Agrawal in Jabalpur, Billy Arjan Singh and Mira Singh in Dudhwa National Park, M. K. Ranjitsinh in Delhi, and Nanda Rama in Bandhavgarh. The late Inder Zutschi in Delhi was a magician at travel arrangements, and we miss him greatly.

In England we are grateful to Nick and Tracy Burdett, who first encouraged us to visit Kanha; to Christian Lax; to Sarah Christie of the Zoological Society of London; to Michael Day of the Tiger Trust; and to Paul Newton of the University of Oxford.

In the United States, we would like to acknowledge the aid of Frances DeLoaché, Helen Horsey, Paul and Juliette Feffer, Richard Ives and Cristina Lindstrom, Ed and Paula Bonlarron, Gary and Colleen Munoz, Ed Darrach, Lyle Foster, Lois Wallace, Bob Seymour, Ed Caesar, Fannie Safier, Ed Ahnert of the Exxon Corporation, Carolyn Hatt of the National Geographic Society, Prof. Philip Lutgendorf of the University of Iowa, Howard Quigley of the Hornocker Wildlife Institute, and Alan Shoemaker of Riverbanks Zoological Park in Columbia, South Carolina.

We are especially grateful to George Schaller for his encouragement, his valuable comments on the manuscript, and his gracious foreword.

Finally, special thanks to the following persons for their encouragement, and interest in this project: Dr. Renata Jaremovic of Biosis Research in New South Wales, Australia, who provided important information and documents relating to her study of ecotourism in Kanha; Irene Boswell in Madagascar; and Claude-Anne Gauthier of the Parc zoologique de Vincennes in Paris.

Preface to the Second Edition

Since this book was first published in April 1999, there have been important developments affecting visitors to Kanha. In this preface to the second edition, we offer an update for the following areas: accommodation and vehicle hire, park entry fees and regulations, improvements at the Kanha Museum, route changes within the park, the tiger show, personnel changes, developments in Project Tiger, the creation of the new state of Chhattisgarh, the poaching crisis, the responsiveness of the park to tourist issues and other concerns, and the utilization of technology at Kanha. We also provide a bibliographical supplement that takes account of significant publications since late 1998. The information is arranged under boldface headings crossreferenced by page number to the text.

Accommodations and Vehicle Hire (page 7) Lodges continue to thrive at Kanha, both on the Mocha and Mukki sides of the park. In Mocha especially, visitors' options have been expanded by the opening of the Tuli Tiger Resort, a luxurious retreat equipped with swimming pool, game room, air-conditioned cottages, an observation machan, and an artificial lake for fishing. At Krishna Jungle Resort, Jabalpur hotelier Neelesh Agrawal has added a handsome new reception building and swimming pool complex, as well as a redecorated dining hall and a brand-new block of guest rooms. Smaller operations near Khatia Gate include Mowgli Resort and Dyna Lodge.

Many new freelancers and vehicle operators are swelling the ranks of Maruti Gypsies and other park transport available for hire. The current rate for park rides by Gypsy is Rs. 10/- per kilometer, with the driver/operator responsible for petrol.

Park Fees and Regulations (page 7) On 15 January 2000, a substantial increase in park fees took effect. Fees are now according to the following schedule.

1. Entry fee (individual)   Indians and citizens   Rs. 20/-
   of S.A.A.R.C. countries
       Citizens of other   Rs. 200/-
   countries
     Entry fee (group)   Indians   Rs. 300/-
   20 students including teachers shall be treated as one group. For larger groups (more than 20 persons) extra charges for each additional subgroup up to 10 persons shall be payable as below:
   - additional entry fee at Rs. 15/- per person
   - additional group entry fee at Rs. 60/- per group

2. Elephant Ride   A maximum of 4 persons shall be allowed at a time.
   Children below 5 years of age shall not be counted.
     Indians and citizens   Rs. 60/- per person per hour
   of S.A.A.R.C. countries   Rs. 40/- per child per hour
   (up to 12 years of age)
     Citizens of other   Rs. 300/- per person per hour
   countries   Rs. 200/- per child per hour
   (up to 12 years of age)

3. Entry Fee for Vehicles
   Car, Gypsy, Jeep,   Rs. 100/-
   Station wagon
   Minibus   Rs. 200/-

4. Camera Fee
   Still camera   Rs. 25/- per day
   Video camera (VHS)   Rs. 200/- per day

5. Filming Fee
   Teleserial, telefilm,   Rs. 6,000/- per day
   teledocumentary
   Cinefilm   Rs. 12,000/- per day

Kanha and Bandhavgarh have instituted a reciprocal arrangement whereby visitors to one park may obtain a 50% reduction in the entry fee to the other, upon presentation of dated receipts. Bandhavgarh has instituted a Rs. 2,000/- fee per day for "premium photography," defined as usage of a lens 500 mm or more. In our opinion, this charge is excessive and should be eliminated.

Note that at Kanha diesel vehicles (models 1997 and later) are now permitted entry, provided they are equipped with 4-wheel drive.

Opening of the 2001-2002 season occurred on 1 October, rather than on the traditional date a month later. Forest Department management will need to assess this change in policy, which is currently on an experimental basis. The drivability of tracks, the potential disturbance to barasingha fawns, and the strain on staff resources are some of the factors that management will want to consider.

Kanha Museum and Millennium Conference (page 11) Starting with the 2000-2001 season, several new rooms were opened at the Kanha Museum. The Old Forest Rest House building at Kanha Village has now been added to the museum complex. One exhibit consists of sixteen attractively lit color panels on the theme of "Pyramids of Kanha." The series as a whole focuses on the ecosystem concept (see pages 33-39). An audio track on a loop features the recordings of Indian bird calls compiled by the Bombay Natural History Society, an audiocassette package published in 1999. A nearby room contains a photo exhibit of 35 bird species.

Park management is planning further expansions of the museum, with the first phase projected to focus on the theme of Kanha's history. Appropriately, these exhibits are also slated for installation in the Old Forest Rest House, itself an historic structure that dates back to 1910. It is hoped that the Centre for Environmental Education in Ahmedabad, which supervised the original installations in the museum, will fabricate the new displays.

In Room 1 of the museum, a selection of more recent research papers is now available, including analyses of biodiversity conservation at Kanha, several specialized studies relating to the barasingha, papers dealing with food habits and population estimates of tigers, and—perhaps most significant—a report by Rajesh Gopal and Aseem Shrivastava on Kanha's efforts to increase public support for the park among residents of the buffer zone.

In June 2001, the park was host to an important "millennium conference" that brought together wildlife managers and experts active in tiger conservation. This occasion witnessed the release of two publications: a paperbound volume entitled *An Anthology of Research Papers* (containing 26 papers relating to Kanha's flora and fauna), as well as an appealingly illustrated booklet, "Tiger Conservation Initiatives: Madhya Pradesh." Digvijay Singh, Chief Minister of Madhya Pradesh, brought Kanha into the world of

Internet by inaugurating a cybercafé at Khatia, which is located in a small building near the outer gate to the park. This structure also contains a new souvenir shop and a small library. The park is to be congratulated on all these initiatives.

Park Map (opposite page 16) In the period 1999-2001, new routes covering approximately 60 km were opened to visitors, thereby relieving the pressure from an increasing number of tourists and vehicles. The new routes are shown on a revised park map in this edition. Two of the most important roads branch off from the main road near Kisli Gate on the western side of the park. The Digdola Road leads northeast up to Sonf Meadow, offering some exceptional landscape views and excellent tiger sighting possibilities. We have seldom travelled this road in the early mornings without seeing tiger sign. Furthermore, tourists on this route can skirt the southern edge of Sonf Meadow, glimpsing this beautiful *maidan* for the first time since the 1992-1993 season, when it was closed in order to foster undisturbed breeding of the barasingha. Stretching south of Kisli is the Indri Road, which traverses Ganghar Nallah and then turns east-northeast after Indri Camp to hook up with the Chimta Camp Road. In Mukki Range, the most scenic new route parallels the Banjar River from Moala Camp to Kivar Dabra Camp for a distance of a little over 5 km.

The Tiger Show (page 25) As expected, the tiger show continues to be a controversial feature of Kanha's tourist setup. Over the past three seasons, we have attended dozens of tiger shows and have found them to be generally orderly and well managed. Park management has recently decided to bar young children from viewing tigers by elephant-back. In our view, this is a prudent step, which was taken in response to a tragic accident in January 2001 involving the fall of a park employee's son from an elephant and the boy's fatal mauling by a tiger. (We should stress that this incident was *not* connected with a tiger show for tourists.) Another positive step is the park's effort to channel tourists to different tiger show venues on days when the park is crowded, thus equalizing the pressures on habitat and personnel alike.

Park management must scrupulously enforce existing regulations and must carefully weigh new rules that will insure safety for all the participants in the tiger show. In fact, given the heightened expectations that the very term "tiger show" inspires, we would advocate changing the very name of the event: perhaps to "tiger tracking." The fieldcraft of Kanha's mahouts, as well as the remarkable interaction between elephants and tigers, are fascinating aspects of the experience of seeing a tiger at Kanha in this fashion, and public expectations should be guided accordingly.

In this regard, it is interesting that park management at Bandhavgarh has erected several signs at Tala Gate clearly designed to keep tourists' expectations on an even keel. As one sign declares, "Tourists will be allowed to see tiger from the elephant only if it is possible to do so without interfering in its natural habitat and behaviour. The park management does not assure any tiger sighting."

Update on The Indian Wolf (pages 106-107). In Bandhavgarh Tiger Reserve on 8 April 2001 at approximately 6:20 P.M., we sighted and photographed three wolves near the Jamunia elephant camp. This was our first sighting of this species. The wolves had just killed a chital, and each animal was carrying a portion of the kill. Questions to mahouts and guides revealed that wolves are now being sighted quite regularly, but nearly always on the periphery of the tourist zone. During the 2000-2001 season, a group of ten wolves was observed on one occasion by Bandhavgarh head mahout E. A. D. Kuttappan.

Personnel (page 130) In Chapter 3, "Kanha's People," we present a collage of the individuals who make the park the unforgettable place it is. Inevitably, in the course of time the cast of characters changes (or assumes new garb). Dr. Rajesh Gopal marked his tenth anniversary as Field Director in April 2001. He was specially recognized with a promotion to the rank of Chief Conservator of Forests, a unique honor for the field director of a tiger reserve. In August 2001, Gopal succeeded P. K. Sen as Director of Project Tiger at the centre in Delhi. The new Field Director at Kanha is Khasegwar Nayak, who knows the park well from his term of service as Deputy Director from 1989 to 1994.

Deputy Director H. S. Negi won the WWF-PATA Award for 1999-2000, in recognition of his initiatives for park-people interface in the buffer zone and for staff motivation in the Phen Satellite Micro Core. Bastaram Nagpure currently serves as Range Officer in Kisli Range; his professional expertise over a long career in Kanha is well described in Vivek Sinha's illustrated memoir, *The Tiger Is a Gentleman: Leaves from a Wildlife Photographer's Diary* (see supplementary bibliography). As usual, staffing rotations have affected the posting of Deputy Rangers, Foresters, and Forest Guards. The park staff as a whole was honored in January 2001 with the Government of India's National Tourism Award for 1999-2000, which cited Kanha Tiger Reserve as "the best-maintained, tourist-friendly national park" in India.

As a high priority for the near future, Kanha Tiger Reserve needs sanction for the services of a full-time medical doctor, a research officer, and a park interpretation officer.

Kanha and the Future (page 170) Over the past five years, the park has made intensive efforts to develop the Phen Wildlife Sanctuary, which was notified and came under Kanha jurisdiction in 1983. This area of forest, comprising 110 km², lies northeast of Supkhar range in the main tiger reserve. As of now, Phen has healthy populations of sambar, wild boar, langur, wild dog, and gaur. On a visit there in December 2001, we saw sign of leopard, jungle cat, and hyena; in addition, staff reports the presence of two adult tigers, one male and one female. During the past few years, Kanha has succeeded in clearing the area of 38 illegal cattle grazing camps, and as a result the vegetation of Phen has swiftly rebounded. Phen's location makes it a key area for the creation of a corridor of protected areas and buffer zone forest, extending from western Chhattisgarh to east-central Madhya Pradesh. If this patch of sal and bamboo jungle can be successfully adjoined to the main tiger reserve, the resulting connectivity will insure a significant improvement in gene flow for many species of fauna.

Project Tiger (page 170) This program at the centre, once acclaimed internationally as a conservation model, has come under increasingly harsh criticism in recent years, and it has even been suggested that the Project be altogether dismantled. Perhaps not coincidentally, the critics' tone turned shriller just as Project Tiger celebrated its 25th anniversary in 1998. Even more striking, P. K. Sen went on record with a dire prediction: if a six-step program of reforms is not promptly implemented, the tiger in India will be doomed in the wild. Sen's six steps, as described in *Tigerlink* 6.2 (October 2000), are as follows:

i.   Split the Ministry of Environment and Forests and create a separate Ministry of Forests;
ii. Create a new anti-poaching force;
iii. Shelter those persons who are protecting natural resources from political interference;
iv. Politically empower those who live on the periphery of forests without binding them to activist manipulators from the metros;
v.   Dedicate 1% of the country's landmass completely to wildlife;
vi. Seal the borders with Nepal and Bangladesh to prevent large-scale smuggling of wildlife derivatives.

Rhetorical claims fly fast and furious. Without Project Tiger's contributions in the 1970s and 1980s, we would probably not have an appreciable number of tigers to worry about, nor would we be visiting places like Kanha to see them. At the same time, blockages in funds disbursement, ill-advised priorities, paralysis in the face of overrun sanctuaries, and a general creakiness have bedevilled Project Tiger's administration from Bikaner House on Shah Jahan Road in Delhi. If P. K. Sen's candour can wake up a few heads in Government, he will have contributed mightily. We wish Rajesh Gopal well. As the new director of the project, he will be serving in a time of challenge.

Meanwhile, as of early 2001, Project Tiger has added several more reserves to its network, bringing the total to 27 (see page 171). The new sanctuaries are listed below.

State	Tiger Reserve
Arunachal Pradesh/Assam	Nameri-Pakhui
Karnataka	Bhadra
Madhya Pradesh	Satpura-Bori-Pachmarhi
Maharashtra	Pench

In addition, plans call for Nagarahole National Park in Karnataka to be renamed in honour of Rajiv Gandhi and joined to Bandipur Tiger Reserve.

Madhya Pradesh and Chhattisgarh (page 172) On 1 November 2000, the new state of Chhattisgarh, comprising much of the eastern and southern regions of Madhya Pradesh, came into existence. The creation of the new state obviously affects statistics for the number of tigers estimated in Madhya Pradesh. It should be noted, however, that Madhya Pradesh has not relinquished its claim to being "the Tiger State," and that three of the major tiger reserves of central India—Kanha, Bandhavgarh, and Panna—still lie within the boundaries, as newly defined, of M.P. Pench Tiger Reserve continues to be partitioned into two sanctuaries, one in Madhya Pradesh and one in Maharashtra. For the chart of tiger reserves on page 171, note that Palamau Tiger Reserve is now located in the new state of Jharkhand rather than in Bihar, while Corbett Tiger Reserve is in Uttaranchal instead of Uttar Pradesh.

Poaching (page 174) The severe poaching threat to the tiger's survival in the wild continues. Probably no published image has driven home the danger more forcefully than a widely reproduced photograph of seven hooligans, defiantly posing for the camera in front of a dead tiger near Bandhavgarh Tiger Reserve in

January 2000. Eerie, ironic echoes of shikar photography, with hunters proudly bestriding tiger carcasses, resound from the page. Whether or not this gang was responsible for the death of the well-known Bandhavgarh tigress Sita (last seen in October 1998) has yet to be determined. What is not in doubt is the effrontery of the gang members, whose identities are reportedly well known in Umaria. Following close on the heels of a record seizure of leopard and tiger parts at Khaga in Uttar Pradesh, this incident spurred the Ministry of Environment and Forests to an unprecedented move: a request for paramilitary forces to deal with wildlife poaching in some states. Meanwhile, *Tigerlink* 6.1 (July 2000) reported that out of a total of 1,048 cases of wildlife offences and 1,325 apprehended offenders for the period 1995-99 in Madhya Pradesh, "only 47 cases have been disposed of by the courts, resulting in just 16 convictions." The Wildlife Protection Society of India (WPSI), under the dedicated and energetic leadership of Executive Director Belinda Wright, continues to play a major enforcement and advocacy role in the anti-poaching effort.

Kanha's Responsiveness (pages 186-197) In the previous edition, we suggested a number of initiatives for consolidation and improvement at Kanha, focusing on the encouragement of ecotourism, buffer zone relations, infrastructure, publications, VIP policy, record keeping, training of guides, response to injured animals, film-making policies, encouragement of research, and monitoring of the tiger show. We can report that the park management has moved on a number of these fronts, but there are still some important areas where action is needed.

Top park officials now hold regular monthly meetings with lodge managers so that concerns on both sides relating to tourism can be aired. A high priority has been set on better relations with peripheral village residents, as described in Gopal and Shrivastava's cogent analysis of the "social buffering of Kanha" (see Supplementary Bibliography below). In this connection, the park has instituted laudable new programs targeted at village children: for example, art competitions and subsidized park visits.

New research publications have been deposited in the Kanha Museum, and several updated leaflets on the park are now available at the orientation centres. The park guides' standards of professionalism, knowledge of natural history, and linguistic proficiency continue to improve. Monitoring of the tiger show, an all-important element in this controversial activity at Kanha, seems generally attentive, as judged by our observations at nearly 100 tiger

shows in the period from January 2000 to December 2001. Kanha now has its own informative and attractively designed site on the World Wide Web:
<http://www.kanhatigerreserve.com>.

Areas in need of further progress include the encouragement of research; re-appraisal and renewal of ecodevelopment initiatives in the buffer zone; a more robust evaluation of the decade-long grass fencing programme on Kanha Meadow; coming to grips with the demands of film-makers; fine tuning of excursion timings (the 90-minute afternoon round from mid-April to the end of the season needs to be extended); and—perhaps most pressing—dealing with the abusive pressure of VIPs (see page 193). We urge the powers-that-be in Delhi and Bhopal to re-think policy so as to allow the park management to husband its resources (and level the playing field for paying tourists). The most senior administrators should strictly limit the categories of "distinguished" visitors who get complimentary joyrides in the national parks.

Technology at Kanha By late 2001, it is clear that technology is playing an increasingly important role in Kanha's conservation mission. Within the past two years, telephone service in Mocha, Khatia, and Kisli has been installed, and as of this writing e-mail facility at Khatiya cybercafé is available. A site on the World Wide Web contributes to public awareness of the tiger reserve, and computer software is now used in the analysis of tiger pugmarks, as well as for statistical analysis of flora and fauna and for Management Information System. Under the leadership of Rajesh Gopal, other applications of technology include the use of digital photography, DNA "fingerprinting" of barasingha, Geographic Information System (GIS) software for mapping of the forest, and the use of information technology in crime detection.

A Note on Chhoti Mada (front cover) As the first edition of this book went to press in 1999, the release of the BBC/National Geographic film *The Tigers of Kanha*, together with an article by Hugh Miles and Chip Houseman in *BBC Wildlife* (April 1999), revealed that the tigress christened "Lakshmi" by the film-makers was actually our old friend Chhoti Mada, photographed in February 1993 for the front cover of this book. Toby Sinclair, an Indian wildlife expert who advised the film-makers on their project, could not tell us what had led them to give the tigress a different name.

We last saw Chhoti Mada fleetingly at Dhawa Dadar on 28 March 1998. We briefly glimpsed the tigress and her three cubs, aged about fifteen months, from the road at a distance of one hundred metres. Then, one by one, the tiger family disappeared into the forest. The film-makers inferred that Chhoti Mada had died defending her cubs, but the real circumstances—as so often with tigers who disappear—can never be known for sure.

From the final litter only one cub, a female named Sundari, has survived. We can now report that Sundari has successfully raised her first litter of two male cubs, whom we dubbed Ram and Lakshman when we first saw them at age four months on 4 January 2000. As of December 2001, the two cubs are independent and are being sighted regularly in the area of Link 9 and Badri Nath. Sundari's territory suggests a case of inheritance: it is virtually the same as her mother's, whose gentle memory lives on at Beniphat and on Bison Road.

Supplementary Bibliography

Deepika Belapurkar. "In Kanha: Where Wildlife Roams Free." *Voyage* 10.10 (January 2002) 24-29.

Eric Bharucha, ed. *Indian Bird Calls* (audiocassettes). Mumbai: Bombay Natural History Society, 1999.

M. Bookbinder, et al. "Ecotourism's Support of Biodiversity Conservation." *Conservation Biology* 12 (1998) 1399-1404.

S. S. Chaudhary. *Ranthambhore Beyond Tigers.* Udaipur: Himanshu Publications, 2000.

E. P. Eric D'Cunha. *Checklist of the Birds of Kanha National Park, M.P.* Privately printed, 1998.

Forestry for Sustainable Development: A Review of Ford Foundation-Supported Community Programs in Asia. New York: Ford Foundation, 1998.

Valerius Geist. *Deer of the World: Their Evolution, Behavior, and Ecology.* Mechanicsburg, PA: Stackpole Books, 1999.

Rajesh Gopal. "The Biology and Ecology of the Hard-Ground Barasingha (*Cervus duvauceli branderi*) in Kanha National Park." Ph.D. dissertation, Sagar University, 1995.

Rajesh Gopal and H. S. Negi. "A Note on Population Estimation of Tigers in Kanha Tiger Reserve (1997)," in *An Anthology of Research*

Papers: Kanha Tiger Reserve. Jabalpur: Amrit Offset, 2001, pp. 151-161.

Rajesh Gopal and Aseem Shrivastava. "Eliciting Public Support for Conservation: The Social Buffering of Kanha," in *An Anthology of Research Papers: Kanha Tiger Reserve.* Jabalpur: Amrit Offset, 2001, pp. 137-143.

Rajesh Gopal and Rakesh Shukla. "Tiger Conservation Initiatives: Madhya Pradesh." Madhya Pradesh Forest Department Pamphlet, 2000.

Rajesh Gopal and Rakesh Shukla. *Management Plan for Kanha Tiger Reserve (for the period 2001-02 to 2010-11).* Mandla, 2001.

Anjali Goswami. *The Effects of Tourism on the Land, the Wildlife, and the Local Population of Bandhavgarh National Park.* Privately printed, 2000.

Richard Grimmett, Carol Inskipp, and Tim Inskipp. *Birds of the Indian Subcontinent.* Delhi: Oxford University Press, 1998.

Ramachandra Guha, ed. *Nature's Spokesman: M. Krishnan and Indian Wildlife.* Delhi: Oxford University Press, 2000.

Sumit Guha. *Environment and Ethnicity in India, 1200-1991.* Cambridge: Cambridge University Press, 1999.

Nicholas Hammond, ed. *Tigers: Artists for Nature in India.* Lavenham: Wildlife Art Gallery, 2000.

Martha Honey. *Ecotourism and Sustainable Development: Who Owns Paradise?* Washington, D.C.: Island Press, 1999.

Jeroo Irani. "Tryst with the Tiger." *Voyage* 10.11 (February 2002) 34-37, 45.

Issues Relating to Species: Tiger. CITES Technical Missions Report, 1999.

M. M. Jamkhindikar. *Of Homo Sapiens and Panthera Leo: A Diary of Experiences in Gir Forest, India.* Mumbai: Tolani Shipping Co., 2000.

K. Ullas Karanth. *The Way of the Tiger.* Stillwater, MN: Voyageur Press, 2001.

K. Ullas Karanth and James D. Nichols. "Estimation of Tiger Densities in India Using Photographic Captures and Recaptures." *Ecology* 79 (1998) 2852-2862.

Anand S. Kathi. *Panoramic Corbett National Park.* Noida: Pelican Creations International, 2001.

Krys Kazmierczak. *A Field Guide to the Birds of the Indian Subcontinent.* New Haven: Yale University Press, 2000.

Isaac Kehimkar. *Common Indian Wild Flowers.* Mumbai: Bombay Natural History Society/Oxford University Press, 2000.

Krushnamegh Kunte. *Butterflies of Peninsular India.* Hyderabad: Universities Press (India) Limited, 2000.

Ranjit Lal. *Enjoying Birds.* Delhi: Clarion Books, 1998.

Peter Matthiessen. *Tigers in the Snow.* New York: North Point Press, 2000.

Subhadra Menon and Pallava Bagla. *Trees of India.* New Delhi: Timeless Books, 2000.

Hugh Miles and Chip Houseman. "Lakshmi's Tale." *BBC Wildlife* 17.4 (April 1998) 14-21.

Carroll Moulton and Ernie J. Hulsey. "Tiger! Tiger!" *Voyage* 9.10 (February 2001) 44-46.

Michael Nichols and Geoffrey C. Ward. *The Year of the Tiger.* Washington, D.C.: National Geographic Society, 1998.

Kristin Nowell. *Far From a Cure: The Tiger Trade Revisited.* TRAFFIC International, 2000.

Sudesh Puranik. *Madhya Bharat Ke Pramukh Vanyajeev.* Balaghat, 2001 (in Hindi).

Mahesh Rangarajan. *Fencing the Forest: Conservation and Ecological Change in India's Central Provinces, 1860-1914.* Delhi: Oxford University Press, 1996.

—————————— , ed. *The Oxford Anthology of Indian Wildlife.* Volume 1: Hunting and Shooting; Volume 2:

Watching and Conserving. New Delhi: Oxford University Press, 1999.

──────────── . *India's Wildlife History: An Introduction*. Delhi: Permanent Black, 2001.

Fateh Singh Rathore and Valmik Thapar. *Wild Tigers of Ranthambhore*. Delhi: Oxford University Press, 2000.

Vasant Saberwal, Mahesh Rangarajan, and Ashish Kothari. *People, Parks & Wildlife: Towards Coexistence*. Hyderabad: Orient Longman Limited, 2000.

Bittu Sahgal and Jennifer Scarlott. "Stranded." *The Amicus Journal*, 23.2 (Summer 2001) 12-17.

P. K. Sen. "The Future of the Tiger in the 21st Century." *Tigerlink* 6.2 (October 2000) 1.

Lynn Sherr. "The Maharajah Wore Stripes." *New York Times*, 7 May 2000, 5:11.

L. A. K. Singh. *Tracking Tigers: Guidelines for Estimating Wild Tiger Populations Using the Pugmark Technique*. New Delhi: WWF, 1999.

S. K. Singh. *Birds of Bandhavgarh Tiger Reserve*. Privately printed, 1998.

Vivek R. Sinha. *The Tiger Is a Gentleman: Leaves from a Wildlife Photographer's Diary*. Bangalore: Wildlife, 1999.

Sheena Sippy and Sanjna Kumar. *The Ultimate Ranthambhore Guide* (2001).

James L. David Smith, Charles McDougal, and Dale Miquelle. "Scent-Marking in Free-Ranging Tigers (*Panthera tigris*)." *Animal Behaviour* 37 (1989) 1-10.

The State of the Tiger. London: Environmental Investigation Agency, 1999.

Valmik Thapar. *The Secret Life of Tigers*. Delhi: Oxford University Press, 1999.

Valmik Thapar, ed. *Saving Wild Tigers, 1900-2000: The Essential Writings*. Delhi: Permanent Black, 2001.

Tiger Conservation Programme: Three Years and Beyond. Delhi: WWF, 1999.

Ronald Tilson, et al., ed. *Securing a Future for the World's Wild Tigers* (Executive Summary of the Year of the Tiger Conference). Washington, D.C.: Save the Tiger Fund, National Fish and Wildlife Foundation, 2000.

Whitney Tilt and Tracy Frish Walmer. *Model for Success: The Save the Tiger Fund 1995-2001.* Washington, D.C.: National Fish and Wildlife Foundation, 2001.

S. K. Tiwari. Wildlife Sanctuaries of Madhya Pradesh. Delhi: APH Publishing Corporation, 1997.

Satyendra Tiwari. "Charger R.I.P.," in *Srishti Creativity in Nature* IV.2 (2001) 20-23.

Satyendra Tiwari and Kay Hassall. "Tiger Mating in Bandhavgarh Tiger Reserve," in Zoos' Print XVI.8 (August 2001) 12-14.

Mark F. Tritsch. *Wildlife of India (Collins Traveller's Guide).* London: Harper Collins, 2001.

The Vanishing Stripes II: A Report by CREW on the Tiger Crisis in Madhya Pradesh. Bhopal: Crusade for Revival of Environment and Wildlife, 2000.

Dieter Zingel. *Tigerland: On Kipling's Tracks in the Heart of India.* Hamburg: Jahn & Ernst Verlag, 1999.

CHAPTER 1

INTRODUCTION TO KANHA

THE SUN IS just up, and Kanha Meadow shimmers. It is November. Only a few days ago, the park has reopened to the public after four months of rest. The monsoon has rejuvenated all nature. At the start of a new season, Kanha is once again a meeting place, an intersection of wildlife and humankind. The rains have renewed Kanha, and Kanha will now nourish and renew her guests.

A gentle, silvery mist still wraps the great vista of the Meadow in its folds. A small party of chital saunters daintily across the road and ambles toward Partak Nallah. Last to cross is a majestic stag. Emerging from the long grass, he stands stock still for a moment, carving a silhouette against grasslands and trees, low hills and horizon and ghostlike sun. He offers an invitation.

1. GEOGRAPHY AND CLIMATE

Location and Habitat

Kanha National Park (which is now officially known as Kanha Tiger Reserve) is located in the Maikal range, the eastern sector of the Satpura Hills of the Central Indian Highlands. The park lies 160 km (100 miles) southeast of Jabalpur in the state of Madhya Pradesh. Kanha is 270 km (170 miles) northeast of the city of Nagpur (Maharashtra), which currently furnishes the nearest air link to the park (direct flights from Mumbai, Delhi, and Hyderabad, with connections to other cities). The exact geographical coordinates of Kanha are as follows. Latitude: 22° 7′ to 22° 27′N; longitude: 80° 26′ to 81° 3′E.

The name *Kanha* itself may be derived from *kanhar*, the local term for the clayey soil in the valley bottoms, or from Kanva, a holy man who once lived there in a forest village. Two river valleys are prominent features of the park's topography: the Banjar in the west and the Halon in the east. Both these rivers are tributaries of the Narmada, which flows through the district headquarters town of Mandla, 64 km (40 miles) to the northwest of the park's western entrance. Kanha's valleys are enclosed by hills topped with plateaux, locally called *dadar*.

Four principal vegetation types have been identified in Kanha: moist deciduous forest, dry deciduous forest, valley meadow, and plateau meadow. The main species in moist deciduous areas (27% of the park area) is the sal tree *(Shorea robusta)*. For a more detailed discussion of vegetation cover types, see Chapter 2, Section 2 (page 39).

Park headquarters, located at Kanha Village in the park's western block, lies at about 600 m (1,900 ft.) above sea level. The plateau at Bamhni Dadar rises to 870 m, or about 2,900 ft. The park is shaped roughly like a figure "8" on its side (see map facing page 16), with a length from west to east of approximately 80 km and a width ranging from 8 to 35 km.

The park consists of a core area of 940 km^2, which is surrounded by a buffer zone of 1,005 km^2, thus comprising a total area of 1,945 km^2. The core area of the park and most of the buffer zone are located in two districts: Mandla to the west and Balaghat to the east. In addition, a small section of the buffer zone in the southeastern sector is part of Rajnandgaon District. There are nearly 150 villages in the buffer zone and over 260 villages within a radius of 10 km.

For management purposes, the park is divided into 5 ranges: Kisli, Kanha, and Mukki in the western block, and Bhaisanghat and Supkhar in the eastern sector. These latter two ranges are closed off entirely to the public. Within Kisli, Kanha, and Mukki ranges, certain roads and areas are also closed to tourists. As of this writing (mid-1998), the percentage of the park's core area open to visitors (227 km^2) is about 25%. The park is served by an extensive network (a little over 700 km) of generally well-maintained roads.

Climate

Kanha enjoys an average annual rainfall of approximately 1,600 mm. There are three seasons: cool and dry (November-February), warm to hot (March-June), and rains (July-October). During the cool season, frost often occurs in the valley meadow areas, with temperatures ranging from a low of –2°C. at night to a high of 32°C. during the day. In November, the *kans* grasses flowering along the *nallahs* (gullies or stream beds) and in marshy areas present a lovely sight. Spider webs glisten and wildflowers abound. During the month of January, many trees shed their leaves.

By the end of February, spring has arrived in Kanha. Pallas *(Butea monosperma)* and silk cotton or semal trees *(Bombax malabaricum)* splash the landscape with their brilliant orange flowers, and birds celebrate the blossoms' nectar in profusion. As daytime temperatures steadily climb to highs of 40-45°C. in May, the grasses begin to wither. Sal trees flush, however, with their new, surf-green leaves. April is perhaps the park's most colourful month, with many tree species in flower. Rainfall is generally low during this period.

The monsoon, during which Kanha receives the bulk of its annual rainfall, swiftly converts the forest from yellow and brown to green. New grasses sprout and grow quickly, reaching a height of more than two feet in July-August. Orchids and creepers proliferate on the forest floor, and the young of gaur, sambar, and barasingha are born into a land of plenty.

2. BRIEF HISTORY

Little is known about Kanha before the middle of the nineteenth century. Presumably, the slash-and-burn (or "bewar") cultivation methods of the Baiga and Gond indigenous peoples stretched back for centuries. According to former field director H. S. Panwar, who surveyed the park's history in his valuable handbook on Kanha, the first forest management rules were instituted in 1862, when cutting of various tree species (teak, sal, saja, shisham, and bija) without official authorization was prohibited. The first extensive natural history notes about the area come from this period, in the form of Captain J. Forsyth's classic *The Highlands of Central India*, a highly readable combination of ethnography, forest survey, and personal memoir (with dashes of *shikar* diary thrown in for good measure).

From about 1865, an area in the current park's western block was officially classified as the Banjar Valley Reserve Forest. In the 1890s, this region of Madhya Pradesh, then called the Central Provinces, was the setting for Rudyard Kipling's *Jungle Book* stories. A. A. Dunbar Brander, a government official and a keenly observant amateur naturalist, focused on the region's wildlife in a landmark publication of 1923, entitled *Wild Animals in Central India*.

In 1933, the Kanha area (which had been excluded from the shooting blocks two years before) was declared a sanctuary. The same status was accorded in the eastern sector to Supkhar in 1935, but within a few years the protection for wildlife in this area was ended, due to the damage caused by the animals to sal saplings, crops, and livestock. Over the next twenty years, shooting of deer and tigers was periodically allowed. In 1955, however, concern about the depletion of tiger numbers resulted in the official designation of Kanha as a national park, some twenty years or so after Corbett became the first national park in India.

During the period 1955-1975, the new national park advanced to the forefront in wildlife research and conservation efforts. In 1963-65, for example, the American scientist George Schaller carried out pioneering research on the Kanha ecosystem. He published the results in 1967 in an influential book entitled *The Deer and the Tiger*. In 1970, the park began a longterm and ultimately successful effort to rescue the hardground barasingha *(Cervus duvauceli branderi)* from extinction. And in 1973 Kanha was designated as one of the original nine reserves under Project Tiger.

This period also witnessed the development of a consensus on some fundamental issues of park management. The core-buffer concept, by which all forestry operations, grazing by outside cattle, and collection of forest produce are banned inside the park's core, was adopted as a basic operating principle. The buffer zone, in contrast to the core area, was designed as a mixed-usage area, intended to insulate the core from disturbance and to minimize the potentially harmful encounters between people and wild animals. Beginning around 1969, in accordance with the core-buffer philosophy, park management began to relocate villages located within the core area, such as Sonf, Bishanpura, and Gorhela. A history of this process of relocations cannot be attempted here, but suffice it to say that there have been ups and downs, with goodwill often jeopardized by lapses in communication and insufficient forward planning. In most wildlife reserves throughout the world, the relationship between a park and its neighbours is a key factor in the ultimate success of any conservation effort, and Kanha is no exception.

During the 1980s, Kanha served as the principal venue for Stanley Breeden and Belinda Wright's award-winning National

Geographic film, *Land of the Tiger*. The success of Project Tiger's first phase was particularly evident at Kanha and at Ranthambhore National Park in Rajasthan, and the annual visitorship to both parks dramatically increased. From 1989 to 1991, an intensive collaboration at Kanha between the Centre for Environmental Education in Ahmedabad and the United States National Park Service (under the auspices of the Indo-U.S. Subcommission on Science and Technology) resulted in the installation of a multi-faceted informational programme at Kanha, consisting of a park museum, two orientation centres, and a variety of publications (see below). By the early 1990s, these new features, together with the park's biodiversity, the expansion of tourist infrastructure, and the reserve's enviable record for research, monitoring, and security, had made Kanha, in the opinion of many observers, the premier national park in India and one of the finest wildlife reserves in the world.

The two most important factors in Kanha's rise to a pre-eminent position in the network of protected areas in India have undoubtedly been its record in tiger conservation and its role in saving the barasingha. Over the past decade, the official census of tigers in Kanha has hovered at about 100. Since 1970, the barasingha population has rebounded from a perilous low of 66 animals to the 400-500 range.

Along with distinction and fame, however, have come challenges, both for the present and for the longer term. Like every reserve today in the "tiger range" states (13 nations besides India, including China, Russia, Nepal, Bangladesh, Indonesia, and the states in the Indochinese region), Kanha continues to face a relentless threat from tiger poaching. Since the early 1990s, the slaughter of the world's greatest cat, lord of the jungle and a timeless symbol of power and majesty in many Asian cultures, has been systematically continuing, largely for the value of tiger bones in traditional medicine preparations. The statistics are chilling. India alone, with 60% of the world's tigers, may be losing as many as *one tiger a day* to poachers. With the world population of the species at fewer than 5,000, the danger of extinction in the wild by the year 2020, if not sooner, is all too real.

Because the vast majority of visitors to Kanha are attracted there by the prospect of seeing India's national animal in its natural habitat, tiger conservation is closely linked to the future of Kanha National Park. Less visible on the surface, but equally critical in the long run, is the level of cooperation between the park and its neighbours, the 150,000 or so inhabitants of "village India" that live on every side. In a participatory economic framework, and with goodwill, the future seems bright, given Kanha's advantages. But, as with nature reserves around a world with an exploding population, hard work and constant effort will be required.

Kanha Timeline

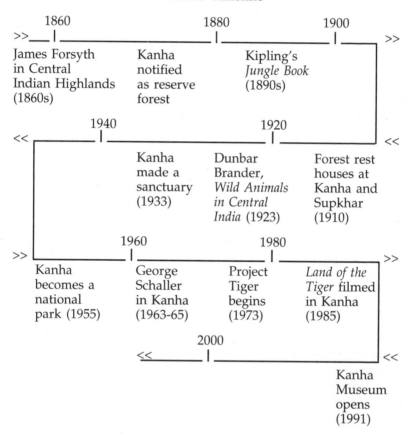

1860	**1880**	**1900**
James Forsyth in Central Indian Highlands (1860s)	Kanha notified as reserve forest	Kipling's *Jungle Book* (1890s)
1940	**1920**	
Kanha made a sanctuary (1933)	Dunbar Brander, *Wild Animals in Central India* (1923)	Forest rest houses at Kanha and Supkhar (1910)
1960	**1980**	
Kanha becomes a national park (1955)	George Schaller in Kanha (1963-65)	Project Tiger begins (1973)	*Land of the Tiger* filmed in Kanha (1985)
2000		
		Kanha Museum opens (1991)

3. BASIC FACTS AT A GLANCE

Travel and Accommodation

The road journey from Nagpur Airport takes approximately 5 hours, depending on route conditions. Good train service exists from the north and west to Jabalpur, which is about 3½ hours away by car from the park. Roughly equidistant to the east is Bilaspur, which serves as a convenient railhead for travellers from Calcutta and other points in eastern India.

The western approach roads, particularly National Highway 7 from Nagpur, are reasonably good. Roughly half way from Nagpur to Kanha is the large town of Seoni, a good spot to buy supplies if you are bringing your own food. If you are coming from Jabalpur, you may stop in Mandla, about 65 km from Kanha's western gate, to do shopping.

There is a wide range of accommodation available in Kanha. On the park's western side, Krishna Jungle Resort, Indian Adventures Wild Chalet, and Kipling Camp are full-service lodges providing room and board as well as vehicles, drivers, and escorts for park rounds. At least two additional lodges—Tuli Tiger Resort in Mocha Village and Mowgli in Khatia—should be operational in late 1999. Less expensive accommodation may be found at Baghira Log Huts near Kisli Gate and at assorted small hotels in Khatia Village. At Mukki, on the eastern side of the park, Royal Tiger Resort and Jungle Lodge are the leading choices. Royal Tiger Resort, a unit of Garuda Resorts, offers the most luxurious accommodation of all. Visitors to Kanha should investigate lodging choices by contacting Madhya Pradesh State Tourism or the private lodge owners. At certain times of the year, especially the Diwali and school holiday periods, advance reservations are essential.

Park Season, Excursion Timings, and Fees

The park is open daily from 1 November to 30 June, although management reserves the option to close earlier if the rains begin before the end of June. The opening hours are scheduled to accord roughly with the seasonal variations in climate, as well as with the length of the day at different seasons. There is always a mid-day break, so that employees may eat lunch and rest and the animals may have a respite, too. Opening hours are as follows:

1 November-15 February	Sunrise to 11 A.M.	3 P.M. to sunset
16 February-30 April	Sunrise to 11 A.M.	4 P.M. to sunset
1 May-30 June	Sunrise to 10 A.M.	5 P.M. to sunset

These hours are subject to change because of special conditions: for example, heavy rain showers may make park roads temporarily hazardous, or official activities such as census taking may be scheduled. In practice, "sunrise" and "sunset" are interpreted as "dawn" and "dusk," with vehicles being admitted at 6:30 A.M., for example, if sunrise occurs at 6:50. The gate attendants tend to be stricter about exit times, since darkness follows sunset quite rapidly at this latitude.

As of 1998, entry fees and regulations are as follows:

Park entry for Indian citizens:	Rs. 10/-
Park entry for foreigners:	Rs. 100/-
Light motor vehicles:	Rs. 10/- per vehicle up to 5 persons and Rs. 2/- for each additional person.
Park entry for student groups:	Rs. 10/- per group

Entry for children below 5 years of age is free.

Permissible capacity of vehicles exclusive of driver and guide is as follows:

Car	5 persons
Jeep	8 persons
Minibus	15 persons
Guide Charge:	Rs. 60/- per round
Elephant Joy Rides:	Rs. 20/- per hour (up to 4 persons)
Tiger Show:	Rs. 50/- per person on elephant back

Photography:

Still Camera	Rs. 10/-
Movie Camera (8 mm)	Rs. 200/-
Movie Camera (16 mm)	Rs. 250/-
Movie Camera (35 mm)	Rs. 1,000/-
Video Camera	Rs. 100/-

Official notice boards direct visitors' attention to the following regulations:

- Heavy vehicles and diesel vehicles are not allowed inside the park.
- Route guide is compulsory.
- Speed limit is 20 km per hour.
- Use of horn or headlights is not allowed.

- Smoking is forbidden inside the park. Forests are vulnerable to fire, and your negligence may cause a widespread fire.
- Visitors are requested not to use flash for photography.
- Foot trekking is strictly prohibited. Do not get down from your vehicle.
- Do not feed the animals, and keep a safe distance from them.
- Do not carry weapons. You are safe when accompanied by a guide, and hunting is banned.
- Do not throw empty tins, boxes, or other litter.
- Keep strictly to the road.
- Supervise young children closely at all times.
- Try to blend with the surroundings. Avoid wearing colours that jar. Do not blow horn, play music, or make loud noises.

Vehicles and Guides

As noted above, no diesel-powered vehicles are allowed in the park, and the speed limit inside the protected area is 20 km per hour. Keep in mind that a vehicle's noise level, the field of vision afforded to passengers, and the speed of travel are critical factors that influence the quality of wildlife sightings. Open vehicles sitting relatively high on the road are best: for example, a Land Rover or a Gypsy Maruti (which is much quieter and more manoeuvrable than a Land Rover). A petrol station is available directly outside Kisli Gate.

If your lodging arrangements do not include transport inside the park, freelance drivers at the main gates (Khatia, Kisli, and Mukki) are often available. A typical park round from Kisli Gate should comprise 40-50 km, with a rate of Rs. 9/- per kilometer (as of mid-1998). Average distance for a round would be somewhat greater from Mukki Gate.

Every visitor to Kanha must sign in, giving name, address, vehicle plate number, and (for foreigners) passport details. Each vehicle is then assigned a park guide. Young men in their twenties and thirties for the most part, the guides are freelancers who have passed a basic written and oral test on their knowledge about the park and its fauna and flora. Their attentiveness and communication skills vary somewhat, but the good Kanha guides are very good indeed, and a rapport between your guide and your driver is to be encouraged. Many Kanha guides have criss-crossed the park daily for ten years or more. To earn extra money, some of them double as forest guards during the monsoon months when the park is closed to tourists.

The guides work on a rotation system and are paid at the end of each round, splitting their fee with the park management. While you are inside the park, your guide has the responsibility of seeing that you obey such regulations as not leaving the vehicle, avoiding closed roads, not driving off the road, and exiting promptly at the proper time. The latter is an especially sensitive rule, since guides can be fined or otherwise disciplined if your vehicle is late. The park management has recently instituted regular workshops for the guides in order to upgrade their language skills with foreign tourists. For the guides, an additional tip is a thoroughly appropriate acknowledgement for attentive service and assistance during a game round.

Informational Facilities

A decade ago, the cooperative efforts of the Centre for Environmental Education in Ahmedabad and the United States National Park Service produced an unusually fine range of informational resources for Kanha visitors—certainly the best in any Indian national park. The interpretation programme is outlined in the following pages.

Two **orientation centres**, one located at Khatia Gate and the other at Mukki Gate, offer informative displays, signs, graphics, and interactive exhibits. For example, the centre at Khatia presents exhibits on predator-prey relationships, wild boar behaviour, Project Tiger, the process of pollination, and the mutual benefits in the relationship between "tick-picking" birds (such as mynas) and deer like the barasingha. Exhibits at Mukki focus on beetles, termites, barasingha, the process of seed dispersal, jungle calls, and the relationship between chital and langur.

Each centre has a sales counter, where park publications, posters, tee-shirts, and other souvenirs are sold. The opening hours of the centres (as of mid-1998) are as follows:

1 Nov - 15 Feb	8 A.M. - 11 A.M.	3:30 P.M. - 5 P.M.
16 Feb - 30 Apr	7:30 A.M. - 10:30 A.M.	4:30 P.M. - 6 P.M.
1 May - 30 Jun	7 A.M. - 10 A.M.	5:30 P.M. - 7 P.M.

The orientation centres are also open in the early evenings almost every day for the screening of wildlife films, for which admission is free.

The **Kanha Museum**, located at park headquarters in Kanha Village, contains fascinating, well-conceived exhibits relating to the entire ecosystem and its fauna and flora. The museum complex consists of six rooms distributed between two buildings. The museum opens daily at 7 A.M. and remains accessible to visitors during park excursion hours throughout the day. Below is a summary of the exhibits.

- **Building A: Room 1 (Research and Display Room)**

  Exhibit 1: Vital Support. Skeletons of wild dog, leopard, tiger, barasingha, and gaur. Similar parts vary in size and shape in different animals, according to the habitat and habits of the species.

  Exhibit 2: Census of the Wild. Links between predators, prey, and vegetation; methods for tiger census and census of the herbivores.

  Exhibit 3: Tiger's Food. Laboratory analysis of droppings to determine the components of the tiger's diet in Kanha.

  Exhibit 4: Incredible Grasses. Resilience and vital importance of the grasslands, which support more living forms and more tiger prey than any other kind of habitat in Kanha; the relationship between grasses and herbivores.

  Exhibit 5: Satellite Images. The role of satellite imaging in wildlife habitat management; graphic showing the habitat suitability for chital in Kanha National Park (see page 36).

  Exhibit 6: Aerial Photos. The use of aerial photography, as well as satellite images, in planning and monitoring corridor links that connect reserves in Madhya Pradesh.

  Exhibit 7: Telemetry. Explanation of radio telemetry and its applications in the study of animal behaviour; graphic showing tiger territories in Kanha National Park (see page 37).

  Exhibit 8: Animals in Action. 8-minute video representing the informative and inspiring images of wildlife photographers and filmmakers, who provide viewers with behind-the-scenes accounts that most of us would never get to see otherwise.

Exhibit 9: Research in Kanha. Display of 11 research papers, including analyses of tiger census and food habits, networks of wildlife reserves, ecological studies on grasslands, the Kanha Interpretation Programme, status of relocated villages, park-people relations, Project Tiger, and birds of Kanha.

- **Building B: Room 2**

  Exhibit 1: Teeth and Jaws. Skulls of tiger, leopard, hyena, wild dog, jackal, sambar, and wild boar; correlation of teeth in a species with its diet.

  Exhibit 2: Horns and Antlers. Antelope have horns, while deer have antlers. The cycle of growth and shedding of antlers, and their function in the social organization of deer.

  Exhibit 3: Claws and Paws. Toes, talons, or paws of langur, monitor lizard, sloth bear, pangolin, chital, vulture, porcupine, peacock, and owl. The design of an animal's paws and claws enables it to hunt, escape, or move efficiently.

- **Building B: Room 3**

  Exhibit 1: Colours Conceal. Illustrations of camouflage: insects on leaves, a tiger's stripes, a leopard's spots, a chital fawn concealed in the grass, the colours of a lapwing's eggs and chicks, bush quails, grasshoppers.

  Exhibit 2: Colours that Confuse. Explanation of mimicry: the ability of one species to imitate the colour, shape, movement, or habits of another.

  Exhibit 3: Colours that Communicate. The role played by colours in pollination, courtship, and survival.

  Exhibit 4: Colour Code. Summary of the significance of colour in the natural world.

- **Building B: Room 4**

  Interactive Exhibit: Jungle Lore. This exhibit is a large-scale model consisting of a tree with a vulture perched on a branch, the remains of a kill, two vultures on the ground, and assorted clues, including tiger pug marks, chital spoor, and fragments of chital hide and antlers. Wall exhibits consist of informational panels covering topics such as pug marks, predator's dragging of prey into cover, fur samples from prey animals, vulture behaviour, blowfly development, and antlers of sambar and chital. Visitors are invited to analyse the scene and to assemble clues to answer the following questions:

* What animal was the prey?
* Where was the kill made?
* Who was the predator?
* Is the killer still around?
* When was the kill made?

[*Answers:* The remnants of skin and antlers, as well as a chital pug mark, show that the prey was a chital; drag marks show that the kill was made in the front of the exhibit and then dragged backwards to a position behind the tree; the predator was a tiger, as indicated by two separate tiger pug marks; the killer has abandoned the carcass, and some vultures have descended to the ground; the kill was made at least 24 hours earlier, as indicated by the presence of maggots on the carcass.]

* **Building B: Room 5**
  Sound and Light Show: Wait Until Dark. Interactive audiovisual show on sounds and movements in the jungle at nighttime, with Hindi and English narration. Show duration is about 15 minutes.

* **Building B: Room 6**
  Man and Environment. This exhibit consists of three large cases, each with a three-dimensional model of the same forest section. Model displays illustrate harmony in nature, the changes caused by development, and current efforts for environmental revival.

The exhibits at the Kanha Museum are supplemented outdoors throughout the park by a series of **wayside exhibits**. In these displays, a durable plate, easily viewed from a vehicle, gives a description of a prominent feature or site. There are nine such wayside exhibits, including displays at Kisli Gate, Kanha Meadow, Shravan Tal, Bishanpura Camp, and Bamhni Dadar. The exhibit at Shravan Tal, which summarizes a famous legend from the *Ramayana*, may serve as an example:

Shravan Tal

Legend has it that Shravan Kumar stopped by this lake with his blind parents while on a pilgrimage to the holy places of India. King Dasharatha, a skilled hunter known for his ability to aim by sound alone, was out on a hunt. Mistaking the sound of water filling in Shravan's pitcher for an animal drinking water, he shot in that direction and killed Shravan. The aggrieved parents placed a curse on him that he too would die like them, without his beloved son at his deathbed.

The interpretation programme at Kanha is rounded out by a variety of useful **publications**, which may be purchased at the orientation centres at Khatia and Mukki. A brief description of this material follows below.

- A 12-page, newspaper-sized brochure entitled *Kanha Chronicle* includes a variety of brief, informative features on the habitat, mammals, and birds of Kanha. At the time of writing, this publication was available in both English and Hindi.

- Also available in both English and Hindi is *A Road Guide to Kanha National Park*, a handy 16-page pamphlet that is keyed to the system of numbered roadside markers you will encounter as you travel through the park. These numbered posts, which have been discreetly placed so as to blend in with the surroundings, direct the tourist's attention to natural and man-made features such as termite hills, patrolling camps, animal tracks, boundary pillars, firelines, observation towers, and local points of interest such as Shravan Tal and Dasharatha Machan. Further information about these features appears in the road guide.

The numbering system for the roadside markers is as follows:

1	Meadow	10	Lapsi Kabar
2	Boundary Pillar	11	Enclosure
3	Patrolling Camp	12	Observation Tower
4	Checkpost	13	Claw Marks
5	Termite Hill	14	Research Plot
6	Animal Track	15	Shravan Tal
7	Migration Corridor	16	Shravan Chita
8	Fireline	17	Dasharatha Machan
9	Water Source		

Most valuable of all is H. S. Panwar's well-illustrated survey of Kanha entitled *Kanha National Park: A Handbook*. Published in 1991, this 136-page book is a mine of information about Kanha. The author had a distinguished term as the park's Field Director during the 1980s, and his knowledge of the ecosystem is still legendary among Kanha's old-timers. Unfortunately, Panwar's book is no longer available in English. The Hindi version, which includes a rudimentary park map, may be purchased at Khatia or Mukki.

The interpretation programme at Kanha is by far the best of any Indian national park, and it should serve as a model for the development of similar programmes elsewhere.

4. GAME DRIVES

There is considerable value in getting your bearings as early during your visit as you can. That way, even if your time at Kanha is limited, you can be sure to tour a variety of habitats (such as meadows and sal forest) and to include a range of important landforms (nallahs, ghats, and dadars) on your route. A sketch map like the one facing page 16 may thus be helpful, if only because it allows you to familiarize yourself with the road system. To the first-time visitor, one park road can look much like any other. However, a visitor who takes the trouble to learn the road network can make efficient use of time. Bear in mind that only 25% of the core area, or about 225 km^2, is open to tourism. In effect, this tourist zone amounts to about half of the park's western section.

(Note: Some park guides use the term "core area" at Kanha to designate the section of the park that is closed to tourists. In this book, however, by "core area" we mean the central portion of the park, in which all forestry operations and grazing by outside cattle are banned. This area, which covers 940 km^2, is surrounded by the buffer zone: see above, page 2.)

Distances Inside the Park

Distances between points inside the park are indicated in red on the route map. For convenient reference, the chart below also shows the distances between major locations.

Distance Chart

From Khatia to:

Kisli	3 km
Kanha Museum	12 km
Sonf	22 km
Shravan Tal	17 km
Mukki (via Kanha)	36 km
Mukki (via Kope Dabri)	38 km
Bamhni Dadar (via Shravan Tal)	41 km
Sondhar (via Kanha)	28 km
Bishanpura	24 km
Gorhela (via Kanha and Aurai)	37 km

From Mukki to:

Kanha Museum	25 km
Kisli (via Kanha)	33 km
Kisli (via Kope Dabri)	35 km
Sonf (via Kanha)	35 km
Bamhni Dadar (via Kanha)	49 km
Shravan Tal	21 km
Sondhar	8 km
Bishanpura	11 km
Gorhela	6 km

Planning your route will always depend, to a certain extent, on the time of year that you visit because of variations in the animals' movement patterns and the changing times of sunrise and sunset.

You will also want to take account of word-of-mouth reports from the guides and drivers about interesting sightings in the past few days. The "bush telegraph" is an important source of information at Kanha, so be prepared to change your route plans accordingly.

Keep in mind that the distances inside the park do not give a full picture of the time needed to cover various routes. You will have to go much slower on certain stretches than on others: for example, when you make the zig-zag ascent on Sal Ghat or when you descend from Bamhni Dadar to Gorhela via Alegi Dadar. In any case, you should observe the park speed limit of 20 km per hour. To get you started map-reading, try the two exercises outlined below:

(a) You're staying for three days in late March on the Mukki side of the park. The guides report that tigers have been sighted nearly every day in the late afternoon on Kanha Meadow. Given the distance from Mukki to Kanha (25 km), how do you plan your afternoon route so that you are in the right place at the right time? Remember that you must exit the park by a few minutes after sunset.

[**Suggestion:** Late March means an afternoon entry time of 4 P.M. Sunset at this time of year is about 6:10, so you must exit by 6:30 at the latest. You therefore have only 2½ hours for the game round. Unless you happen on a superb sighting on the way, the best plan is to proceed from Mukki straight to Kanha Meadow on the main road via Sondhar Camp and Sondhar Tank. Take the eastern route around Bishanpura Meadow and go straight up to the Nakti Ghati trijunction, where you will turn right, climb to Beniphat, and then reach Kanha Meadow via either Bari Chuhri Rd. or Lukua Chappar.]

(b) Soon after sunrise in mid-November, you spot a tigress on the Sonf Road, just south of the junction with Sal Ghat. The animal heads off into the jungle slowly. You can tell by the position of the sun that the tigress is travelling northeast. She is evidently hunting or marking her territory. How might you use the park's road network to maximize the chances for another sighting of the same animal?

[**Suggestion:** Draw an imaginary line at 45° to the Sonf Road. You will see that the route of the tigress will probably intersect both Link 9 and Link 8. Proceed at a moderate pace up to Bhapsa Bahara and then turn right to check up on the chances for another sighting.]

Using Your Senses to Find a Tiger

The American ethologist George Schaller wrote that tigers hunt primarily by sight and hearing, with the sense of smell as a poor third in importance. It is a striking coincidence that your eyes and ears (and, significantly less often, your sense of smell) are the best senses to use when *you* are hunting a tiger with your camera in hand.

Tigers are fond of using roads to patrol their territories or to seek indications of prey, so seeing a tiger on the road is not uncommon, especially during the early morning (sunrise +90 minutes) or the late afternoon (sunset –90 minutes). But the road network covers only a tiny fraction of the park's surface area, and roads offer little or no cover, which is one of the tiger's most basic needs.

Quite often, then, tigers move through deep jungle, long grass, bamboo thickets, or along the edge (called the "ecotone") of forest and open meadow. Tigers love the deep gullies or nallahs made by watercourses, which offer them cool shade as well as excellent opportunities for the ambush of an unwary deer. (Chital, for example, are often drawn to such spots, since they must drink once a day.) Even when they are nearby, tigers can be so silent and perfectly camouflaged in their surroundings that it is said that for each tiger you spot in the jungle, five tigers have already seen you. So, if you are not lucky enough to see a tiger ambling down a road or sitting out in the open, how can you improve your chances of a sighting?

The key to successful tiger spotting lies in the jungle's reactions to the animal's movement. When the king of the forest is on the move, his kingdom is as responsive as the court of any of the great Mughal emperors or the monarchs of Vijayanagar. Peacocks blare, sambar bell, spotted deer call, langurs explode in cough-like alarms, jungle fowl screech, bison whistle softly, and barking deer emit the impossibly raucous bark for which they are named (it can be heard at distances of a kilometre or more). The continuous repetition of such calls, as well as their combination from two or more species in the same small area of forest, is a very good sign that a tiger is moving nearby. Because of langurs' exceptionally keen sight and their privileged vantage point, langur alarm calls are especially reliable.

Using your ears to listen to what other animals are saying, then, is a good method of locating a tiger. Ask your driver or guide to identify alarm calls as they occur, and train your sense of hearing to remain alert. Needless to say, this is one reason why you should not pass the time in idle chatter during a game drive; in fact, a minimum of conversation may insure a maximum number of sightings.

Training your eyes on other animals is helpful as well—tempting as it may be to eyeball the landscape uninterruptedly for a glimpse of those orange and black stripes. Too much concentration on trying to see a tiger can be frustrating: after all, the pattern of the big cat's coat has evolved in an almost perfect match with the tawny and dark palette of the long grasses and the dappled light of sal forest and bamboo thicket. Keep an eye on the chital or spotted deer, by far the most common large mammal in Kanha. When they sense danger, chital react with a distinctive body posture. Ceasing to graze, they stand with head up, stock still, with ears erect and swivelled to sense movement. Like langurs in the trees, chital on the ground often stare in the direction of the perceived threat. As the threat level increases, their stubby tails go up, so that the white underside functions as a signal flag. Depending on the terrain and other factors (possibly including an instinctive sense of the predator's intentions), chital may slowly drift away from the area, or they may flee with long, rushing leaps.

Sambar behaviour resembles that of chital, but since sambar live in a denser habitat and move around in smaller parties or are solitary, you should keep some differences in mind. A sambar may stand stock still merely because a vehicle is passing, for example. But if the tail is up and the animal repeatedly strikes the ground with one of its forefeet, or if it stares fixedly at some point inside the forest, it is quite possible that something other than the vehicle—a nearby tiger or leopard—is the cause for the deer's alarm.

Observing the behaviour of chital and sambar may thus yield productive clues to a tiger's presence. These deer are major items in the tiger's diet at Kanha, so it is no surprise that their instinct for survival triggers alertness mechanisms, from which interested humans on the sidelines can profit.

Besides the larger mammals, many birds as well offer clues in this game of detection. We have already mentioned the peacock's abrupt, single-note blare or honk, which can be readily distinguished from the harsh, echoing rise and fall of its normal cry.

Peacocks will also suddenly take flight when alarmed, as will waterfowl. The Indian Roller (*Coracias bengalensis*), one of Kanha's most common, beautifully coloured birds, is sometimes said to have a sharp, click-like alarm call. Tree Pies may suddenly break out into raucous chattering when alarmed. Lapwings, well described as "ceaselessly vigilant" by the great ornithologist Sálim Ali, emit a loud, screechy alarm call of four or five notes that signals their displeasure with a wide range of disturbances.

Most prominent of all are vultures and crows, whose presence on a single tree or a group of trees in a small, defined area frequently signals a kill by a predator on the ground. If the scavenging birds are collected on the ground, however, it is a reasonable assumption that the kill has been consumed or abandoned and that the predator has left the scene.

The existence of a kill site may also be suspected if jackals appear. But one should remember that jackals are efficient hunters in their own right, as well as scavengers, so that their presence in an area should always be weighed in combination with other clues. If a kill is very close by, it can be directly identified by smell.

Using your senses to focus on the other animals of the jungle, including many bird species, can be of prime importance in locating a tiger. Hearing, sight, and smell (the latter to a relatively small degree) may all aid the vehicle-bound tiger tracker who is prepared to use jungle craft for a sighting. But what about the signals given directly by the king of the jungle himself, or by his *maharani* the tigress? In short, what about the tiger's famous roar?

By the standards of the animal kingdom, tigers are relatively silent. Although the *a-a-oh-oun* of a tiger reverberating around Kanha Meadow at sunset is an unforgettable sound, tigers do not roar with the frequency of lions, for example. They are capable of making a variety of softer calls. These vocalizations, like the tiger's ear position, tail movements, and body posture, can express a spectrum of different moods or needs. For example, the soft exhalation of air designated by the German term *prusten* seems associated with pleasure or satisfaction. A tigress uses an unobtrusive contact call to summon her cubs. Tigers may roar, grunt, or moan softly when calling out for a mate. When a chance encounter leads to a fight, a tiger may roar at high volume; when only mildly disturbed, it may produce a muted, sinister grumble or growl. Such a sound may also accompany the facial grimace or *flehmen* (also a German term) that a tiger uses when a special organ,

Pug Marks

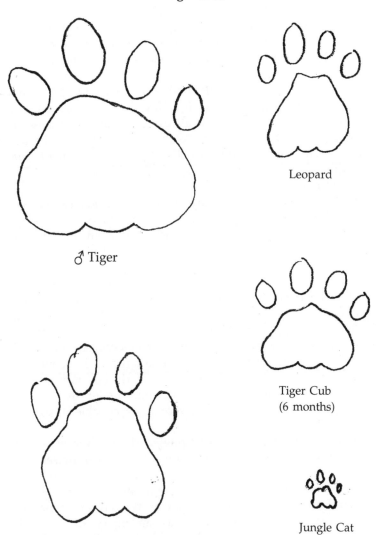

♂ Tiger

Leopard

Tiger Cub
(6 months)

♀ Tiger

Jungle Cat

[Scale: approximately $^1/_3$ actual size]

located on the roof of the animal's mouth, operates to evaluate scent.

The sounds directly produced by tigers are not likely to be nearly as important to the tracker as the visible traces of the animal's travel on the ground. Reading these signs in their totality is a complex, challenging task that can demand the effort and accumulated experience of a lifetime. The casual tourist cannot aspire to the skill of a tracker such as Jim Corbett, the legendary hunter of man-eating tigers in the 1920s, or to the expertise of the Baiga and Gond tribals still living within Kanha today. A broken stalk of grass, a drag mark at the road's edge: apparently minuscule changes in the landscape can speak loud and clear to an experienced observer.

However, even an amateur may be aided by evidence of "tiger sign," as tracks, droppings, and other indications of a tiger's presence are called. By far the most prominent evidence is furnished by the impressions left by the pads and toes of a tiger's feet. These impressions are called **pug marks**.

If an imaginary square were placed around the extremities of an adult male tiger's pug mark, the dimensions might measure anywhere from 14 to 17 cm (5½ - 7 inches) on each side. A typical adult female's pug marks would square off within a range of 11½ - 15 cm (or 4½ - 6 inches). Exceptions may occur, of course. On several occasions in 1994, we sighted one large male nicknamed Saddam Hussein by the Kanha mahouts. Early one morning we measured his pug marks in the soft mud under the Sulcum River bridge on Sijhora Road. They were an improbable 20 x 20 cm (or 8 x 8 inches).

Careful examination of a tiger's pug marks can reveal several kinds of information: sex, direction and rate of travel, presence of dependent cubs with a mother, and other activities such as drinking, rolling, sitting, or even making a kill. If the impressions on the substrate are very clear, one may even tell if the animal has some unusual characteristics, such as an injury or a highly distinctive identifying trait. Some trackers can even tell the approximate time that tiger pug marks were made.

How Many Tigers Are There?

The casual visitor is not likely to enter into the complex (and hotly contested) area of using pug marks to census the number of individual tigers in a protected area. Nevertheless, the brief summary below of how pug marks have been used in this way may be of interest. Readers wishing to skip over this discussion should proceed directly to the section headed "Tiger Sightings and the Tiger Show" (page 25).

The issue of tiger census, which has provoked such controversy since the late 1980s, presents several inter-related problems. When Project Tiger was accused by some critics of publishing grossly inflated estimates of the number of tigers within protected areas, it was duly noted that census techniques were largely developed by park management, and management is inevitably subjected to political pressures. For some years, Project Tiger and Forest Department officials responded to their critics with a single, ostensibly scientific chain of reasoning. Their premise was that, just as tigers have unique facial markings above the eyes, no two tigers have identical pug marks. In the same way that human beings can be accurately identified by fingerprints (and, more recently, by their DNA), so could each and every tiger be told apart from every other individual by its pug marks.

The concept that pug marks never lie was widely supported for years by many (but not all) experts across a wide spectrum, ranging from Jim Corbett onwards to H. S. Panwar, Kanha's energetic field director in the 1980s. (In fact, an article by Panwar entitled "A Note on Tiger Census: A Technique Based on Pug Mark Tracings" is one of the research papers on display in Room 1 of the Kanha Museum.) Field biologists joined trackers and park managers to applaud the method's potential. Even today, the ability of Dr. Charles McDougal, a tiger expert based at Tiger Tops in Nepal's Royal Chitwan National Park, to distinguish the pug marks of individual tigers continues to hold many of McDougal's colleagues in awe.

Yet Billy Arjan Singh, one of India's most famous tiger-wallahs, has incisively criticized the basic premise of the use of pug marks in tiger census, as has Fateh Singh Rathore, former Field Director of Ranthambhore, who served for years in the jungle and became a distinguished photographer as well. These skeptics argue that soil conditions, as well as the outlines of the pug marks themselves, may be very deceptive. More troubling still for the critics has been the implementation of the census on a practical level, since—even if the basic premise were correct—the actual observation and tracing of pug marks on glass plates by thousands of minimally trained personnel, as well as by volunteers and raw recruits, would leave a very substantial margin of error.

In 1993 Dr. Ullas Karanth, a well-known field biologist based in Nagarahole National Park in southern Karnataka, published a study showing that a group of experienced wildlife managers could not arrive at the correct identification of sample sets of tiger pug marks. The pug marks of 4 individual tigers were used in the study. The experts offered the following estimates for the "population" being counted: 6, 7, 13, 23, and 24! Karanth's blind test prompted a few more ironic retellings of the famous story about the six blind men who tried to figure out the elephant.

With the support of the Wildlife Conservation Society in New York (whose research arm is headed by George Schaller), Karanth has recently developed two alternative approaches to tiger census. The first is a direct camera trap method, in which pictures from a variety of angles are taken automatically when an infrared beam is broken. The stripe patterns of the animals are then compared. Interestingly, some basic features of this technique were pioneered as early as the 1920s by the photographer F. W. Champion, whose book *With a Camera in Tigerland* still makes for entertaining reading.

Karanth's second method derives from a theoretical model in which predator-prey density ratios are analyzed and extrapolation from sample transect counts is employed to estimate populations within an entire protected area. The aim here, as with the first technique, is to specify population **ranges**, rather than exact numbers. Even more important, as Karanth stresses, is the spotting of trends: upward, downward, or stable. Both of Karanth's techniques have significant advantages, but neither has escaped criticism from his scientific colleagues.

In the computer age, ever subtler and more nuanced differentiation of stripe patterns, cheek marking, and pug marks may be possible. But we are also in a time of critical threat to the tiger's very survival in the wild, with some pessimists predicting extinction early in the twenty-first century for all five subspecies. It is doubtful that counting precise numbers for populations of fewer than 100 tigers should consume so much energy and so many resources. If the poaching threat to the tiger can be surmounted and the scattered populations stabilized, there might be greater scope for meticulous debates over census figures. At present, however, such debates have the air of fiddling while Rome burns.

In any event, the case of Kanha is relatively uncontroversial. For this is India's best-protected, best-equipped, and best-monitored reserve under the Project Tiger umbrella. Often in the spotlight,

Kanha's managers have worked hard to maintain credibility. Their reports of tiger census over the years have met with general acceptance. Based on our own visits to the park since 1990, our direct observation of tigers and tiger sign, and our interviews with park personnel and independent observers, we see no reason to doubt the official claim of approximately 100 tigers at Kanha. (As of this writing, the most recent census was held in May 1997.)

Tiger Sightings and the Tiger Show

If you are lucky enough to sight one of the 100 or so tigers in Kanha from your vehicle, here are some practical suggestions to make the most of your experience.

1. DO NOT drive too close. The tiger should not feel threatened by your presence. Generally, a distance of 30 metres (100 ft.) can offer a good sighting. Some tigers are quite used to vehicles, and they may approach much nearer of their own accord. If this happens, remain calm and quiet. Tigers rarely charge vehicles without provocation, and they virtually never come into physical contact with them. A show of aggression is overwhelmingly likely to be a "mock charge," in which the tiger will rear up short or swerve aside after having made its point.

2. You will get better photos and learn more about the tiger's behaviour if you and your driver resist the temptation to follow or move parallel to a moving tiger during the sighting. If the tiger is in view for a considerable time and is moving, drive slowly to a point that is within a respectful distance in order to keep pace, and then stop.

3. NEVER crowd a tiger off the road, or permit your driver or guide to intercept the animal or prevent a road-cross. Tigers are by nature suspicious of disturbance in open areas where they lack cover, and there should be no interference with their efforts to travel to different parts of their range.

4. NEVER toss or throw an object at a tiger, and never try to provoke it for "more dramatic" photos by shouting at the animal. This sort of behaviour is so counterproductive and silly that the admonition may seem needless, but people do actually behave like this upon occasion.

5. If the tiger is genuinely irritated by your presence, it will find a way to leave the scene rapidly. If you want to

appreciate and admire one of the most spectacular mammals left on this planet, it is in your own interest to be quiet and non-threatening. You are in no danger.

6. That being said, all bets are off if you are foolish enough to get out of your vehicle. Then you certainly are in danger, whether or not you have the tiger actually in view. NEVER get down from your vehicle anywhere inside the park without the permission of your guide. Do not "hang out" of the vehicle, with legs, arms, or other body parts extending over the side.

7. For a more enjoyable sighting, try to identify what the tiger is doing. Also attempt to anticipate its movements (this is especially important if you are taking video footage). Is it resting, scent-marking, stalking, or possibly just moving from one point to another in its home range? Are potential prey in the vicinity? How is the tiger reacting to one or more vehicles? Does it seem to be heading steadily or purposefully in a single direction? Finally—perhaps most important of all—is the tiger male or female? If it is female, are its udders swollen, indicating that small cubs may be hidden nearby? Your park guide may be very helpful in answering these and other questions.

8. All tiger and leopard sightings by vehicle should be recorded in the special registers maintained for this purpose at Kisli and at Mukki. Be sure to supply accurate data in the correct columns, including the time and place of the sighting, the sex of the animal (if known), your vehicle plate number, and the name of your guide.

In addition to sightings by vehicle, Kanha also offers its visitors the chance of seeing tigers by elephant back. In fact, the **tiger show**, as it is locally referred to, offers most tourists their best chance of seeing a tiger in Kanha.

Early in the morning at Kanha, Kisli, and Gorhela Camp on the Mukki side of the park, the park mahouts and their elephants begin tracking operations. Tracking may be suspended or cancelled if special circumstances warrant, but the park makes considerable efforts to insure that the trackers look for tigers with reasonable regularity. If the mahouts are successful in finding a cooperative tiger (namely, one that is content to sit still for a considerable time), they send a wireless message to headquarters. Visitors are then allowed to drive to the nearest road position, whence they are taken into the jungle on elephant back to view the tiger. The mahouts are successful roughly 60% of the time.

What sounds like a simple system has, in fact, developed with astonishing complexity, and the first-time visitor to Kanha may be excused if he or she is bewildered by some of the twists and turns in the procedure. Some helpful hints follow below. Since most tiger shows originate at park headquarters in Kanha Village, our suggestions are specifically tailored for Kanha. The system is somewhat more informal and flexible at Kisli and in Mukki Range.

1. The park management uses a token system to establish the priority of vehicles for the tiger show. Tokens (which are really slips of paper indicating the number plate of tourist vehicles) are issued to the vehicle, rather than to the individual person. Therefore, a single token in the queue may be valid for a group that fills a minibus.

2. A token is only issued if the mahouts and the park officials decide that there will indeed be a tiger show. However, vehicles are permitted to "preregister" for a slot in the order starting at 6:30 or 6:45 A.M. at Kanha Village. If you are interested in getting a token later in the morning, you are well advised to drive straight to Kanha and then to request your guide to put your vehicle number on the list.

3. After preregistering, take advantage of the spectacular early-morning views of Kanha Meadow (and, incidentally, of some of the best time for birding) by driving in such areas as Bari Chuhri, Schaller Hide, Bison Road, Shravan Tal, Sijhora Road (up to the Sulcum River bridge), and the lower part of Link 7 (see map facing page 16). You can check back for "tiger news" at Kanha Village at 8 A.M. and 9 A.M., when wireless messages from the mahouts in the field are scheduled to be reported. Kanha Village also furnishes tea and light snacks, as well as rest room facilities. After 7 A.M. you may tour the highly informative exhibits in the Kanha Museum (see pages 11 to 13).

4. If there is to be a tiger show, your park guide will be issued an official token for your vehicle. Vehicles are dispatched to the venue in shifts in order to prevent crowding on the road and general confusion or disorder. The elephants at Kanha track within a radius of several kilometres from the

Meadow, so it should not take your vehicle long to reach the site.

5.   When you arrive at the tiger show venue, you should remain in your vehicle until the guide gives you the signal to get down and board the elephant. Get cameras and film ready. Elephants accommodate four adults on the howdah or platform. It is especially important that you obey the mahout's instructions.

6.   After you are seated, make sure that the bar across the howdah is hooked securely. Remain seated at all times, and pay special attention to the supervision of small children. Do not make loud noises. Protect your eyes, spectacles, and equipment when you are riding through thick jungle.

7.   The amount of viewing time permitted by the mahout will depend on circumstances, such as the number of people waiting, the tiger's behaviour, and the amount of time that the elephant has been working already. Average viewing time at a tiger show is about five minutes. Your mahout will turn the elephant so that riders on both sides have an equal chance to take photographs.

8.   If the tiger starts to move, the mahouts will often follow, and your time on the elephant will be extended. Such tracking is almost invariably exciting. But this eventuality has its downside as well, because if a tiger is determined to disappear into the jungle, the mahouts will call off the pursuit. If you are next in the queue by the roadside, you will miss the show entirely.

9.   The tiger show offers visitors some excellent chances for photography, since photographing a tiger from elephant back (provided that your mount is reasonably steady) generally allows you to get a closer shot than you can get from a vehicle. (Most of the tiger photographs in this book were taken from elephant back.) Tigers may occasionally be observed on a kill or with cubs—scenes that would rarely be observed from a vehicle.

It is easy to see that such a system depends to a high degree on the forbearance and good judgment of many participants—not least of all, the elephant and the tiger. In our personal experience of the tiger show, there is no danger to the visitor or undue disturbance to the habitat if strict rules of conduct are followed. Unfortunately, misbehaviour by tourists and mahouts became so common some years back that the show was banned in 1994 on the recommendation of the Tiger Steering Committee, a group of a dozen tiger experts set up by Project Tiger in New Delhi. In the spring of 1996, the tiger show was reintroduced, this time with significant administrative changes designed to prevent abuses. Although critics still object that the tiger show is artificial and intrusive, in our opinion it plays a valuable role in Kanha's public relations, since it furnishes most visitors their best chance of seeing a tiger in the wild. On the tiger show, see also Chapter 2 (page 97) and Chapter 4 (page 197).

More than Just Tigers

Kanha is more than just tigers, although it is hard to convince the first-time tourist of this, especially if he or she has travelled to the park with hopes firmly fixed on a tiger sighting. We should point out here that many of the clues offered above to using the senses of sight and hearing are valid and helpful for locating the other two major predator species in the park: the leopard and the wild dog (or dhole).

Leopards are primarily nocturnal, although they may operate by day in deep forest cover. Wild dogs cover large areas of varied terrain and often hunt by day. We have had wild dog sightings at all hours of the morning and afternoon, as well as at sunrise and sunset. Both leopards and wild dogs trigger alarm calls, with an interesting variant in the case of langur monkeys' response to leopards. The langur is the mainstay of the leopard's diet in Kanha, and the big cat's climbing ability often causes langurs to jump excitedly from branch to branch as well as to give their alarm calls. When alarmed by a tiger, langurs are more apt to call from a stationary perch.

The presence of wild dogs may occasionally be suspected from the absence of all potential prey species in an area. Wild dogs are coursers (as opposed to stalkers), who pursue their quarry with skill and unflagging determination. One February morning in 1993, we were riding in the Paparphat area around 11 A.M. We had just commented on how unusually quiet the area around Sandukhol was—with not a chital, a langur, or a wild boar in sight for several kilometres. When the *talao* came into view, the reason was evident: a pack of seven wild dogs lay comfortably ensconced around the waterhole, enjoying a late-morning siesta.

If there are no signs of the king of the jungle or the secondary predators, open your eyes and ears to other intriguing features of the flora and fauna. Remember that the ecosystem is a seamless whole: grasses, insects, birds, trees, and mammals are all linked together in a fascinating, variegated mosaic (see Chapter 2). In particular, birders may wish to plan their routes in advance by noting the following locations on the park map (see page 16): Kanha Meadow (especially Manhar Nallah Road, Schaller Hide, and Shravan Tal), the waterhole on Bari Chuhri Road, Nakti Ghati, Bamhni Dadar, the small ponds to the west of Bishanpura Meadow, and Sondhar Tank.

Field Guides and Wildlife Photography

Two field guides are basic companions for a visit to Kanha: S. H. Prater's *The Book of Indian Animals* (third edition, 1971) and Sálim Ali's *The Book of Indian Birds* (twelfth edition, 1996). Both are available from the Bombay Natural History Society and are also sold at many book shops and tourist hotels in the larger cities. Besides these basic reference works, a number of specialized studies exist on trees, reptiles, and butterflies, as well as on individual species of mammals: see the bibliography at the end of this volume.

The subject of wildlife photography embraces a wide range of individual preferences. In general, you will require at least a 200 mm zoom lens to get anything more than general landscape pictures at Kanha. Ideally, it is best to outfit yourself with a minimum of two lenses: for example, 28-80 mm for wide-angle shots and a zoom lens (100-300 mm) for close-ups of animals and the larger birds. Video camera charges at Kanha are reasonable: several years ago, the daily fee was reduced from Rs. 200/- to Rs. 100/- (compared with a daily video camera fee at Dudhwa National Park of Rs. 500/-). Be sure to protect your camera, lenses, and film from the dust. Bring a supply of plastic bags, and don't change lenses or film in bright sunlight or while moving in an open vehicle. Bean bags, monopods, and tripods may be useful for stability, depending on your equipment and the quality of the images for which you are aiming.

When visiting Kanha, it's a good idea to bring more film than you think you will need. (One morning in April 1998, we used five rolls during a single tiger show that lasted nearly an hour!) Don't forget to pack at least one extra camera battery. Remember that the use of flash is prohibited inside the park.

It is virtually impossible to get a good shot of an animal if your vehicle is moving or if the engine is on, causing vibration. Insist that your driver stop and turn off the motor. If you're really serious about photography with a zoom lens, try to arrange a private vehicle, since other people may cause camera shake, even if they shift position only slightly in their seats.

Try to tour the park in an open car, such as a Maruti Gypsy or a Land Rover. Inside a closed car, your opportunities for photography will be far more limited.

At the lodge or hotel, always store your film in a cool place. Because of the tiger's favoured habitat (forest cover or "edge"), you should be prepared to use film with an ASA range of 64 (such as Kodachrome slides) all the way through 100, 200, 400, or even 1000 ASA (for slides and prints). Fast film is especially useful at sunrise or sunset, or if a tiger is located in deep shade.

CHAPTER 2

THE KANHA ECOSYSTEM

No BIOLOGICAL COMMUNITY on earth exists in isolation. Human beings have acquired an especially vivid awareness of this truth in the past quarter of a century. Concern about pollution of air, land, and water has become acute throughout much of the world, and the threats to endangered species have received worldwide media attention.

It is within the context of an "escape from civilization"— or of a "return to nature"—that many tourists all over the planet make their first visit to a national park. At a sanctuary such as Kanha, visitors are not likely to be disappointed. They may gain an especially rewarding appreciation of the park, however, if they look at it as an **ecosystem**. This term, coined by the British plant biologist A. G. Tansley in 1935, has been defined as "all the living organisms in a particular environment, together with the physical environment itself." Ultimately, as we will see in Chapter 4 (page 186), tourists themselves are a component of the ecosystem comprising Kanha.

In this chapter, we examine the idea of an ecosystem in Section 1. One of the most basic links among species in such a system is the transfer of energy in the food chain (see the illustration of the energy pyramid on page 34). Another important set of relationships stems from certain keystone species. Conservation of the tiger, for example, is a critical environmental issue for India now, not just because of this creature's own magnificence, but because of the value of the species to whole ecosystems.

In Section 2, we give a brief overview of Kanha's vegetation: habitats, grasslands, and trees. Section 3 offers detailed descriptions of the major mammals in the park. These are divided into two groups: the 15 species most commonly seen by tourists, and another 15 that are more rarely glimpsed (including 4 species of bats). Section 4 is devoted to the birds and reptiles.

In the chapter as a whole, we are acutely conscious of the limitations of this profile of an ecosystem. We have little to say, for example, about geology, amphibians, wildflowers, butterflies, and lesser life forms such as termites, millipedes, spiders, beetles, and ants. These are all part of the ecosystem as well. Perhaps, in a future edition of this book, we can expand the portrait of Kanha to do them more justice.

1. THE ECOSYSTEM CONCEPT

Producers and Consumers

Ecosystems exist in many different sizes and shapes. They may range, for example, from a small pond to a vast desert. Within any particular ecosystem, water, soil, plants, and animals interact. Mineral nutrients are recycled between living and non-living components of the system. Plants absorb energy, and the process of photosynthesis helps them to grow. These plants are often called *producers*. They make their own food.

If we use a geometrical shape to illustrate some of the most important relationships within an ecosystem, the producers would be at the base of a pyramid. Herbivores, or vegetation-eaters, are considered *primary consumers*. At Kanha, these include the four species of deer (sambar, barasingha, chital, and barking deer), as well as the antelope (nilgai, blackbuck, chowsingha) and the gaur. Vegetation is also an important part in the diet of langurs, sloth bears, and wild boar. Primary consumers sustain themselves by eating plants, exclusively or for the most part. They are on the next-higher level of the pyramid, above the producers.

One level above the primary consumers are the *secondary consumers*, who are sometimes called predators or carnivores. Although these species may sometimes eat plant matter, their diet is primarily other animals. Carnivores themselves are often further subdivided into two categories: primary and secondary. Primary carnivores, such as mongooses and foxes, eat only (or mostly) herbivores. Secondary carnivores, such as tigers and leopards, may eat other carnivores as well as herbivores.

The Food Chain and Energy Transfer

The relationships of producers, herbivores, and primary and secondary carnivores are set out in the diagram of the food chain below. This diagram, in the shape of a pyramid, shows how energy is transferred among the various levels of an ecosystem.

From the bottom to the top of the pyramid, an energy transfer takes place at each level. However, at each stage in an upward direction, there is also an energy loss. Only a small percentage of the energy captured from the sun by the Kanha grasslands, for example, is used by the chital in the park. Furthermore, many body parts of chital are not digestible by tigers, leopards, or wild dogs, so only a small percentage of the energy that is available from these herbivores gets transferred to the carnivores. This is why the "food chain" of an ecosystem is commonly represented in the shape of a pyramid. It is also the reason that there are many fewer carnivores than herbivores in a typical ecosystem.

The **food chain** is a sequence in which energy is transferred from one set of organisms to another. A highly simplified food chain for the Kanha ecosystem is shown in the **energy pyramid** below. The levels in the pyramid show steps in the transfer of energy.

The Energy Pyramid

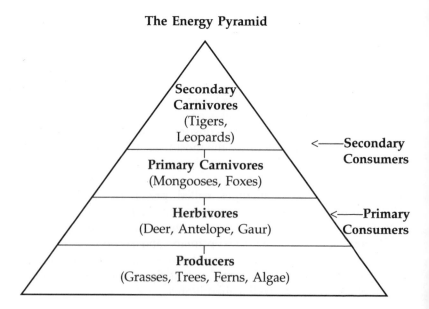

To a certain extent, the pyramid shape, despite its appeal as a graphic representation of some basic facts about ecosystem dynamics, is misleading. Most species seldom move in a straight line up and down the food (or "trophic") levels. A more common pattern is for a species to feed on several items at the next-lower level, and to be preyed on in turn by several different species at the next-higher level.

Furthermore, the pyramid does not show the vital recycling operations accomplished by species that feed on dead plants and animal wastes. These species, which include jackals, vultures, dung beetles, worms, fungi, and bacteria, break down complex tissues and other organic matter. Such species are sometimes called *decomposers*.

Why is it important to think of Kanha as an ecosystem? In the first place, the concept of *linkage* among all the components of a system enables the visitor to understand some key relationships. An outstanding example of such links is the connection between tiger densities and suitable habitat for chital, which are the tiger's most important prey in the park. During the 1980s, the park management surveyed the core area and classified over 120 subdivisions of Kanha according to the suitability of habitat for chital. (If the same evaluation were carried out today, the results would not be very different.) On page 36, we show a map derived from an exhibit in the Kanha Museum presenting the results of this analysis. A brief comparison of this map with the map of tiger territories on page 37 emphasizes the correlation between prey density and predator density.

Certain relationships within an ecosystem are less obvious, however. For example, Kanha is home to two species of largely diurnal ungulates that live in open grasslands: the blackbuck and the barasingha. Each of these is a spectacular animal, and there is no record to our knowledge of friction or aggression between these species. Yet there is a built-in conflict between the antelope and the deer *within the Kanha ecosystem*. Blackbuck are short-grass grazers, while barasingha favour long grass, not only for forage but for the protection of their fawns against predators. As of this writing (mid-1998), blackbuck numbers have fallen to a miniscule level in Kanha. Yet any attempt to restore this species within the ecosystem will come at the direct expense of the barasingha. Open meadows are at a premium in Kanha, and many grassland areas are already suffering from regression due to overgrazing by chital, the park's

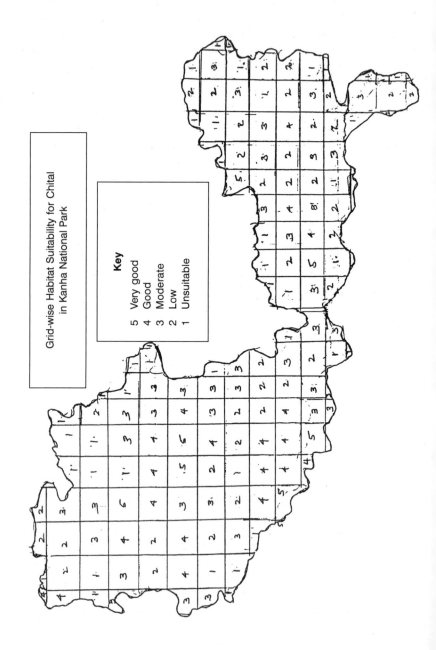

Grid-wise Habitat Suitability for Chital in Kanha National Park

Key

5 Very good
4 Good
3 Moderate
2 Low
1 Unsuitable

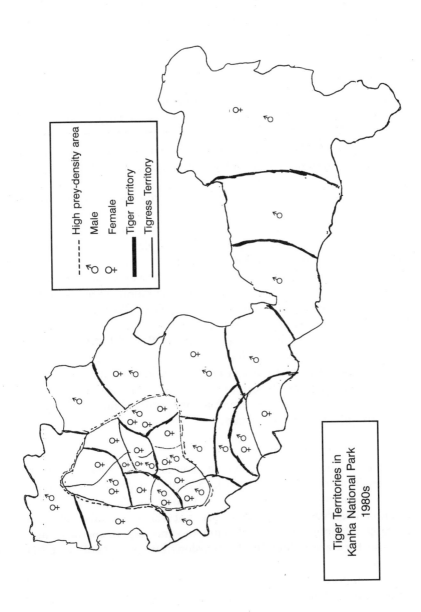

Tiger Territories in
Kanha National Park
1980s

High prey-density area
♂ Male
♀ Female
Tiger Territory
Tigress Territory

most common ungulate. Kanha managers, whose scope and resources for intervention are limited, must choose between the barasingha and the blackbuck in restoration schemes. Given the hard-ground barasingha's precarious status as an endangered species, the choice is clear: the park must try to foster the barasingha population, almost certainly at the expense of the blackbuck.

Keystone Species

Associated with the ecosystem concept is the idea of *keystone species*. These are species that determine the ability of large numbers of other species within a given ecosystem or region to maintain themselves and thrive. If a keystone species is allowed to disappear from an ecosystem, many other species may decline or be lost as well.

Top predators such as the tiger are among the most important keystone species. Decreases in the population of tigers may result in a snowball effect within the ecosystem: herbivores such as chital may multiply disproportionately, for example, and the effects on vegetation may be catastrophic.

Keystone species are not restricted, however, to the large carnivores or the charismatic animals commonly seen on WWF posters. For instance, the Indian Flying Fox *(Pteropus giganteus)*, along with about 50 other fruit bats in its genus, is vitally linked to numerous plant species in the tropics of the Old World. Many species of plants are totally dependent on these bats for pollination and seed dispersal. In a number of cases throughout the Pacific and Indian Ocean regions, these plants have important economic value. Among their products, for example, are fruits, ebony, mahogany, and various dyes and medicines.

Change: A Constant Factor

Ecosystems not only involve a complex network of inter-relationships, but they are also in a continual process of change. As the American ecologist Frank Golley of the University of Georgia observes: "Ecosystems are not stable, because of their unstable components of soil, climate, and organisms and also because they are vulnerable to invasions by components of other systems."

It is important to appreciate the dynamic, shifting nature of ecosystems because, all too often, visitors and managers alike are tempted to settle for oversimplified descriptions. Why are tigers more common in Kanha Meadow this year than last? Why has cooperative hunting by jackals on the Meadow increased over the past few years? What might have caused the sal trees to bloom earlier in any given year or to be attacked by a borer? If the wild dog population should increase for several years in a row, what would be the effect on Kanha leopards? What impact will the steadily growing number of tourists and their vehicles be likely to have on Kanha's vegetation, mammals, and birds?

These questions are only samples of the ongoing queries that spring from the varying climate conditions, accumulated observations, and tourist visitorship every season in Kanha, as well as from ever-continuing progress in ecological studies.

2. THE VEGETATION

Kanha's flora, or plant life, is the underpinning of the park's entire ecosystem. Tigers could not live here without prey, such as chital, sambar, wild boar, and barasingha. These animals, in turn, could not subsist without the forage that the plant life furnishes them. Langurs, sloth bears, and birds depend on fruits, flowers, nectar, and forbs for survival. Insects, spiders, and trees have a complex, interdependent set of relationships, in which spiders help to regulate the defoliant pressures on trees by controlling the insect population. Termites, whose digestive system turns decaying vegetation into soil-enriching nutrients, are a major item in the sloth bear's diet, exemplifying dynamic linkages among insects, plant life, and one of the park's major mammals. In these and many other similar examples, an ecosystem approach is, as always, the key to a more sensitive, accurate understanding and appreciation of the park.

Habitats

There have been various descriptions of the habitats in Kanha Tiger Reserve. The Kanha Management Plan of 1988-89, for example, distinguished ten vegetation cover types within the park's core area as follows. Figures in parentheses give the percentage of the core area for each type.

1. Sal (defined as a zone with over 50% sal trees, *Shorea robusta*): mostly in valleys (18.08%)

2. Sal/bamboo: mainly lower slopes (5.07%)
3. Mixed sal, together with jamun, saja, and other species (13.21%)
4. Mixed sal/bamboo (7.34%)
5. Mixed: upper plateaux areas (16.05%)
6. Mixed bamboo (24.8%)
7. Valley grasslands (6.4%)
8. Dadar (plateau) grasslands (2.61%)
9. Grasslands with mixed forest tree species (2.88%)
10. Agriculture and human habitation (3.5%)

Another, more immediately helpful classification of Kanha habitats is that of Canadian biologist Renata Jaremovic, who is now based in Australia and who carried out a research project in Kanha in the mid-1990s. She identifies the following six readily recognizable habitats within the park, together with the major mammals that make use of them.

1. **Sal Forest:** Chital, sambar, wild boar, langur, tiger, leopard, jungle cat, sloth bear, wild dog.
2. **Sal/Mixed Bamboo:** Sambar, gaur, wild boar, langur, tiger, leopard.
3. **Miscellaneous Mixed Bamboo:** Same species as above.
4. **Miscellaneous Mixed Deciduous:** Sambar, gaur, chowsingha, sloth bear, langur, tiger, leopard.
5. **Grassland:** Chital, barasingha, blackbuck, chowsingha (on plateaux), wild boar, langur, tiger, wild dog.
6. **Habitation:** Used by species accustomed to humans.

The sal tree *(Shorea robusta)* and various species of bamboo (especially *Dendrocalamus strictus*) are the most prominent features of Kanha's extensive flora. These species have complex, distinctive flowering patterns, with sal blooming annually over a period of several months and deciduous throughout the year, and many bamboo species flowering only once during an extremely long life cycle that may span several decades.

Officials have estimated that Kanha is home to more than 600 species of flowering plants. A list of 50 water plants was included in the Kanha Management Plan of 1988-89 (Kotwal and Parihar, 1989). Aquatic plants such as water lilies are of considerable importance to the barasingha. In *Kanha National Park: A Handbook* (1991), H. S. Panwar points out that Kanha's rich flora is largely due to the variety of landforms and soil types, as well as to the substantial amount of annual rainfall, which averages about 1,600 mm.

Grasslands

Considerable research has been carried out on the Kanha grasslands. An exhibit in the Kanha Museum entitled "Incredible Grasses" effectively draws attention to the role of grasses as "silent superstars." The exhibit stresses the amazing resilience of these species to drought, frost, and fire. As food and shelter providers, grasses yield bounty to a broad range of life forms. An acre of grassland in Kanha, in fact, supports more living forms than does any other kind of habitat. Insects, birds, herbivores, and carnivores: all make efficient use of the grasslands. Grasses do not need insect or bird pollinators, despite the hospitality they furnish to these guests, because the wind is sufficient to pollinate grasses.

Despite repeated trampling and grazing, grasses have an impressive regenerative ability—within limits. When grasslands deteriorate into a regressive state, park management is faced with various choices regarding intervention. Among these options are carefully controlled burning, weed eradication, the clearing of invasive woodland species (such as lendia, pallas, and tendu trees), and the enclosing of areas to permit regeneration.

The Kanha Management Plan of 1988-89 identified 16 distinct communities of grasslands distributed throughout the park. These regions account for 112 km^2 or 11.9% of the total core area. The grasslands have been formed as a result of either the abandonment or the relocation of villages. Some grasslands are naturally maintained because of frost; others must be continually monitored. Some examples of the Kanha grassland communities are listed below. (For locations, see park map facing page 16.)

Species	Location
Themeda triandra + Dicanthium annulatum	Bamhni Dadar
Saccharum spontaneum + Eragrostis uniloides + Ischaemum indicum + Dimeria ornithopoda + Imperata cylindrica	Kanha Meadow
Themeda triandra + Themeda quadrivalvis	Kodai Dadar
Heteropogon contortus + Themeda triandra	Sondhar, Ghorela, Mundi Dadar
Heteropogon contortus + Saccharum spontaneum	Sonf

With reference to the above classification of grasslands species, it is important to note a second distinction. Bamhni Dadar, Kodai Dadar, and Mundi Dadar are plateau habitats, and their higher elevation markedly differentiates them from valley grassland habitats, such as Sonf, Sondhar, Gorhela, and Kanha Meadow.

Trees

Some common trees of Kanha are listed in the chart below, which gives their botanical as well as their familiar names.

Common Name	Botanical Name
Amaltas	*Cassia fistula*
Aonla	*Emblica officinalis*
Arjun (Kohwa)	*Terminalia arjuna*
Bahera	*Terminalia bellarica*
Banyan	*Ficus bengalensis*
Ber	*Ziziphus mauritiana*
Bija	*Pterocarpus marsupium*
Dhawa	*Anogeissus latifolia*
Haldu	*Adina cardifolia*
Harra	*Terminalia chebula*
Imli (Tamarind)	*Tamarindus indica*
Jamun	*Syzygium cuminii*
Kasahi	*Bridelia squamosa*
Kosum	*Schleichera oleosa*
Kulu	*Sterculia urens*
Lendia	*Lagerstroema parviflora*
Mahua	*Madhuca indica*
Mahul	*Bauhinia vahlii*
Mango	*Mangifera indica*
Pallas	*Butea monosperma*
Peepal	*Ficus religiosa*
Pukhri	*Ficus virens*
Saja	*Terminalia tomentosa*
Sal	*Shorea robusta*
Salai (Frankincense)	*Boswellia serrata*
Semal (Silk Cotton)	*Bombax malabaricum*
Sendur	*Mallotus philippensis*
Teak	*Tectona grandis*

Common Name	Botanical Name
Tendu	*Diospyros melanoxylon*
Thwar	*Bauhinia roxburghiana*
Umer	*Ficus glumerata*

Guides to Indian trees include the following: P. V. Bole and Yogini Vaghani, *Field Guide to the Common Trees of India* (1986); Pippa Mukherjee, *Common Trees of India* (1983); K. S. Sahni, *The Book of Indian Trees* (1998); and H. Santapau, *Common Trees* (1966).

3. THE MAJOR MAMMALS

In this section, we give species accounts for 15 major mammals in Kanha Tiger Reserve. We have personally observed and photographed all of these species (Category A), either within the core area or the buffer zone. At least ten of these species, including the tiger, are commonly seen in the course of a visit of two or three days to the park. Several other species have been included, although they are glimpsed comparatively rarely, because of their intrinsic interest and/or the important roles that they play in the ecosystem.

These detailed accounts are followed by very brief notes for 15 additional species of mammals that are rarely seen but are known to be present at Kanha (Category B). However, it is important to note that these two categories, even when taken together, do not constitute a comprehensive listing of all the mammals at Kanha. Regrettably, the park does not make official checklists of mammals or birds available. In *Kanha National Park: A Handbook* (1991), H. S. Panwar, a former field director, mentions the Leopard Cat *(Felis bengalensis)* as occurring in Kanha, but we were unable to obtain confirmation of recent sightings for this mammal. It is quite likely that additional species of bats occur in the park, over and above the four we have included in Category B.

The chart below lists in alphabetical order the species that receive detailed discussion in this section, together with their scientific and Hindi names. At the end of each species account, we offer advice for photographers, in addition to some tips for locating the species in the park. In the box on page 45, the 30 species of Kanha mammals are tabulated according to the classification system of orders and families used by biologists. A glance at this table will show how many of Kanha's mammals are related to each other.

Major Mammals of Kanha Tiger Reserve: Category A

Common Name	Scientific Name	Hindi Name
Barasingha	*Cervus duvauceli branderi*	barasingha
Barking Deer (Muntjac)	*Muntiacus muntjak*	kakar
Blackbuck	*Antilope cervicapra*	harna(i), mrig, krishnasara
Chital	*Axis axis*	chital
Gaur (Indian Bison)	*Bos gaurus*	gaur
Hyena	*Hyaena hyaena*	lakkar baghar
Jackal	*Canis aureus*	gidhar
Jungle Cat	*Felis chaus*	jangli billi
Langur	*Presbytis entellus*	langur
Leopard	*Panthera pardus*	tendua
Sambar	*Cervus unicolor*	sambar
Sloth Bear	*Melursus ursinus*	bhalu
Tiger	*Panthera tigris*	sher, bagh
Wild Boar	*Sus scrofa*	suar
Wild Dog	*Cuon alpinus*	dhole, jangli kutta

Other Mammals: Category B

Small Indian Civet	Nilgai (Blue Bull)
Common Palm Civet (Toddy Cat)	Chowsingha (Four-horned Antelope)
Common (Gray) Mongoose	Indian Pangolin
Indian Wolf	Indian Flying Fox
Indian Fox	Fulvous Fruit Bat
Ratel (Honey Badger)	Greater False Vampire
Indian Porcupine	Indian Pipistrelle
Indian Hare	

Families of Mammals at Kanha

Order Carnivora (Carnivores)	
Family Canidae (Dogs)	Wild Dog, Jackal, Indian Fox, Indian Wolf
Felidae (Cats)	Tiger, Leopard, Jungle Cat
Ursidae (Bears)	Sloth Bear
Mustelidae (Weasels, etc.)	Ratel (Honey Badger)
Herpestidae (Mongooses)	Common (Gray) Mongoose
Viverridae (Civets, etc.)	Common Palm Civet, Small Indian Civet
Hyaenidae (Hyenas)	Striped Hyena
Order Artiodactyla (Even-toed Ungulates)	
Family Cervidae (Deer)	Sambar, Barasingha, Chital, Barking Deer
Bovidae (Cattle, Antelope, Goats)	
Subfamily Bovinae	Nilgai, Chowsingha, Gaur
Subfamily Antilopinae	Blackbuck
Suidae (Pigs)	Wild Boar
Order Rodentia (Rodents)	
Family Hystricidae (Porcupines)	Indian Porcupine
Order Primata (Primates)	
Family Cercopithecidae (Monkeys)	Common Langur
Order Pholidata (Pangolins)	
Family Manidae (Pangolins)	Indian Pangolin
Order Lagomorpha (Lagomorphs)	
Family Leporidae (Rabbits, Hares)	Indian Hare
Order Chiroptera (Bats)	
Suborder Megachiroptera	
Family Pteropodidae (Old World Fruit Bats)	Fulvous Fruit Bat, Indian Flying Fox
Suborder Microchiroptera	
Family Megadermatidae (False Vampire Bats)	Greater False Vampire
Family Vespertilionidae (Evening Bats)	Indian Pipistrelle

Barasingha

The name barasingha means "twelve-tined," although the impressive racks of antlers on the stags of this species may develop twenty points or more. Three subspecies of this majestic deer are now recognized: a northern race in Uttar Pradesh and Nepal (*Cervus duvauceli duvauceli*); an eastern race in Assam (*Cervus duvauceli ranjitsinhi*); and the southern or hard-ground barasingha of Madhya Pradesh (*Cervus duvauceli branderi*). The hard-ground barasingha, found only at Kanha, represents one of the park's outstanding contributions to conservation in the past thirty years. From a low of 66 animals in 1970, the barasingha population has rebounded to 325-350. It is fair to say that Kanha has rescued the barasingha of Middle India from extinction. A combination of careful stewardship, good science, and decisive administration made this dramatic success story possible.

Barasingha are a glowing, medium shade of brown. Full-grown stags measure about 130 cm (somewhat over 4 feet) at the shoulder and weigh approximately 180 kg (400 lb). Females are somewhat smaller and lighter, although the chief difference between the sexes for most of the year does not depend on size or weight but rather on the male's splendid antlers, which are often bedecked with tussocks of grass. Barasingha are closely related to the brow-antlered deer or thamin (*Cervus eldi*), whose principal distribution lies farther east in Myanmar, Thailand, and Vietnam. Unlike chital and sambar stags, whose antler development is normally limited to the six points that they attain by the age of three or four, male barasingha up to the age of nine or ten years replace the antlers that they shed annually with a continually larger rack. During the rutting season in Kanha in 1969-70, M. K. Ranjitsinh recorded a pair of antlers with a total of 22 points and a weight of 5.65 kg (12 lb.) when shed. In *The Book of Indian Animals*, S. H. Prater reported the length of average barasingha antlers as 75 cm (30 in.) around the curve, with a record of 104 cm (41 in.). The orientation of the brow tine to the angle of the beam, as well as the curved outline of the beam before its emission of vertical tines, is integral to the distinctive pattern of antlers in barasingha. An adult stag's head of antlers and his deliberate, unhurried gait result in a carriage for this animal that is unlike that of any other in Kanha. Altogether, the barasingha has justly been praised as one of the most beautiful deer in the world.

During the rutting season, which at Kanha reaches a peak in the coldest months (December-January), barasingha stags develop a swollen neck surrounded by a pronounced ruff of hair. At this time the pelage is dark brown; after the rut, the coat progressively lightens. The transition from the winter to the summer coat often makes the deer look a bit untidy, with the hair peeling off in patches. (The barasingha's inherent dignity is such, however, that even in this condition they do not look ungainly!) The ears of both stags and hinds are large and rounded, with long white or pale yellow hair on the inside. Sometimes spots are visible on adult barasingha of both sexes, as well as on fawns.

The barasingha rut occurs at different seasons of the year, depending on the habitat. The winter timing of the barasingha rut at Kanha is scarcely accidental, since it insures that, after a gestation period of 8+ months, the fawns are born at roughly the mid-point of the rains in August-September, when fodder is plentiful and the long grass affords effective concealment for offspring. Just after they shed their velvet, the antlers of stags are reddish in colour; they soon turn to brown. The larger, more dominant stags, who come into hard antler earliest, do most of the mating, and battles between stags for access to a harem are not uncommon. A luxurious mud wallow (an important adjunct to the rut) is often the prerogative of the victorious male. The barasingha stag's rutting call, which has been compared to the braying of a wild ass and is sometimes known as "bugling," is one of the animal's most distinctive vocalizations. (It may be heard on the soundtrack of Belinda Wright and Stanley Breeden's classic film, *Land of the Tiger*.)

Barasingha are highly gregarious animals, and next to the chital they are the most diurnal of the deer species at Kanha. The common name "swamp deer" is really more appropriate for the northern race of *Cervus duvauceli*: at Dudhwa National Park, for example, you may see large aggregations of these deer, numbering 50-100, foraging on marshy ground. Although barasingha at Kanha may often be sighted in such habitat—for example, feeding in the marshes opposite Sondhar Tank or immersed up to their necks in Shravan Tal while they forage for lotus, weeds, and sedges—the hard-ground barasingha's preferred habitat is grassy *maidans* (meadows). As one might expect, the hooves of the southern race have adapted to this change in habitat, being less elongated, splayed, and spongy than those of the swamp deer of the marshy *terai* in northern India.

Barasingha are almost exclusively grazers, with a selective preference for certain perennial grasses (for example, *Saccharum spontaneum* and *Themeda triandra*). More than any other factor, the availability of suitable species and the length of the grass for the vital activities of foraging and fawning have affected the fortunes of this deer. In his account of the crisis of critically low hard-ground barasingha numbers at the end of the 1960s, M. K. Ranjitsinh (who played a leading role in the recovery of the species) asserts that the degradation of grassland habitat—rather than disease, poaching, or predation—was the key cause of low fawn production. Repeated annual burning of the grasslands, along with diversion of grassy meadows to agricultural purposes and competition for food from a rapidly increasing chital population, were also important contributing factors to the barasingha crisis.

Ranjitsinh cogently describes how management interventions at Kanha helped to restore the barasingha. These steps included construction of a large enclosure, strict control over grass burning, and the augmentation of grasslands areas achieved through the relocation of villages such as Sonf and Bishanpura. Careful efforts have been made throughout the years to redistribute the growing barasingha population at Kanha in order to protect the animals from the threat of epidemics, as well as to insulate them from disturbance. A 10 km-long migration corridor was created to link Kanha with Bishanpura Meadow, and, beginning in 1994, Sonf Meadow was closed to the public so that the barasingha there might mate and raise their fawns undisturbed.

At Kanha, the tiger is the principal threat to barasingha. The adult deer's size makes it a prime candidate for the attention of a large predator, and tiger predation on barasingha fawns has been amply documented. Barasingha, who are equipped with an excellent sense of smell as well as with good eyesight and hearing, exhibit alertness in very much the same ways as chital, with erect head posture, cocked ears, and a raised tail that exposes the white underside. Like chital, barasingha may audibly stamp a foreleg on the ground to express apprehension. The alarm call is a bark-like roar, which may be frequently repeated, rising in pitch and intensity to a scream. Ranjitsinh reports that barasingha seem to allow tigers a closer approach than do any other prey species. Schaller commented that, while the barasingha on Kanha Meadow during his research seemed acclimatized to human beings, their general tendency was to avoid situations that would lead to encounters with tigers—an aim in which they were aided by their acute sense of smell and the relatively open areas preferred by the deer.

The sustained campaign at Kanha on behalf of the barasingha continues to this day. Field Director Rajesh Gopal conducted research in the early 1990s on the deer's feeding ecology, and he presented the results in a Ph.D. dissertation. Even now, barasingha numbers are carefully monitored, and Kanha's forest guards have standing orders to report the circumstances surrounding the death of any barasingha in the park directly to the Field Director's office.

Although Sonf Meadow, which has been a barasingha stronghold since shortly after the relocation of the village in 1969, remains off-limits to the public, there are a number of locations in Kanha where you may sight this striking species of deer. Barasingha are often visible on Kanha Meadow, particularly on the northern edge (Koila Bhatta Road) and in the vicinity of Shravan Tal. Early to mid-morning are the best times for you to look for them. Another excellent place to look is Sondhar Tank, anytime from early morning to mid-afternoon. Depending on the weather, the time of year, and the rainfall, you may be able to sight barasingha on Bishanpura Meadow as well. These deer are virtually always found in open areas. They are quite tolerant of other species, so you may often glimpse them in the company of chital, blackbuck, and langur, and occasionally together with gaur or wild boar.

Photography: The barasingha's diurnal habits and preference for open territory make it comparatively easy to photograph. Although these deer are not nearly as skittish as sambar, you should approach them cautiously and quietly. During many seasons, we have observed barasingha males in mid-morning in the north-eastern sector of Kanha Meadow, filing toward Shravan Tal in stately procession for their daily bath. Stopping our vehicle about twenty metres shy of the deer's road-crossing point, we were able to get good pictures with a telephoto lens. When the animals are in the water at Shravan Tal, they are at some distance from the road and consequently difficult to photograph. Occasionally, however, you can find a singleton barasingha or a small party of these deer "taking the waters" at the anicut on Manhar Nallah Road (toward the western end of Kanha Meadow), where close photography is possible. On elephant back from Gorhela, head for Sondhar Tank, where you will frequently find barasingha, either at the tank itself or in the marshy patches across the road on the western side. Here you have a good chance of sighting the females, whose rich coloration and graceful proportions make them the equal of any male, we think, in the photographer's lens.

Barking Deer (Muntjac)

The barking deer is the smallest of the four members of the deer family that are regularly seen in the park. Barking deer *(Muntiacus muntjak,* Hindi *kakar)* range up to 22 kg (48-50 lb.) for an adult male, with a height at the shoulder of 51-76 cm (20-30 inches). This deer is coloured a deep, glowing chestnut brown. The antlers resemble small, slightly curved spikes, and they seldom exceed 10 cm (4 in.) in length. Barking deer antlers are based on bony, hair-covered projections called pedicels, which extend down the face of males. Males also use their tusk-like upper canines (about 2.5 cm or 1 inch long) to defend themselves. A barking deer's slow movement while grazing accentuates the rather squat proportions of its body: no one could describe it as majestic, like the barasingha, or graceful, like the chital. But at top speed in flight, the barking deer is surprisingly lithe and agile.

In both their habitat and social behaviour, barking deer more nearly resemble sambar than they do any other relatives in the deer family. They prefer thickly forested areas and are comfortable on steep hillsides, although occasionally they will appear at the edge of the forest or even venture into level, open clearings in order to forage. Thus you will virtually never glimpse this species in the great meadows of Kanha, or in the same places where you will see chital and barasingha. Barking deer are territorial, but the average area that they will defend seldom exceeds three or four hectares (up to 10 acres). Stags will not ordinarily tolerate the presence of other males in their area.

Also like the sambar, the barking deer is not a very gregarious animal. The social organization of this species, in fact, is closer to that of human beings than any other common mammal in Kanha. Barking deer normally pair for life, and they are found in small family parties—typically a male, a female, and one young. In this, their closest counterparts among Kanha mammals are jackals, who live in small family groups. Jackals, however, usually have litters of two to four pups.

Barking deer subsist on a diet of grasses, leaves, and wild fruits. They are eligible prey for all the major predators of the park, although their small size does not make them an efficient kill for tigers. We once sighted a pack of eight wild dogs very close to Sondhar Tank around 8:30 in the morning. From their purposeful movement—fanning out and then coming together in a single direction—it was an easy guess that they were hunting. Taking note of the direction, we drove around to Minkur Nallah Road, arriving at the junction about 20 minutes later. Within less than half an hour, the dogs had killed and eaten a barking deer male, leaving only the freshly detached head for vultures. A mother and her fawn stood by, about fifty feet from the carcass.

The most unusual feature of this small mammal, without doubt, is its alarm call, which gave the species its popular name and is utterly at variance with its size. The barking deer alarm call has been variously described as a snorting bark or an echoing roar. Despite the muffling effects of forest habitat, the call reverberates for a considerable distance. At a much lower pitch than the calls of either a sambar or a chital, this harsh sound is almost comically at odds with the modest appearance of the animal producing it. In our experience, a barking deer call may signal any one of the three major predators in the park: tiger, leopard, or wild dog. The call is quite reliable, since barking deer are not spooked nearly as easily as chital. As Jim Corbett remarked in *Jungle Lore* (1953): "Of all the animals in the jungle, the kakar gives the impression of being most on his toes. . . . I know of no better friend that a man . . . can have in a jungle than a kakar."

We have not heard a barking deer call signal the presence of jackals. It would be interesting to know if jackals occasionally prey on barking deer young, the way they do on chital fawns. Probably the muntjac is shielded from this danger by its preference for comparatively thick jungle.

Barking deer are active at all times of day and night. The best time to spot them, however, is from mid-morning to late afternoon, when the light is favourable for peering into deep jungle by the edge of the road. Since barking deer are not as crepuscular (or active around sunrise and sunset) as sambar, you have a good chance of seeing them—provided that you are going through the right habitat—during the middle of the day, when many other animals (most notably the tiger) are hard to see. Good areas for barking deer in Kanha include the Kisli-Kanha Main Road, Sal Ghat, and the Paparphat network of roads, as well as Links 7 and 8 (north of Kanha Meadow) and the wooded areas of Mukki Range (such as Sondhar Tank and the Mahavir Road).

Photography: Getting a good picture of a barking deer is a matter of luck, even more than is the case with most other Kanha mammals. These animals are small, and their coloration provides good camouflage with their habitual surroundings. If you spot a barking deer near the road, the chances are that the animal will freeze for 5-10 seconds before bounding suddenly into the jungle. For a forest animal, a barking deer can run off with surprising speed, and you will be left only with the memory of a white, upraised tail tuft. One way to approach this challenge is to have your camera ready at hand (with an 80-200mm lens and 200 or 400 ASA film, preferably) and to be positioned in your vehicle so that you can take a roadside shot at very short notice. Knowing the barking deer's habitual "timetable" and recognizing the habitat's suitability should be a help. We have found the Kanha guides to be excellent in spotting this species, which is quite a challenge even to an experienced spotter.

At the start of a barking deer sighting, keep in mind that there may easily be more than one animal in the immediate vicinity: often the mate, a fawn, or a yearling may be within the same small patch of forest. Use a little caution, and you may find that the deer peacefully grazes parallel to the road or even approaches a bit closer. Sightings by elephant, of course, offer the best chance for good pictures of this species.

Blackbuck

The blackbuck (*Antilope cervicapra*, Hindi *harna/harni*, *mrig*, *krishnasara*) is surely one of the world's most beautiful antelopes. Blackbuck numbers have drastically dwindled since we first visited the park in 1990. At that time, there were several dozen blackbuck, and they could be seen every day on Kanha Meadow, as well as inside the enclosure that was originally built to protect the barasingha. In the afternoons, one could observe the blackbuck at Phuta Talao on the north side of Kanha Meadow—a charming spot that has, sadly, been off-limits to tourists for some five years or more. Although at the time of writing there were only two blackbuck left in Kanha, we include a description of this elegant, graceful animal here in the hope that a small population may be sustained, or even increased, in the future.

For zoological purists, the blackbuck is the only true antelope, although it is related to ten other genera in the subfamily *Antilopinae* (including the springbok and the gerenuk in Africa, as well as the various gazelle species). The blackbuck probably evolved within the Indian subcontinent, and for centuries it has been venerated by religious custom and pictured in Indian art, especially of the Mughal period. Blackbuck are depicted in the cave paintings at Ajanta, dating from the sixth and seventh centuries A.D. One thousand years later, the Mughal emperor Jehangir (ruled 1605-1637) was so affected by the death of his favourite blackbuck that he constructed a memorial and decreed that the antelope's natal area should become a protected reserve. Indian sages are commonly portrayed in art as sitting on the skins of blackbuck, and the antelope is still regarded by villagers around the Little and Great Ranns of Kutch as a symbol of fertility.

At Kanha, the blackbuck is one of three species of antelope, the other two being the rarely glimpsed nilgai (*Boselaphus tragocamelus*) and the chowsingha (*Tetracerus quadricornis*) (see pages 108-109). More closely related to the blackbuck than either of these is the chinkara, or Indian gazelle *(Gazella gazella)*, which is not present at Kanha but may be seen at other national parks in Madhya Pradesh, including Pench and Panna.

Adult blackbuck males stand 80 cm (32 in.) at the shoulder and weigh an average of 40 kg (90 lb.). As juveniles, they are coloured yellowish brown (like females), but after the age of three or so the coat of the males darkens. In a mature male, the neck, the back, the sides, part of the face, and the outside of the animal's legs are brown to black in a pattern that presents a striking contrast to the white chest, abdomen, rump, and tail. Like other male antelope, blackbuck carry permanent horns, which are not shed annually (as are deer antlers). The horns on a male blackbuck are some of the most spectacular in the whole animal kingdom. Ringed and spiralled, they diverge from their base to form a "V" above the male's head. In adult bucks, the horns have three or four complete spirals. Record horn lengths, from north-western India, exceed 80 cm (31 in.), thus making the blackbuck one of the very few ungulates whose maximum horn length may surpass its height at the shoulder.

There are rare cases on record of females with horns, as well as of melanism and albinism in blackbuck. The appearance of blackbuck females is normally in striking contrast to that of the males: hornless and more slightly built, females are light brown in the places where the males are dark brown or black, and white in the remaining portions.

Blackbuck are gregarious, diurnal animals whose favourite habitat is open, short-grass plains. Such an environment favours their keen eyesight, as well as their extraordinary speed. Along with American pronghorn (*Antilocapra americana*), blackbuck are probably the fastest ungulates on earth: they have been clocked at 90 km per hour (56 mph). The running prowess of both species almost certainly evolved as an anti-predation defence: in the case of the blackbuck, to the danger posed by the cheetah (*Acinonyx jubatus*), now sadly extinct in India for more than half a century; and, in the case of the pronghorn, to cursorial predators of the genus *Acinonyx* that are known to have roamed the North American plains some ten thousand years ago before the late Pleistocene extinctions.

Blackbuck males are territorial, occupying and defending an area up to 20 ha. In large blackbuck aggregations, however, as in Velavadar Blackbuck National Park in Gujarat, such territories may be much smaller, ranging down to less than 1 ha. Males challenge each other for access to females, with the victor commonly taking possession of a harem, herding his females, and warding off other males. The most aggressive, dominant males typically exhibit the darkest color. Although the horns are dangerous weapons, most observers agree that they are seldom used in earnest, sparring being confined to brief matches. Males mark their territory by rubbing the pungent secretions from their preorbital glands on grass stems and twigs, and also by defecating regularly at dung sites. Breeding may take place throughout the year, and females give birth after a gestation period of 6+ months. Blackbuck are able to outrun tigers and wild dogs with ease, and the only important predation in most locales on this species is by jackals and wolves (jackals kill mostly fawns). Oddly enough, at Kanha a significant number of blackbuck in the enclosure just outside park headquarters fell victim to pythons.

Ironically, the decline of the blackbuck at Kanha has been closely related to the park's efforts in behalf of the barasingha. Blackbuck prefer short grasslands, but barasingha need a habitat with taller grass, especially in order to conceal their fawns against predators (see page 47). Countrywide, blackbuck numbers several centuries ago have been estimated at four million strong. George Schaller commented that the blackbuck was probably once "the most abundant wild hoofed animal in India." Although the blackbuck has generally profited from agricultural development, its preference for open habitat has made it a prime target for hunting, and numbers have drastically declined. Despite such inroads, there may be as many as 30,000 of these antelope remaining in India today.

Photography: At the time of writing, there were only two blackbuck (both males) remaining in Kanha. During the 1997-98 season, these animals could be seen quite regularly on Kanha Meadow. The best place to look for them was the Circular Road, which leads from the western side of the meadow to Schaller Hide and thence to Shravan Tal. The most important factors for photography were the position of the sun (glare in the open habitat may be considerable) and our proximity to the blackbuck.

Chital

Many people consider the chital or spotted deer *(Axis axis)* to be the most beautiful of all the deer species in the world. Along with the tiger, the chital is certainly a prime symbol of Kanha. It is the most numerous large mammal in the park, with a population currently exceeding 25,000, and its vital role there—along with that of its other relatives in the deer family—was signaled in the title of George Schaller's classic study of the Kanha ecosystem, *The Deer and the Tiger* (1967).

In the late 1980s, the park management did an interesting study of the suitability of all the habitat in Kanha for chital. This study focused on the health of the grasslands and the year-round availability of water—two prime requirements for this species. The results of this research were summarized in a graphic displayed in the museum at park headquarters in Kanha Village. It is no coincidence that the best areas for chital in Kanha show a high correlation with the density of tiger territories in the park (see maps on pages 36-37).

The diet of chital consists of grass, shrubs, vines, young bamboo shoots, the sprouting leaves of trees, and various fruits. Mahua, aonla, and ber fruits are especially preferred. The chital's association with the langur is especially important with regard to some of these food items (see below). The breadth of the diet and the chital's tolerance of human beings are probably the two outstanding factors underlying this deer's successful colonization of virtually the entire subcontinent.

Chital are the most gregarious or group-loving of Kanha's four species of deer. At most times of day from dawn to sunset, you will see them in the park's great valley meadows—Kanha, Sonf, Bishanpura, Sondhar, and Kudh— grazing or ruminating in parties that number from 8-12 to several dozen. Occasionally, very large herds of several hundred animals have been observed.

Chital also live in forested areas, so you may encounter them almost anywhere in the park, except on steep hillsides. These deer are active both by day and by night. They graze most often in the open meadows during the early morning and early evening, and in the heat of the day they often seek the shade of trees.

The composition of chital parties varies. Some groups are all-bachelor herds, while others consist primarily of does and fawns, with a dominant stag and one or two other males. You may also see mixed parties, with males, females, and young associating together.

The chital, as its Hindi name implies, is dappled with white spots on a rufous, medium-brown coat. Prime stags stand about three feet tall at the shoulder and may weigh close to 90 kg (200 lb.). Does are built more slimly and gracefully: many of them scale only a little more than half this weight.

The peak of the rutting season in Kanha is summertime (May-July), just before the onset of the rains. Since the gestation period is approximately 7+ months, many chital fawns are born in winter, from December to February. If you visit the park during this period, you will delight in seeing the females with very small fawns scampering at their heels. One fawn is the norm, although very occasionally you will find that a doe has given birth to twins.

The coloration of chital is yet another example of how nature has subtly calibrated the complex balance between predators and prey. If the tiger's dark stripes and the combination of orange and white on its coat and underparts give it exceptional camouflage within its habitat, the same may be said for the chital's brown and white pelage and its pattern of spots. A chital's movement through tall grass or in dappled light along the forest floor may be quite difficult to detect. In fact, even experienced wildlife spotters may occasionally mistake a chital for a tiger at a distance!

As with all deer species except the North American caribou or reindeer *(Rangifer tarandus)*, in which both sexes are antlered, only chital males grow antlers. These start as small spikes and then develop a maximum growth of three tines (or branches) on each side of the animal's head, resulting in six points. The two forward branches or brow tines are set nearly at right angles to the beam. Loss of condition in the antlers is one sign of an aging stag; another is the darker coloration of the deer's coat, especially around the neck.

Deer go through an annual cycle, growing antlers only to shed them and regrow them. Furthermore, the antlers themselves change in structure and appearance during this cycle. Antelope, by contrast, possess permanent horns. Thus, in Kanha, animals such as the nilgai, the blackbuck, and the rarely glimpsed chowsingha keep their horns for life, and the horns do not change their appearance .much, once maximum growth has been achieved.

Since the chital is the animal you will see most often in Kanha, it furnishes a good example of the functions that antlers serve in all deer, including the two other large species that are commonly seen in the park: sambar and barasingha. (The far smaller and more solitary barking deer, which exhibits comparatively undeveloped antlers, is something of an exception: see page 50).

The antler cycle begins with new growth of hollow bone, covered with keratin, the horn-like substance of which nails and hair are made. The antlers are covered with a thin layer of soft, sensitive skin, overlaid in turn with fine hair. A term that is often used for this covering is "velvet." At this stage, the blood vessels inside the antlers are tender and vulnerable. When a chital stag is in velvet, he will seldom use his antlers to spar with another male, since to do so might result in bleeding or in other damage.

As the mating system or rut approaches during the hotter months of May and June, chital lose the velvet covering on their antlers. This happens after the blood supply to the antler is reduced, owing to the growth of a bony ring or "burr" just above the join of the antler with its base, or pedicel. Chital hasten the process of losing the velvet by rubbing their antlers on smooth tree bark or on other vegetation. When the velvet has completely peeled off, deer are said to be in "hard antler." Chital stags are now ready to spar with each other for dominance over females. Their harsh, bugling calls ring out over the meadows during the rut.

After the rut, chital shed their antlers. Worn down by conflicts with other stags and by breeding activity, males may be less capable of the sustained bursts of speed necessary to outrun predators. Shedding the antlers may provide them with some additional security, since now they resemble females.

Although there is a definite peak season to the rut, some chital stags in Kanha breed throughout the year. Therefore, it is possible for you, during a single visit, to see males at almost every stage of antler development. Likewise, although you will probably see the greatest number of fawns toward the end of winter, you may catch sight of young chital at any season when the park is open (1 November – 30 June).

Chital associate freely with many of the forest residents of Kanha, including barasingha, blackbuck, wild boar, gaur, peacock, sloth bear, and sambar. But their most special association is with langur. As the British field biologist Paul Newton has shown, the two species are found together more often than mere random chance would predict, and there seems to be a definite scientific foundation for a "chital-langur relationship." Whether or not this association truly fulfills the requirements of "mutualism" (a relationship in which two quite different species cooperate for the mutual benefit of each) is still open to debate. But it is clear that chital profit from their close association with langur monkeys by a) consuming fruits and other vegetation that falls from the trees while monkeys are foraging; and b) benefiting from the alarm calls of langur, whose privileged position in the trees allows them a wide range of view for predators.

The eagerness of chital to consume some of the leaves and fruits that lie just beyond their reach in the trees is beyond question, since we have frequently observed spotted deer standing on their hindlegs to reach such delicacies. The langur, no doubt, throw forage down to the ground as discarded food, rather than with any deliberate consideration for the deer. The monkeys may benefit in turn from the relationship by escaping from predators at the expense of the more numerous, ground-dwelling deer (see page 71). We were once able to photograph a chital with a langur on its back, and M. K. Ranjitsinh writes of having observed such a scene several times, most often with no attempt by the chital to drive off the monkey.

As you travel through the park, why not make your own estimate of the frequency of the association between langur and chital? Every once in a while, when you see the two species together, stop your vehicle and pause for five or ten minutes to observe the interaction between the deer and the monkeys. One place you will usually find the two species together is just inside the Kisli Gate at the park's western edge; another is the start of Bari

Chuhri Road on the southern side of the great Kanha Meadow, as you wind around toward Chhoti Chuhri and come to the large pukhri tree on the right-hand side of the track.

The chital's alarm call is a single, piercing, high-pitched yelp. It resembles the sound "Ow!" given out shrilly at high volume by a small child who has just been pinched hard. This call's value to the tiger seeker in Kanha (and in most other tiger reserves) can scarcely be overestimated, since the sound carries for a considerable distance and is quite a reliable indicator that a major predator is on the move (see page 18).

Chital also signal the threat of tigers, leopards, wild dogs, and jackals by their body posture. A chital who is "alert" will typically exhibit a head-up position, staring fixedly in one particular direction. Raising the tail so that the white underside is visible signifies an increased level of alarm, as does the repeated stamping of a forefoot on the ground with a slow, deliberate rhythm. Chital will often display these alarm signals without running from their position. As with gazelles, impala, and other antelope in Africa, chital seem to possess an uncanny intuition about a predator's intentions. Whereas they may loudly signal the approach or presence of a threat, their failure to run or withdraw may result from a sixth sense that the predator is merely "passing through," with no intention of hunting or killing. Time and again, we have seen chital who have given out urgent, repeated alarms, yet who have not taken to their heels. On the other hand, chital may react to a predator more silently. They may slowly but quite steadily fade away from an area where they have been grazing contentedly only minutes beforehand—presumably after they have caught a tiger or leopard's scent with their keen sense of smell.

The chital has a formidable list of enemies. This deer is a staple item in the diet of the park's top three predators: tiger, leopard, and wild dog. In addition, jackals prey on chital fawns. We have seen single jackals, as well as small packs, hunt young chital, and we have witnessed two jackal kills of fawns in Bandhavgarh N.P. You should bear in mind that chital alarm calls—most especially in open meadow habitat—may be motivated by jackal, as well as by the larger predators. We have witnessed two tiger kills of chital (one of a stag and one of a doe, both on Kanha Meadow), as well as two wild dog kills (both of chital does: one on Kanha Meadow and one on the Kanha-Kisli main road very near Kisli Gate). The tiger kills occurred in early morning and late afternoon, the wild dog kills in mid- to late morning.

The chital's primary safety factors, of course, are their numbers, their acute sense of smell, their association with the langur, and their prolific reproduction. The last, in particular, probably more than compensates for the offtake due to predation.

Photography: Although the photography of chital might seem like an easy proposition, given these animals' common occurrence in the park, they can be surprisingly difficult to capture on film. Rather like peacocks, who tend to fade away when a vehicle approaches with photographers poised, chital often look eminently accessible, only to prove elusive as one composes a picture and focuses. Deer that are initially located on the road or very close to it will almost always prove skittish when a vehicle enters the range of their "flight distance," or the minimum distance at which they will flee from danger. We have found that the best strategy is cautiously to approach a small party of deer located at a short distance (say 10-20 m) from the track, stop the vehicle, and wait for the chital to drift back toward the road, if such is their inclination. Parties feeding in conjunction with langur around vegetation located close to the road offer promising subjects, since chital are reluctant to forsake good foraging sites. Occasionally, a close look at chital will reveal some interesting oddities: for example, in April 1998 we photographed a chital stag with thirteen points, an extraordinary variation of the usual six. During the winter months, one may very occasionally spot a mother with twins, instead of the usual singleton fawn.

Gaur (Indian Bison)

Gaur (*Bos gaurus*) are the largest wild cattle in the world. An adult male is the embodiment of muscular strength. Standing nearly six feet at the shoulder, their heads majestically crowned with sturdy, sweeping horns, full-grown bulls may weigh up to 900 kg (2,000 lb.). The name "Indian Bison" is often used for gaur, but they are really wild cattle, whose closest relatives are the yak and the Indonesian banteng, rather than the bison of North America. The distribution of gaur in India is almost totally in the central and southern parts of the country, south of the Narmada River. Kanha thus lies at the northern edge of the gaur's range. Recent enumerations in Kanha suggest that there are about 1,000 gaur in the park.

Mature gaur are darkish brown. The coat of bulls often turns black with age. The lower legs of both sexes have "white socks," sometimes tinged with pale yellow. Newborn young are coloured yellowish gold and progressively darken to light and then reddish brown. Both male and female gaur have horns, with the horns of the female configured in a tighter arc than those of the male. In good condition, the horns display a lustrous contrast of hues, with the lower part tinted salmon-orange and the upper section ashy to brownish-grey. In addition to the wide sweep of their horns, mature males have a distinctive ridge that extends roughly half way from the neck down the back. This "dorsal ridge," as it is known, suddenly drops off in a way that gives added emphasis to the animal's formidable musculature. Males also display a short dewlap, or fold of skin, below the chin, as well as a longer one on the chest.

Bamboo thickets and hillsides are the key habitat features that can help you to locate gaur in Kanha. Essentially grazers rather than browsers, gaur eat bamboo shoots, green grass, fallen beanpods, and the leaves (sometimes even the bark) of various trees, including sal, saja, and aonla. Gaur are also partial to salt licks. They often descend from higher elevations to more open meadow areas during the hot, dry months of April-June. Good places to look for gaur in Kanha during the months between November and March include the following: Paparphat area near Jamun Talao, Bija Dadar, Nakti Ghati, and (on the eastern side of the park) the roads connecting Gorhela, Andha Kuan Camp, and Sondhar.

Gaur commonly live in small herds numbering 8-20 animals, although larger concentrations have occasionally been documented in Kanha. A herd consists of cows and calves, except during the rutting season, when a dominant bull controls the herd's movements and mates with the cows. The height of the rut in Kanha is during the coldest months, December-January. This means that, just as with barasingha fawns, gaur calves are born at the peak of the rainy season, in August-September. Another similarity with Kanha's deer species is the sparring between young gaur bulls. These encounters, partly playful and partly aggressive, afford the males a chance to develop the strength and condition they will need in order to assume the role of dominance in a herd.

Aside from the rutting season, adult males tend to keep to themselves. Sometimes they are spotted in small, all-male parties of 2-5 animals. With increasing age, male gaur often become solitary.

Gaur are fairly silent animals, although their feeding is sometimes noisy, due to their large size. They have two principal calls: first, a horn-like challenge call, given off by males who approach and then circle each other in an aggressive encounter; and second, a whistling alarm call, which is rather incongruously high-pitched, given the gaur's huge size. In this regard, the gaur is the reverse of the barking deer—a pint-sized animal that is capable of an echoing roar when alarmed (see page 51). Experts disagree about the gaur's powers of sight, with some observers claiming that the animal possesses only moderate vision and others fully convinced that it can spot movement and colour from distances up to 150 m (500 ft.). No one, however, disputes the gaur's exceptionally keen sense of smell.

Because of their size, predation on gaur is limited to only one important species: the tiger. Gaur are especially vulnerable to the loss of calves to tigers, and the cows' conduct in a herd with young calves is noticeably cautious and protective. Capt. Navneet Singh, who has closely observed the species in Kanha for over a decade, notes that gaur configure themselves in a circle to rest, watching every approach for a hint of danger. Do adult gaur ever fall prey to tigers? Surprisingly often, according to Navneet Singh. As with lions in Africa, who regularly prey on buffalo that may be three times their own weight, tigers attack adult gaur in combats that must be some of the most violent prey-predator encounters in the entire mammal kingdom.

One important difference in this comparison should be noted, however. Lions are social animals, and lion attacks on a buffalo usually involve several lions' hunting cooperatively. Tigers, almost without exception, stalk and kill alone. To attack and hold such a large animal, tigers may bite at the hock or ankle joint of a gaur, rather than going at first for the killing bite at the base of the neck or the choking grip on the throat.

Although the gaur is a far less agile animal than the tiger, the bovid's horns and hooves still present serious threats to the big cat. If sambar and chital are abundant, one might wonder why a tiger would risk such a dangerous fight. One possible answer might be the energy-benefit ratio characteristic of predators, whereby large carnivores, especially, are likely—all other factors being equal—to concentrate their effort on prey that gives the maximum reward for the energy expended. Given the fact that up to 95% of tiger hunts or stalks end in failure, success in bringing down a gaur is a handsome pay-off. In some habitats, such as Nagarahole N.P. in southern India, the gaur plays a major role in the tiger's diet.

Gaur are notably shy and reclusive by nature, so at the beginning of a gaur sighting, you should take care not to make any noise or sudden movements. In our experience, it is best to have the vehicle stop at least 30 m (100 ft.) from the herd, allow the animals to accustom themselves to your presence, and then move forward slowly and discreetly. Gaur will often pause to inspect you and then slowly but firmly move off into the forest. Occasionally, however, you will come across a herd that pays no attention whatever to human intruders. Such gaur may cross the road within 3 metres or less of your vehicle.

Photography: As with sambar and barking deer, gaur are often sighted in the shady conditions of sal and bamboo forest. Their large size and occasional habituation to vehicles make distance less of a problem than it can be for photographing other mammals. When you spot a herd close to the road, there is a chance that they will cross and you will be able to get an unobstructed view of the animals in the open. Sunshine glinting on the glossy black coat of a bull gaur is a memorable sight, so do not neglect to follow up reports of gaur sightings in the open meadows.

Hyena

Like the sloth bear (see page 82), the hyena (*Hyaena hyaena*, Hindi *lakkar baghar*) is a major mammal in Kanha that is very rarely glimpsed. Little is known about the animal's habits in this ecosystem, but studies of the species elsewhere can be used, to a certain extent at least, to infer certain basic patterns of the hyena's social organization and behaviour.

Hyenas, along with their smaller cousin the aardwolf, comprise a separate family among carnivores called the Hyaenidae. Of the three species of hyena—striped, spotted, and brown—the striped hyena is the most widely distributed geographically. The species ranges from Africa through the Middle East into the Indian subcontinent and southeast Asia. Such wide distribution across a range of habitats is one index of the adaptability of this species.

An adult male striped hyena weighs approximately 40 kg (85-90 lb.) with the females scaling about 5-10 kg less. The coat of the hyena may range from gray to sandy brown. The head is large and the forequarters are far better developed than the hindquarters, thus resulting in the hyena's distinctive, loping gait. The vertical stripes are usually well defined.

Unlike their gregarious relatives the spotted hyenas of Africa (*Crocuta crocuta*), who live in clans that may range up to 30 individuals, striped hyenas are fairly solitary and much more silent animals. Spotted hyenas, whose behaviour has been intensively studied, have a matriarchal social structure, and adult females are commonly larger and heavier than males. Although we know that this is not the case with the striped hyena, the social organization of the species is poorly understood. One study from Israel by Liora Kolska Horwitz and Julian Kerbis (*Israel Land and Nature* 16.4: Summer 1991) suggests that the nucleus of striped hyena existence is the den. In one such lair, located on the cliffs above the Dead Sea valley, 90% of the bones analyzed by the researchers were from domestic animals (sheep, goats, camels, cows, dogs, donkeys, mules, and horses). Bones from wild animals included those of Nubian ibex, gazelle, porcupine, brown hare, Syrian hyrax, fox, wild boar, desert hedgehog, hyena, and various shrews, rodents, snakes, lizards, and birds—indicating a remarkably varied diet. Inside the den, which the researchers estimated had been active for at least twenty years, was a latrine area.

Striped hyenas have quietly accommodated themselves to coexistence with humans. Like the wolf and the fox, hyenas or their tracks are more commonly sighted at Kanha in the buffer zone than within the park itself. They are predominantly nocturnal animals, and it is presumed that they rely mainly on scavenging for food. Another comparison with the spotted hyena of Africa is relevant here, however. Spotted hyenas were long held to be scavengers too, until wildlife biologist Hans Kruuk produced the first full-scale scientific study of the species in 1972. Among Kruuk's surprising conclusions was that, in certain habitats at least, the spotted hyena was not only a formidable predator but also actually killed more than it scavenged.

Might this be the case with the striped hyena as well? Probably the picture is a complex one, answering to the requirements and dynamics of specific habitats. Since the striped hyena does not have the advantage of cooperative hunting, it is highly unlikely that it would challenge a tiger. Yet a pair of hyenas might well mount a challenge to a leopard at a kill made by the cat. And the role of hyenas as predators on smaller herbivores at Kanha, such as chital and barking deer, remains to be investigated.

Our single hyena sighting at Kanha occurred in March 1997 in the buffer zone near the village of Danwar, about two hours after sunset. We have seen hyena tracks on several occasions. The fresh sets of pug marks, observed early in the morning, were very close to two lodges on the western side of the park: Kipling Camp and Indian Adventures Wild Chalet.

Photography: This animal is sighted so seldom at Kanha that "going for" pictures of hyena does not make much sense for most visitors. The determined photograph hound is best advised to hire a Gypsy or other 4-wheel drive vehicle and a good driver who can negotiate the roads around the buffer zone at night. Some of these can be in pretty rough condition, so be prepared for a bumpy ride. Setting out after dark, take a ride from Mocha around to Mukki, for example, or ride up to the village of Tatri and then go along the road to Baihar. Take along a spotlight and load your camera with film of 1600 ASA. You just might get lucky!

Jackal

The golden jackal (*Canis aureus*, Hindi *gidhar*) is one of the most intriguing small predators in Kanha. Jackals are supremely versatile animals, adapting themselves well to their comparatively low position in the pecking order of carnivores and eking out a living in the shadow of tigers, leopards, hyenas, and wild dogs. They have a well-deserved reputation as scavengers, and together with vultures (who are often their rivals for pickings at a kill) they perform an important function in the natural cycle by disposing of the remains of kills. This behavioural trait is even more important when jackals live near (or actually within) human habitations, as they often do in India. Like leopards, jackals seem to have accustomed themselves to coexistence with human beings. Less well known is the role of jackals as hunters and killers in their own right. In Kanha, this has been especially noticeable with respect to jackal predation on the fawns of chital and blackbuck.

The golden jackal stands about 38-43 cm (15-17 in.) high at the shoulder, with the head and body measuring 61-76 cm (2-2 ½ ft.), excluding the tail, which may add another 30 cm to the animal's profile. A good-sized adult male may weigh up to 11 kg (25 lb.). The colour is a subtle and attractive, variegated mixture of black, buff, silver, and dark brown. The coloration affords good camouflage in open, grassy terrain, as well as in lightly forested jungle. The short, bushy tail is such an appealing mixture of hues as to be an ornament to the animal. Besides its fine appearance, the golden jackal is also notable for its movement. Far from skulking or slinking, the movement of jackals is almost comical, with a mincing, prancing step that can, on occasion, accelerate to a streaking, extremely graceful run.

The jackal has a social organization that offers the closest parallel within Kanha to the patterns of human society. Jackals pair for life, and normally both males and females participate in the rearing of the young, who are called pups. Litters average three or four young. Like wild dogs, jackals raise their pups in underground dens.

It is relatively easy to sight jackals in Kanha, since they prefer the open meadows and the edge of the jungle. Since these animals live in family groups, you will often come across more than one jackal: a typical sighting involves a pair, with or without pups. Normally jackals are silent during the day, but at dawn or dusk you may hear their high-pitched, whining call as they yowl in chorus—cries that somewhat resemble those of seagulls. These calls may be territorial, indicating jackal families' positions to other families. More than once in Kanha, and on several occasions in Bandhavgarh, we have seen jackals stalk and kill chital fawns. Keep in mind that a chital alarm call may well be triggered by the threat of jackals to the deer's young.

The activity of jackals, especially in conjunction with vultures and crows overhead, may also signal the presence of a kill by a larger predator. Jackals are amazingly agile in stealing fragments of a kill; they manage both to elude the wrath of an irritated tiger and to chase away eager vultures.

The golden jackal is sympatric or coresident in East Africa with the black-backed jackal (*Canis mesomelas*). The American field biologist Patricia Moehlman has studied both species there and revealed an interesting pattern in the jackals' social structure: in many cases, pups do not disperse from their parents after a year, as was previously thought, but remain with the family group and help in the rearing of the next year's litter. The reasons for this "helping" behaviour by older siblings are still poorly understood. It would be interesting to know if this pattern is true of the golden jackal in India as well.

Photography: Jackals are relatively easy to photograph, due to their diurnal habits, marked curiosity, and habituation of open areas. Animals will often venture very close to a vehicle, and with reasonable discretion you should be able to get good shots with 100-200 ASA film and a moderate zoom lens.

Jungle Cat

The jungle cat *(Felis chaus,* Hindi *jangli billi)* is the smallest feline in Kanha. Coloured sandy grey, this cat's head and body are about 61 cm (2 ft.) long. The tail, which averages about 30 cm in length, is quite short in proportion to the body. The tail of the jungle cat exhibits black rings toward the end and is tipped in black. Adult males may weigh up to 5-6 kg (12-14 lb.).

Jungle cats are widely distributed, ranging from Egypt and Turkey through the Middle East to South Asia and the Indochinese peninsula. In Kanha, they prefer open terrain and lightly forested areas. We have sighted this small mammal several times in Kanha Meadow during mid-morning: jungle cats seem to be relatively more diurnal in their habits than tigers and leopards. Jungle cats are extremely speedy, agile, and strong for their size. They live on small mammals and birds, and there are many reports of their bold confrontations with more powerful rivals (for example, crested serpent eagles) who might have been expected to intimidate them.

Like the African wild cat *(Felis libyca),* jungle cats in India will readily interbreed with domestic cats, and we have known several lodge cats around Kanha whose markings strongly suggested a forest ancestry, at least on one side of the family.

Spotting a jungle cat in Kanha is largely a matter of luck, since the preferred habitat of the animal, as well as its small size and coloration, makes it difficult to see. Even relatively short meadow grass affords the jungle cat excellent camouflage, as do leaf litter and small shrubs on the forest floor. Jungle cats are usually quite shy, so sightings are brief. On two occasions, however, we were able to observe this animal at length in Kanha.

The first was an early morning sighting in February 1994 at Partak Puliya, the entrance to Kanha Meadow (see map facing page 16). A jungle cat sat two metres from the edge of the road, sunning himself in the open. The vehicle made no difference at all to this animal; in fact, he seemed so intoxicated by the warmth of the sun's rays that it took him quite some time to lift his head and open one eye for a picture! On a second occasion, in March 1997, we spotted a jungle cat at twilight as we were returning to Kisli through the Kanha Ghat. This animal walked at least 100 m down the middle of the twisting road, oblivious to the vehicle as we followed him slowly.

Photography: If you are lucky enough to have a good sighting, keep in mind that you will normally need at least a 200 mm lens to photograph the jungle cat properly. Light may be relatively poor, in which case you should use film of 200 or 400 ASA. The photograph that appears in this book was taken by the authors in Keoladeo National Park, the world-famous bird sanctuary at Bharatpur. Surprisingly, this jungle cat allowed himself to be approached on foot, and the photograph was taken at a distance of only 5 metres.

Langur

The Common or Hanuman Langur affords an outstanding example of the Indian tradition of respect for nature and veneration of wildlife. Every langur is Hanuman, and monkeys are seldom molested, even around habitations and in urban areas. Other examples of animals that have had a long tradition of worship and protection in India are the cow, the elephant, the blackbuck, and—of course—the tiger. One may also compare the veneration in various parts of India for crocodiles, parrots, cranes, nilgai, and even jackals; note, likewise, the religious sentiment for the banyan and peepal trees. The identification of the langur with Hanuman seems most appropriate—since much of the Hindu mythology for this god casts him in the role of an intermediary between sky and earth, gods and men. The development of an anthropomorphic view of langur behaviour is understandable: like the god whom he represents, the langur is strong, agile, resourceful, and speedy (Maruti, "son of the wind," as he is called in the *Ramayana*).

Langurs are found all over India and in Sri Lanka. In *The Book of Indian Animals*, S. H. Prater mentions 14 or more separate races. The shape of the head and the colour phase, in particular, vary considerably, depending on geography. The Common Langur (*Presbytis entellus,* Hindi *langur)* has a good claim to being considered as the nominate race. The name *langur* comes from a Sanskrit word meaning "long tail." The animal's scientific name is a revealing example of how biological taxonomy (classification) often refers to either the appearance of the species, a behavioural characteristic, or both. The Greek word *presbytis* means "old lady," while the Latin proper name *Entellus* is an allusion to a minor character in Virgil's ancient Roman epic, the *Aeneid*. Entellus is an aging boxer, whose strength and endurance help him to defeat a much younger rival. The allusion signals the remarkable strength of the Common Langur for its size. (The men who coined the scientific names for langurs seem to have been steeped in Greek and Roman literature: other species names include Anchises, Iulus, Aeneas, Elissa, Priam, and Thersites!)

The Common Langur is 60-75 cm (2-2 ½ ft.) high when seated; it weighs from 9 to 16 kg (20-35 lb.), although the weight may reach over 20 kg in the North. Its most striking feature is certainly the tail, which measures 90-105 cm (3-3 ½ ft.). Silvery gray, it has a black face and dark hands and feet. Langurs are more arboreal (tree-living) than terrestrial (ground-living), but the percentage of time spent on the ground seems highest (about 40%) in the Common Langur. Langurs are vegetarian, following a diet of wild fruits, berries, leaves, shoots, buds, and flowers.

These monkeys commonly live in troops of 10-30 animals, the core of which consists (as in lion society) of related females. Such troops, usually coordinated by only one fully adult male, are noticeably territorial, with areas in Kanha averaging about 40-70 hectares (or around ½ km²). Young males leave the troop of their birth and join all-male nomadic bands. The average size of such bands is somewhat smaller than the size of breeding troops. British researcher Paul Newton, working at Kanha in the early 1980s, found that the mean troop size in his study area (Kanha Meadow) was 21.7, while the mean all-male band size was 14.0. Fights between rogue males and family (breeding) troops, or even between two family troops, are fairly common. Occasionally, one or more takeover males are successful in dislodging the dominant male of a breeding troop.

Mating in Kanha seems concentrated in summer during the monsoon, with the young born just before the beginning of spring after a gestation period of about 6 months. Interestingly, in light of their interspecific association with chital (see below), the peak in the birth season for both langur and chital occurs at the same time of year. As in other species of group-living primates, very small langur babies are often passed from their mothers to other females, who take great interest and care in examining and handling them.

Langurs start their day with the sun, when they may be seen at the top of the roosting tree enjoying the first slanting rays. From mid-morning to late afternoon, they often descend to the ground to feed, although feeding in the trees also occurs during the daylight hours. Although an exact count of these animals in Kanha is impossible, the park's population has been estimated at about 6,000, and they may be sighted in almost any area that is open to the public. At any given time during our visits, there have been four or five troops residing on Kanha Meadow alone.

The langur's contact call is a sustained, echoing hoot or whoop, repeated several times in quick succession. In contrast, the alarm call is a loud, choking, cough-like sound, staccato and guttural in intonation. Alarm calls differ for males, females, and young: the calls of males cover several notes, while those of females are given on a single pitch. The calls of infants sound like a high-pitched, sharply emitted whine or bleat. The alarm calls of a langur are the most reliable of any signals in the jungle for the presence of a predator, due to the monkey's keen vision and its position in the trees. Langurs even issue alarm calls at night.

For langurs, the most feared and deadly predator is the leopard, owing to this cat's tree-climbing ability, but tigers, wild dogs, snakes, and eagles will also cause them to call. Experienced guides can judge from the pacing and intensity of the calls whether langur are calling for tiger, leopard, or wild dog. One may compare the alarm calls of African vervet monkeys (Cercopithecus aethiops), who have been shown to emit different types of call according to the threat presented by different predators (such as leopards, martial eagles, and pythons). The size of a langur does not make it a particularly suitable kill for a tiger, but we have witnessed a kill by a tigress on Kanha Meadow—a langur simply did not move fast enough up a tree when the tigress passed beneath it. With one swipe of her paw, the tigress killed the monkey. She ate it immediately, finishing her meal in fifteen minutes.

It has long been noticed that langur troops are often in the company of chital—suggesting that there may be some mutual benefit to both species from their association. Paul Newton's studies in Kanha established that chital and langur are found together significantly more often than could be expected from random chance. Is the langur-chital relationship an authentic example of mutualism, in the fashion that is sometimes suggested for impalas and baboons in Africa or the cooperation there between the honey badger (Mellivora capensis) and the Honeyguide Bird (Indicator indicator)? For mutualism to be confirmed, there would have to be specific, concrete advantages on each side.

For the chital, the benefits are more obvious: langur discard fruits and leaves from the trees, which are then picked up and eaten by chital; and alarm calls also warn chital and other ungulates of a predator in the vicinity. What benefits do langur derive from the relationship? When the monkeys are on the ground in association with a large party of chital, the deer's keen sense of smell may warn both species of approaching danger. In the case of tigers and wild dogs, langur may also benefit from a byproduct of association with the more numerous, ground-dwelling deer: it is a chital, rather than a langur, that is likely to end up as the prey animal if a kill is made.

We noted earlier the similarity of langur troops to lion prides. Infanticide among langurs presents another striking parallel between the behaviour of these primates and lion society. Males who succeed in taking over a troop often enhance their own breeding opportunities by killing infant offspring sired by their predecessors, since females who lose young will come into estrus more rapidly than females who rear their infants to weaning. Sarah Hrdy, who investigated infanticide in langurs in the Mount Abu area of Rajasthan, reported that out of 32 takeovers by invading males, more than 50% were accompanied by the disappearance of infants. Significantly as well, infanticide in langurs has only been noted when males enter the troop from outside it.

However, many mysteries remain. For example, some males do not exhibit the infanticidal trait at all. Paul Newton's research at Kanha ·militates against the hypothesis that infanticide is pathological behaviour caused by crowding in degraded habitat. Further research is needed, but Newton has suggested that troop composition (for example, the presence of just one male or of several in a breeding troop) rather than density may predict the distribution of infanticide among langur populations.

Other species of monkey in which the same phenomenon has been observed include the Purple-faced leaf monkey in Sri Lanka (Semnopithecus vetulus), the Silvered leaf monkey in Malaysia (Semnopithecus cristatus), the Redtail monkey (Cercopithecus ascanius) and the Blue monkey (Cercopithecus mitis) in Uganda, and several species of howler monkeys in Central and South America. Infanticide is also a much-researched topic for rodents of the squirrel family: for example, among Belding's ground squirrels (Spermophilus beldingi) and Black-tailed prairie dogs (Cynomys ludovicianus). In the latter species, in fact, infanticide is the major cause of juvenile mortality. Lest it be assumed that infanticide is always the act of brutish males, in Black-tailed prairie dogs the leading marauders are lactating females, who kill the unweaned offspring of close kin! For infanticide among tigers, see page 91.

An intriguing strategy that female langurs seem to have developed in order to defend against infanticide by males is "pseudo-estrous behaviour." In this form of deceit, a pregnant female solicits a takeover male sexually, thereby inducing him to tolerate her subsequent offspring. Lionesses, too, have evolved adaptations to the waste of their maternal investment caused by infanticidal males. After losing their cubs in a takeover, for example, some females mate for an average period of 4-5 months without becoming pregnant, while others come into estrus every few weeks but fail to ovulate. Such protective mechanisms, presumably, shield a lioness against desertion by takeover males, as well as help to bond the new males to the pride.

Photography: Langur photography is one of the joys of bringing a camera to Kanha. These animals are diurnal, easily found, and reasonably approachable. Their playful antics and rapidly shifting moods provide entertaining subjects for the still photographer and the video enthusiast alike. Mothers with young infants are especially intriguing, as are the dominant troop males, who will warn you if you approach too near. The effects of sunlight on the langur's steel-gray coat are often extremely striking, and the association of the monkeys with chital offers fascinating opportunities for observations (and photographs) of interaction between species.

Leopard

The leopard (*Panthera pardus*, Hindi *tendua*) is probably the most successful of the world's thirty-seven species of wild cats. Three major criteria for the success of a species in the wild are its widespread geographical distribution, its adaptation to many different sorts of habitat, and its coexistence with human beings. The leopard today enjoys the widest range of any wild cat in the world; in fact, it has one of the largest ranges of any terrestrial mammal. Leopards are found in nearly all countries in Africa, throughout the Middle East, and in much of the rest of Asia. The population in sub-Saharan Africa alone may number over half a million animals. In 1992, the Wildlife Institute of India estimated a total population in India of nearly 15,000 leopards, approximately half of which occur in protected areas. Except for some extremely rare subspecies such as the Amur leopard in the Russian Far

East, the leopard does not seem to be critically endangered in most parts of its range, including the Indian subcontinent—although who knows what the situation might be today if the fashion craze for leopard-skin coats had continued longer than it did.

Far more leopards than tigers remain in India. Paradoxically, however, leopards are seen a great deal less frequently than their larger cousins in protected areas, due to their nocturnal habits and secretive nature. Furthermore, there has been a disappointingly small amount of research by wildlife biologists on the leopard in India—certainly by comparison with the tiger or even with the African leopard, which has been the subject of several recent book-length studies. The most informative of these are Lex Hes, *The Leopards of Londolozi* (1991), which reports on leopards in a private reserve adjoining Kruger National Park in South Africa and which includes stunning photographs; and Jonathan Scott, *The Leopard's Tale* (1985), which offers a keenly observed and beautifully illustrated account of a leopard family in Kenya's Masai Mara, a reserve that is roughly the size of Kanha. It is especially surprising that even in Sri Lanka, where the absence of tigers has had the effect of encouraging more diurnal habits in leopards, very little research about leopard behaviour has been undertaken.

Partly because leopards are in the unenviable position of always taking a back seat to tigers, they are the victims of some unflattering stereotypes. In the famous phrase of Jim Corbett in the preface to his first book, *Man-Eaters of Kumaon,* the tiger is "a large-hearted gentleman with boundless courage." The reputation of the leopard has been quite different, however. Another of Corbett's best-known books was *The Man-Eating Leopard of Rudraprayag,* in which he recounted his efforts to "bring to book" a man-eater that claimed over 125 lives in the early 1920s. Corbett had a healthy respect for the strength and cunning of the species, but he left no doubt that his affections lay with the tiger. Even S. H. Prater, in *The Book of Indian Animals,* refers to the leopard as "a greater potential scourge [than the tiger] on human life and property."

The hunter-naturalist R. G. Burton, writing in the *Journal of the Bombay Natural History Society* in 1918, also furnished a typical commentary on leopard behaviour: "Their conduct is frequently characterized by extreme boldness and by extreme timidity." Burton phrased the most common stereotype for this animal rather tactfully: for a century or more, the *shikari* literature presented leopards as fearsome yet despicable, blending brazenness and cowardice in a bizarre and quite unpredictable mixture.

Leopards do, in fact, claim more human victims every year in India than any other species except the elephant, as M. K. Ranjitsinh has pointed out. A man-eating leopard operated in Mandla District in the late 1960s. In 1990 in Kanha, we saw a man-killing leopard confined in a primitive holding pen in Kanha Village. We were told that the hapless animal would be given to a zoo, once an institution willing to accept such an offender could be identified.

Destructive encounters with humans seem a bit different with leopards than with tigers. Normally, tigers go out of their way to avoid people. The leopard's greater adaptability to human surroundings, however, involves disadvantages as well as advantages: cattle-lifting raids by leopards, for example, can be major sources of conflict on the periphery of villages, and leopards are notorious for their audacious attacks on domestic dogs, whose flesh they apparently regard as a great delicacy.

The reasons for the rather unflattering, stereotyped image of leopards are not far to seek. The tawny spotted coat of this cat, which is beautifully covered with small, dark, closely set markings called rosettes, affords even better camouflage in forest habitat than is enjoyed by the tiger. The strength of leopards, which allows them to climb trees while carrying prey that is heavier than their own body weight (for example, a well-built chital stag), makes them extremely formidable predators. They are stealthy, speedy, and amazingly agile animals, gifted with phenomenal powers of sight and hearing. For the most part, leopards are silent (though see below on their small repertory of calls).

Finally, even more than the tiger, leopards are usually nocturnal animals, active from just before dusk to just after dawn. (Do keep in mind, however, that it is possible to see a leopard at virtually any time of day in Kanha: we have had sightings in the early and late morning, as well as in the mid-afternoon and at dusk.) The versatility and all-around competence of leopards might have been expected to evoke human admiration. Perhaps it is all too human, however, to cherish resentment when we are outsmarted by a resident of the jungle—as we so frequently are by the leopard.

In Africa, leopards and lions are deadly enemies. The Indian lion, of course, has been reduced to only one population—the lions of the Gir Forest in Gujarat. It would be interesting to learn more about lion-leopard interaction there. Whatever the facts, it is certain that leopards and tigers have an uneasy coexistence at best in the protected areas where both are present.

In Kanha, most (but not all) leopard sightings in our experience have been in areas that are not densely populated by tigers: for example, Paparphat, Nakti Ghati, and Bija Dadar on the western side of the park, as well as throughout the Mukki range on the south-eastern side (see map facing page 16). Leopards are also quite active at night in the buffer zone, where tigers are seldom seen. Chuck McDougal, who has observed large carnivore behaviour in Nepal's Royal Chitwan National Park for three decades, reported (in 1988) extensive leopard mortality there, which he attributes to severe competition between tigers and leopards for food.

Tigers, quite simply, do not enjoy having their access to prey interfered with, and since an adult male tiger may outweigh a male leopard by a ratio of 4:1, the results of a violent confrontation between the two species will almost always be in the tiger's favour. In 1991, the Indian photographer Rajesh Bedi published the first photograph of a tiger feeding on a leopard, which the larger cat had killed in Corbett National Park. Besides keeping out of the tiger's way, a leopard also has to contend with wild dogs, whose numbers may pose an awesome threat, and also with hyenas, whose scavenging at kills may force even a leopard to withdraw.

On the other hand, in areas with sufficient prey to go around, tigers and leopards (as well as wild dogs) seem to coexist with less strain. Such is the case in Nagarahole National Park in southern Karnataka, where the prey base is ample. Resident wildlife biologist K. Ullas Karanth, whose innovative methodologies for tiger census have attracted wide notice since the early 1990s, compares Nagarahole to the meat counter of a large supermarket, with gaur and sambar ("big-ticket items") for the tigers, langur and chital for the leopards, and a variety of small to mid-size prey for wild dogs. Even in Kanha, one of our leopard sightings (in 1993) occurred near Kanha Meadow at the junction of Link 7 and Bhavan Dabra Road (see map facing page 16), an area where at least three tigers were known to be operating at the same time. In March 1998, there were repeated leopard sightings and evidence of leopard presence (pug marks) along the Kanha-Kisli main road, between Kanha Ghat and Bandari Chappar. During the same period and in the same area, four tigers were sighted regularly. These examples suggest that the so-called "rules" of territory and species distribution may vary quite widely, depending upon the habitat and on the constantly changing dynamics of prey and predator populations.

The subspecies of leopard in the Indian subcontinent is known as *Panthera pardus fusca;* the Latin word *fusca* means "dark". (A separate subspecies, *P. pardus kotiya,* is recognized for Sri Lanka.) The coat of Indian leopards, in fact, does seem somewhat darker than the colour, for example, of leopards in East Africa or South Africa. The Indian leopard is a bit smaller on average than its African cousin. Male leopards in India range up to just over 2.15 m (7 ft.) in length (including the tail) and have an average weight of 55 kg (120 lb.). Female leopards average 30 cm (1 ft.) shorter in length and about 14 kg (30 lb.) less in weight. Melanistic or black leopards occur very rarely in India and have never, to our knowledge, been recorded in Kanha. They are commonest in Malaysia and Indonesia. Like white tigers, black leopards owe their colour to a recessive gene. They possess rosettes, which can be clearly seen in the proper light.

Like leopards everywhere, Kanha leopards can adapt to an extremely varied diet, ranging from small rodents, lizards, and hares to jungle fowl, peafowl, chital, barking deer, and even porcupines. Besides the chital, the favored prey of leopards in Kanha is certainly the langur. The two species together probably account for over 75% of the leopard's total intake of food. Just as there is little love lost between tigers and leopards, langurs regard the spotted cat as a deadly enemy—and they surely lose more of their numbers to leopards than to tigers, due to the leopard's superb camouflage, patient stalking, and tree-climbing agility. Langur alarm calls for a threat from a leopard are especially intense, insistent, and continuous, and the calls are very often accompanied by movement among tree branches or between trees.

Alerted by urgent langur calls, we once waited more than an hour on a February afternoon in 1993 near Kanha Meadow before a leopard showed himself, dashing across the track about 60 m away and then pausing just inside the jungle, until he could inspect us, before melting into the forest. The sighting lasted barely two minutes, but it was memorable.

Leopards and tigers share many of the same behavioural patterns. Essentially solitary animals, male leopards usually separate from their mates, leaving the females to bring up the cubs.

Tigress on Kanha Meadow near Schaller Hide (May 1996)

Chhoti Mada, just off Bison Road

Banseri, Chhoti Mada's mother

The Sunapani Tigress near Desi Nallah

Male cub at Sunapani, aged about 2 years

Female cub at Sunapani

Young male tiger under a banyan tree

Mother with cub on Kanha Meadow

Tigress marking on the way up
from Nakti Ghati to Beniphat

The Chuhri Tigress soon after giving birth (May 1996)

Chuhri cubs after their peacock exploit (see page 146)

Male tiger with sambar kill

Leopard in camouflage near Chimta Camp Road

Wild Dog on Kanha Meadow

Golden Jackal

Females are sexually mature by the age of three years. The gestation period is slightly shorter than for the tiger, lasting 90 days on average, as opposed to 105 days. The litter normally consists of two or three young, who are carefully concealed by the mother in a secluded den (rocky caves are especially favoured) for their first few months of life. Predation by tigers, hyenas, wild dogs, and other leopards probably accounts for a mortality rate of 50% during the cubs' first year. The cubs disperse from the mother when they are about two years old. Longevity in the wild is similar for leopards and tigers, averaging 10-12 years. (Zoo animals, of course, may live considerably longer.)

Leopards use Kanha's system of roads rather less often than tigers, but you should still keep your eyes peeled for leopard pug marks (see the illustration on page 21 for a comparison with tiger pug marks). You may find it difficult to distinguish leopard pug marks from those made by a tiger cub. If the marks have been made by a tiger cub, however, the pug marks of its mother will most often be visible nearby.

Just like tigers, leopards are territorial. The size of a leopard's territory may vary greatly, depending on the prey density in a particular area and on the numbers and spacing of its primary competitors, tigers and wild dogs. Leopards, again like tigers, possess an elaborate scent marking system, which involves spraying, scratching, depositing foeces, and rubbing the face and other body parts on tree limbs and grassy areas. One of this system's principal purposes is to minimize chance meetings that may turn into aggressive or even fatal encounters.

Little information is available about the size of leopard territories in Kanha, although it is almost certain that, as with tiger territories, they vary in size within the park because of prey density and other factors. Research carried out in Sri Lanka (Wilpattu National Park) and in Nepal (Royal Chitwan National Park) during the 1970s suggested that leopards had territories averaging 10 square kilometres. The park estimate of approximately 75 leopards in Kanha seems to have been derived from leopard pug marks observed incidentally in the course of tiger census, as well as from intermittent reports of sightings.

Aside from the yowls and snarls they may give when fighting, leopards have a comparatively small group of calls. Even these are not well understood by scientists. The most distinctive noise a leopard makes is a low, sustained, growling call, which is often compared to the sawing of wood. Experts disagree, however, about the purpose of this call. Some believe that it is territorial, while others think it is a contact call to a mate. Although they are capable of roaring (like lions, tigers, and jaguars), leopards rarely do so. They have been occasionally reported to make softer, less rasping calls like the pook and the *prusten* of a tiger (see page 89).

Considering its importance as the second-ranking predator in the park, the status of the leopard in Kanha is quite poorly understood. Although the park management recently asserted that the leopard population was about 75 or so, no one really knows how many leopards there are. Even more important, there is no reliable information on whether the population is increasing, decreasing, or remaining stable. Significant changes in the leopard population would be important for at least two reasons. First, such changes would inevitably suggest an impact on the dynamics of tigers and wild dogs, and perhaps other species as well. And second, a marked upward trend would almost certainly force more leopards into the buffer zone, where conflicts with human beings—such as preying on cattle and goats—are an ever-present possibility. For these reasons alone, more research on leopards in Kanha is urgently needed.

Photography: The leopard is one of the most difficult animals to photograph in Kanha. Leopards are shy and secretive; sightings are often at dawn or at dusk; and the animal is very seldom seen out in the open. Besides the challenge of low light, the photographer must also cope with the rapid movement of the animal: unlike tigers, leopards seldom sit still long enough to be "working for Kodak." Despite their formidable strength, leopards are considerably smaller than tigers, and using a zoom lens to compensate for distance adds to the difficulty of photographing a highly mobile subject in poor light conditions. For an example of the leopard's unparalleled camouflage in Kanha, see the photograph taken from our vehicle on the Chimta Camp Road in March 1997 in late afternoon.

Seeing a leopard in Kanha, much less photographing it, takes luck. In the first five months of the 1997-98 season (1 Nov–31 Mar), there were only 56 leopard sightings reported at Kisli Gate: an average of approximately one sighting every three days. During the same period, 485 tiger sightings (exclusive of cubs) were reported. At Mukki Gate, 7 leopard sightings and 43 tiger sightings were reported for the same time period. Although these sighting records are only rough indications (given the occurrence of duplicate entries), they yield a ratio of 8+ tiger sightings for every leopard sighting in Kanha.

Sambar

The sambar (*Cervus unicolor*, Hindi *sambar*) is the largest deer in Asia and is widely distributed on the continent. A sambar stag stands between 1.2 and 1.5 m (4-5 ft.) at the shoulder and may weigh over 320 kg (700 lb.). The stag's rack of antlers is sturdy and impressive, measuring 1 m (3+ ft.) on a well-developed head. In India and elsewhere throughout the tiger's range, sambar are the most important members of the deer family as prey for the big cat. Depending on the size of a sambar kill, a tiger may feed comfortably for up to a week.

In Kanha, for example, George Schaller's studies established that tigers in the mid-1960s were preying on sambar more frequently than the ratio of sambar to the total ungulate population would have predicted. The proliferation of dense bamboo thickets in some areas of the park since that time has afforded additional habitat for sambar, and it is a reasonable inference that the population of these deer in Kanha has more than held its own against tiger predation, even though sambar are comparatively slow to reproduce and have a long gestation period (eight months).

The scientific name (or "Latin name") of this deer—*Cervus unicolor*—means "deer of one colour" and accurately describes the animal's monochromatic appearance overall. Sambar coloration ranges through a spectrum of browns (sometimes tinged with grey or yellow) from pale to dark, and the shady forest habitat adds to a viewer's impression of a sambar's muted, almost subdued appearance. Other details of the sambar's coat include the dense ruff of shaggy hair around the neck of both sexes (but especially in males), paler underparts, and a hairless patch or "sore spot" that is sometimes found on the base of the neck. The latter is still poorly understood: it may be linked to the activity of parasites or to a process of glandular secretion.

Because of their large size, sambar need especially effective camouflage. Anyone who has been riding along a track in Kanha in the early morning and has missed spotting a sambar three metres in from the road can testify that camouflage has evolved most successfully for this species.

Sambar are also strikingly silent animals. In *The Book of Indian Animals* (a reference work that is still invaluable), S. H. Prater points out that "the capacity of so heavy an animal to move silently through dense jungle is amazing." It is also noteworthy that sambar, unlike chital and barasingha, do not give a rutting call during the mating season (November-January in Kanha). Communication is confined to scent marking (see below) and to a blaring, honk-like alarm call which—like the roar of a barking deer—travels amazingly far through dense forest. Like chital, sambar also express alertness by stamping a front hoof on the ground and raising their tail.

Sambar and their far smaller cousins, barking deer, are basically forest animals. Sambar are more active at night than by day (unlike barking deer, which are commonly encountered during the middle of the day as well as at dusk and at dawn). Overall, we have found that the best time to look for sambar is during the first hour of the morning park round. On the western side of the park, the Kisli-Kanha main road, the Paparphat area, and the road from Jamun Talao to Nakti Ghati offer good sambar locations. The Mukki Range has a number of good areas: for example, Mahavir Road, Andhahari Jhap, and the road network west of Bishanpura Maidan.

The social organization of sambar also resembles that of barking deer far more than that of the group-living chital or barasingha. Sambar are either solitary or live in small parties comprised of a stag, several hinds, and their young (fawns and yearlings). It is not uncommon to see solitary adult stags, who live on their own except during the rut, or mating season. You may also see a hind either alone or accompanied by one or two young.

Stags reach full maturity and develop all six points of their antlers by the time they are four years old. Besides using their antlers as weapons in fights for control of territory and for access to hinds during the rut, sambar thrash or rub their antlers against saplings and other vegetation. This may be an example of redirected aggression, as M. K. Ranjitsinh has argued, or it may play a role in communication, somewhat like the scent from the preorbital glands that sambar are fond of rubbing on vegetation. For many species of ungulates like deer, in fact, scent marking fulfills a complex communication function; this system is as important, perhaps, as scent marking among carnivores, although much more field research is needed to establish its mechanisms.

Sambar live over a vast geographical region, ranging from India and Myanmar, Malaysia, and parts of China to the islands of Sumatra, Borneo, and Taiwan. It is therefore no surprise that the diet of this adaptable species is quite diverse. In Kanha, sambar feed on grass, wild fruits, and the foliage of trees such as sal, saja, mahua, and aonla. They are also partial to the fruits and the bark of the haldu tree. In Kanha and in other Indian national parks such as Corbett, sambar will readily visit salt licks.

Of the four major deer species in Kanha, sambar and barasingha are the most at home in water. During extremely hot, dry weather (April-June), when food is scarce elsewhere, sambar will congregate at waterholes, wading in up to the head and neck to eat sedge. In 1984, while Belinda Wright and Stanley Breeden were filming their classic documentary *The Land of the Tiger,* a large male tiger known as Genghis perfected a technique of charging into the water to prey on sambar in the lakes at Ranthambhore National Park in Rajasthan. Wright and Breeden were able to include in their film some of the most dramatic footage ever taken of a tiger in the wild—including a struggle between Genghis and a crocodile over a sambar carcass. Valmik Thapar photographed an epic battle between a sambar stag and the famous Ranthambhore tigress named Noon (the sambar survived the combat).

Less dramatic, but equally memorable in our minds, was our own first sighting of a wild tigress in February 1989. It was Nuri, the daughter of Noon in Ranthambhore, and the location was the edge of one of those same lakes. Out for a late-afternoon promenade, Nuri was making no effort to stalk or to conceal herself as she strode around the lake. We were nearly 1 km away when the blare of a sambar alarm call alerted us to her presence. Even after several hundred other tiger sightings in Indian parks, the memory of this first *darshan* remains indelible.

The most spectacular sambar we have sighted in Kanha was on the steeply sloping, open strip of ground that serves as the fireline between Mandla and Balaghat districts, about half way between Nakti Ghati and Bishanpura on the main Kanha-Mukki Road. As we climbed the hill and looked to the right around 7:30 in the morning, a sambar stag stood motionless in golden, slanting light. Even though he was at least 75 m away, his size and majestic rack of antlers were breathtaking. As is often the case with sambar, he stood stock still for a considerable time. Then, judging that we were beyond his flight distance, he quietly returned to grazing.

Photography: Sambar are relatively difficult to photograph because of their monochromatic coloration, their camouflage with the habitat, and their preferred time of day for moving around (early morning or late afternoon). On the other hand, even if they are spotted very close to the road, they tend to freeze for 15 seconds or more, provided you do not penetrate the range of their flight distance. Using 200 or 400 ASA film, you should be able to get a decent shot. Remember that the use of flash in the park is forbidden.

Sloth Bear

The sloth bear *(Melursus ursinus,* Hindi *bhalu)* is one of the most fascinating large mammals in Kanha. The distinctive, large pug marks of this species may be seen fairly often in the early morning before too many vehicles have disturbed the roads. But the animal itself, which is almost wholly nocturnal at Kanha, is seldom observed. Lovers of deep forest, bears seldom bother with making themselves available to tourists and photographers. In nearly ten years of visits to the park, we have had only one sloth bear sighting when the animal was near enough to the road and the light was good enough to make photography possible. It is fair to say that the sloth bear (along with the hyena, perhaps) is truly Kanha's mystery animal. If you keep score on such matters, a good sloth bear sighting might be rated the equivalent of 10 tigers (or 5 leopards).

Adult male sloth bears measure 65-85 cm (2-2¾ ft.) at the shoulder, with a total body length of 140-170 cm (4½-5½ ft.) and a weight of 125-145 kg (275-320 lb.). Adult females are somewhat smaller and lighter. The sloth bear has a long, black coat, shaggy and coarse in texture; a long, flexible snout and naked lips; and a prominent white or creamy brown U- or V-shaped chest mark. The gestation period is about 7 months, with mating concentrated during the hot weather and young (typically 2 cubs) born in winter. Sloth bears, unlike other species of bear, do not become dormant, but rather retire to dens for seclusion and the protection of the young. Mothers, which have been photographed carrying young cubs on their back, tend the offspring for 2-3 years. A. A. Dunbar Brander, who opened his classic survey of Indian wildlife (*Wild Animals in Central India*) with a chapter on the sloth bear, states that the animal, while gifted with a reasonably strong sense of smell, has poor eyesight and hearing.

Sloth bears in Kanha are omnivores rather than carnivores, subsisting on a diet of ants and termites, as well as honey, eggs, carrion, grubs, flowers such as mahua, and various fruits and fruit remnants (seeds and peelings), including mango, jamun, and amaltas (laburnum); they consume the latter especially during the hot months of April-June.

Among the relatively small number of species in the family *Ursidae* (seven worldwide), the sloth bear has developed some unique adaptations that distinguish it from any other bear. It takes its common name from its ability to hang upside down like a sloth, owing to the long, curved formation of its claws. As a specialized adaptation for its diet, the sloth bear lacks two inner upper incisors that are found in other bears. Longevity of the species in the wild is unknown, but in captivity sloth bears have been known to live up to 40 years.

The sloth bear is proverbial for its courage, its ingenuity in foraging, and its pugnacious temperament. No other animal, including a gaur or a tiger, is more unpredictable or dangerous to an unarmed human being on foot in the forest. At the start of a nature walk in Royal Chitwan N. P. in Nepal, where sloth bears are more commonly sighted than at Kanha, our guide gave the following succinct advice: in case of a tiger, freeze and be silent, but in case of a sloth bear, make all the noise you can, and pray that the disturbance will frighten the animal away. Despite this unpredictability of the species, human beings have taken a melancholy revenge on sloth bears by "training" them as performing entertainers. As recently as 1984, a photograph of one such bear appeared in David Macdonald's standard reference work, *The Encyclopedia of Mammals*, with a caption asserting that such a sight nowadays in India is rare. Unfortunately, not rare enough: we have seen itinerant captive bears several times on highways, most recently in March 1999 near Fatehpur Sikri.

Photography: For the reasons given in the first paragraph of this section, we can scarcely presume to offer any advice on sloth bear photography. If you get a good picture of a sloth bear in Kanha, please send it to us, so that we may include it (and credit your good fortune) in a subsequent edition of this book!

Tiger

The tiger *(Panthera tigris,* Hindi *sher, bagh)* is the largest of all thirty-seven species of wild cats. Along with the lion, the leopard, the snow leopard, and the jaguar, the tiger is classified in the genus *Panthera,* which comprises the group of "big cats" that are capable of roaring, owing to a modification of the hyoid bone. Tigers are the only big cat with stripes, which have evidently evolved for the sake of camouflage in the animal's wide range of habitats. Stripes, like the spots and rosettes on many other felid species, break up the image of an animal's body in long grass or in the dappled light of the forest; according to one theory, the stripes of tigers are actually elongated spots.

Like the puma or cougar of the Americas *(Felis concolor)* and the leopard of the Old World *(Panthera pardus),* the tiger has a wide geographical range, although it is not nearly so widespread as it was a century ago (see map on page 85). Today there are fourteen tiger range states: Bangladesh, Bhutan, Cambodia, China, India, Indonesia, Laos, Malaysia, Myanmar, Nepal, North Korea, Russia, Thailand, and Vietnam. These countries are the custodians of the five remaining subspecies of tigers, amounting to a total of probably fewer than 5,000 animals. These figures compare with eight known subspecies at the turn of the last century, with a tiger population of 40,000 or so in India alone. All five extant subspecies of tiger are now officially classified as endangered.

What is a subspecies? The American field biologist and big cat expert John Seidensticker has proposed three criteria for the definition of members of a subspecies: 1) sharing a unique geographical range; 2) possessing identifiable physical characteristics; and 3) having a unique natural history relative to other subspecies within the species. The concept of subspecies is somewhat controversial, and searching questions have been posed recently about the evidence and methods used to classify tigers. Recent DNA work shows that no real differences exist between subspecies. British biologist Andrew Kitchener has pointed out, moreover, that 7 of the 8 tiger subspecies were originally described (or defined) on the basis of only 11 specimens in all. The length of the body and the length of the tail were the outstanding features considered, and little attention was paid to the complexities of body

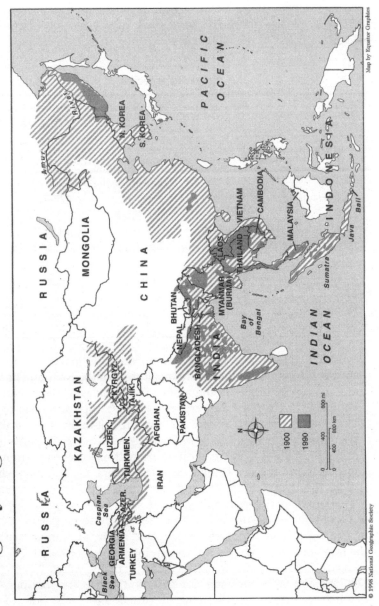

Range of Tigers

Map by Equator Graphics

© 1998 National Geographic Society

size, coloration, and pelage. Kitchener suspects that variations *within* populations may be more significant than variations *between* populations. Virtually all the literature on tigers today, however, continues to use the eight traditional subspecies for discussion. These are listed in the table below.

Tiger Subspecies

Scientific Name	Common Name	Where Found	Population Estimate
Panthera tigris tigris	Royal Bengal	India, Nepal, Bangladesh	2,500-3,000
P. tigris altaica	Amur, Siberian	Russian Far East	425-500
P. tigris sumatrae	Sumatran	Indonesia	400-500
P. tigris corbetti	Indochinese	Thailand, Laos, Vietnam	1,200-1,800
P. tigris amoyensis	South China	China	20-30
P. tigris balica	Bali	Indonesia	Extinct (1940s)
P. tigris virgata	Caspian	Central Asia	Extinct (1970s)
P. tigris sondaica	Javan	Indonesia	Extinct (1980s)

As this table shows, wild tigers can thrive in a wide variety of habitats, ranging from the coniferous forests of the Russian Far East to the tall grass jungles at the foot of the Himalayas, the mangrove swamps of the Sunderbans, and the steamy, tropical forests of the island of Sumatra. Related to this distribution are striking variations in the size and weight of tigers. Unlike leopards and pumas, individual tigers may differ dramatically, depending on the subspecies and the sex. Female Sumatran tigers, for example, which weigh 75-110 kg (165-240 lb.) and measure 2.2 m (7+ ft.) on average, are dwarfed by Siberian males, which may scale over 300 kg (660 lb.) and which measure over 3.3 m (10½ ft.) between pegs.

The tiger is at the apex of the food chain at Kanha (see the diagram on page 34). Males weigh 180-230 kg (400-500 lb.) and measure 2.8-3 m (9-9½ ft.) on average. Females weigh 100-160 kg (220-350 lb.) and measure 2.4-2.65 m (7¾-8½ ft.). Besides the distinctive stripes, whose pattern differs on each side of an individual's body, the back side of a tiger's ears displays striking white spots on a black field. The most persuasive explanation for these markings, which are common to a number of other wild cat species, is that they facilitate the following of a mother by cubs in long grass.

Individual tigers may also be identified by their unique patterns of cheek and eyebrow markings. Using this method for identification, however, takes considerable care and practice. As with sidestripe markings, patterns are readily subject to distortion in photographs, depending on lighting conditions, the angle of view, and the effect of posture and musculature on the appearance of the tiger's coat at any particular moment.

Tigers have three basic requirements: sufficient water, shelter, and prey. Tigers need to drink regularly, and they use dense vegetative cover for resting and for concealment while hunting. Not surprisingly, tiger density varies considerably according to the habitat's prey density. For example, in areas with very high prey density, such as south India's Nagarahole National Park, tiger density has been estimated at an abundant 11.65 animals per 100 km². This compares with a figure (calculated in the early 1990s) of 6.92 tigers per 100 km² at Kanha. At the other end of the scale, there may be as few as 1.3 tigers per *thousand* square kilometers in the Sikhote Alin area of Siberia.

Despite their excellent camouflage and enormous power, tigers are successful only once in every 10-20 attempts to stalk and kill prey. At Kanha, the mainstay of the tiger's diet consists of sambar, chital, barasingha, and wild boar. Tigers will occasionally attack gaur (especially the calves), as well as small prey such as barking deer and porcupines. We have watched a tigress catch and eat a langur on Kanha Meadow. We have also witnessed a year-old tiger cub's inept assault on a peacock, which escaped.

Tigers have two principal methods of dispatching their prey: a bite on the nape of the neck that severs the vertebral column (commonly used with smaller prey) and suffocation by means of a throat bite (used with prey weighing more than half the tiger's own weight). In two chital kills that we have witnessed, one tigress seized a doe by the back of the neck, while another one suffocated a full-grown chital stag with a stranglehold on the throat. With a throat bite, the grip may be maintained for several minutes. After the kill, a tiger will normally carry or drag its prey into thick cover in order to protect it from other predators and from scavengers.

In the case of large ungulate prey such as deer, tigers typically begin to feed from the rump.

The precise composition of a tiger's diet is obviously affected by the habitat, as is its killing rate. It has been shown that for large predators such as tigers and lions, the efficient expenditure of energy favours the taking of large prey whenever possible. In places such as Kanha and Ranthambhore, this means the sambar. Additional factors influencing prey selection are the presence and numbers of co-predators. In habitats with very high prey density such as Nagarahole N.P. in south India, the average size of tiger prey (adult male chital, sambar, wild boar, and young gaur) was recently shown to be 90+ kg (200 lb.), with a selective bias toward animals in the range of 175 kg (385 lb.) and up. In contrast, leopards and wild dogs favoured prey in the 30-175 kg (65-385 lb.) weight class. In such habitats as Nagarahole, prey availability in the size classes suitable for each major predator is not a limiting resource.

How much does an adult tiger need to eat? A tiger's kill rate will vary, of course, with the size of the prey taken, the ratio of edible to inedible parts, and whether or not the prey is shared with conspecifics or appropriated by another tiger. Tigers must kill more in terms of prey weight than the amount actually eaten: for example, more than 25% of a chital stag's total weight may consist of inedible parts such as the bones and the rumen contents. On average, it has been calculated that an adult tigress needs to take a fair-sized prey (full-grown chital and up) 40-50 times a year, or once every 7-8 days. A tigress with cubs must kill more often. During the two-year period of offspring dependency, a female with two young needs 60-70 kills a year, or one every 5-6 days. Tigers may remain at a kill for three days or more. Average consumption of meat for an adult tiger has been estimated at 15-18 kg (33-40 lb.) per day, although tigers have been occasionally known to consume up to 34 kg (75 lb.) in a single night.

Tigers are equipped with excellent vision and hearing, as well as with a complex olfactory system about which we know little. Vision and hearing have been usually assumed to play the key roles in hunting, although it seems unlikely that tigers do not employ their sophisticated sense of smell, used so often for other purposes on a daily basis, in locating and stalking prey. We do know that smell and scent-marking are critical factors in the communications system of tigers. To keep in touch with what other tigers are doing, and to advertise their own presence, both male and female tigers spray urine mixed with scent from the anal glands, deposit fœces, scrape the ground, and scratch trees. The information that tigers glean from these "calling cards" allows them to avoid potentially dangerous confrontations; it also facilitates the sexes' consorting to mate when females are in estrus. Scent marks adhere to vegetation for a surprisingly long time: George Schaller reported, for example, that scent on tree trunks persisted for three to four weeks in the absence of heavy rains.

Tigers possess two sensory enhancements, neither of which is unique to this species. The first is the *tapetum lucidum* (Latin for "bright carpet"), a reflective patch in the retina of the eye which maximizes vision in poor light (and which causes the eyes of tigers, like those of deer and many other mammals, to shine in the dark). The second is the vomeronasal organ (VNO), sometimes called Jacobson's organ, which is located in the roof of the mouth. A tiger's use of the VNO is most obvious in the grimace known as *flehmen*, in which the animal wrinkles its nose and extends its tongue. There is evidence that the VNO in males is especially adapted for ascertaining and evaluating the sexual receptivity of females.

Other components of the communications repertory of tigers include calls, body and ear posture, and tail movements. In *The Deer and the Tiger*, George Schaller noted the following vocalizations: purring, *prusten* (a gentle, puffing sound of air rapidly expelled through the nostrils), pooking (a loud, clear call that is a bit flatter than a sambar alarm), grunting, miaowing, whoofing, moaning, and roaring. Aggression may often be conveyed by body language: for example, head carried low, back muscles tensed, ears laid back, and tail swinging from side to side.

The social organization of tigers has received a good deal of study, but we still have much to learn. Despite the elaborate system of scent marking, which makes communication possible, tigers have evolved as basically solitary: almost certainly, this feature is an adaptation to seeking and securing prey dispersed in a forest habitat. (Contrast, for example, group-living lions on the open savannah.) The basic social unit among tigers is a mother and her cubs, which remain with her for 20-24 months after birth. Both males and females are territorial, in that they regularly patrol a "beat" that they will aggressively defend against other tigers, especially those of the same sex. At Kanha and in other national parks, tigers often use park roads to patrol their territories, and they may cover 16-32 km (10-20 miles) in a single night.

A tiger's **territory,** or the area that it will actively defend against intrusion, may be distinguished from a larger area called its **home range,** or the region that the animal travels over to find food and shelter, to locate mates, and to raise its young. The typical home ranges of male tigers are considerably larger than those of females. At Nepal's Royal Chitwan National Park in the 1970s, for example, Mel Sunquist found that the home ranges of females measured approximately 20 km² (8 square miles), as against 60-100 km² (23-40 square miles) for males. In the 1960s at Kanha, George Schaller reported a home range for a tigress of 25 square miles and one for a male tiger of 30 square miles, but these figures were based on a population estimate of 10-15 adult tigers (not including transients) in a total area of about 300 km² (120 square miles), or less than a third of the park's core area today. In the Russian Far East, where prey is widely scattered, home ranges are a great deal larger. For a female tiger, the primary factor in territoriality seems to be access to prey and a secure area for the raising of a litter. For males, the more important factor may be access to females, rather than food.

At Kanha, the territory of a male tiger will typically contain those of several females: see the map on page 37. Although this map shows female territories as non-overlapping, it is probable that the home ranges, at least, of Kanha females overlap each other considerably. Some researchers have found that, soon after dispersal, the home ranges of daughters are adjacent to, or overlapping with, those of mothers. Male offspring typically range much farther afield in the attempt to lay claim to or take over a territory of their own. Until they succeed, they are often classified as "transients" or "floaters," who occupy a peripheral position on the basic territorial map of tiger distribution within a region at any given time.

It is important to remember that tiger territories are dynamic, rather than static, spaces, constantly shifting over time in accordance with multiple factors. For example, fluctuations in prey density will inevitably have an impact on the density and distribution of tigers in any given population. Relationships with co-predators, such as leopards and wild dogs, will also affect the size of tiger territories.

These dynamics received a dramatic illustration recently at Yellowstone National Park in the USA, where the reintroduction of wolves in 1995 after half a century's absence reshaped the ecosystem within two years. The newly arrived wolves—who are, like tigers, at the apex of the food chain in their ecosystem—had a major impact on the Yellowstone coyotes *(Canis latrans)*, who were suddenly demoted to the position of second-ranking predator. The coyote population was cut in half, with a concomitant increase in rodents, while elk were forced to become far more vigilant.

Consorting to mate is the only regularly recurring association between male and female tigers. Reports from the field and from zoos suggest that the estrus cycle differs considerably for wild and captive females, with intervals of 15-20 days reported for free-living tigresses and cycles of 45-60 days recorded for zoo animals. The average length of the heat period appears to be about five days. Despite anecdotal evidence of seasonality in mating, with a peak occurring during the cold months and early warm weather (November to April), conception and birth can occur at any time of the year. Copulation lasts only 15-30 seconds but may be repeated at frequent intervals over a period of five or six days (in a pattern similar to that of lions). The roars and snarls of the tigress are at least partially due to the risk and pain she incurs. As in other felids, the heavier male, mounting from behind, grasps the female in his jaws by the nape of the neck, a position that exposes her to potentially fatal injury. Meanwhile, small spines on the male's sexual organ are thought to induce ovulation in the female, making conception possible but rendering copulation painful. Should a tigress lose her litter, estrus occurs very soon thereafter (mean of 17 days)—a biological fact that is closely related to the phenomenon of tiger infanticide (see below).

Tigers are born blind and helpless after a gestation period of approximately 105 days. As with many carnivores, the tiger's relatively brief gestation is an adaptation for the pregnant female's necessity of pursuing and killing prey. The average tiger litter size is 2-3 cubs. Although litters as large as seven are mentioned in the literature, we could find no one at Kanha who had seen a litter of even four young (Schaller reported two cases of 4-cub litters in 1964). Mothers give birth in a carefully chosen, secluded den, from which the cubs rarely emerge until they are three months old. Juvenile mortality has been reported as high: according to one study, 34% during the first year of life and a further 17% in the second. A common cause of cub death is infanticide: one may compare the same phenomenon in the very different social systems of langurs (see page 71) and lions. Infanticide in tigers, monkeys, and lions seems to have the same root cause. Since females who lose their offspring come into estrus sooner than mothers who rear infants to weaning, a usurping or "takeover" male will enhance his own opportunities to breed if he eliminates the offspring of competitors.

Female tigers become sexually mature when they are about three years old (as opposed to males, which are thought not to mature until they are four or five). With an interbirth interval of 20-30 months and a longevity of up to 15 years or so in the wild, females have an average reproductive life span of 6.1 years, with a range up to 12.5 years. Sita, a well-known tigress in Bandhavgarh National Park who has graced the cover of *National Geographic*, produced six litters between early 1986 and September 1996: of her 18 cubs that were documented, 7 died in the first two years of life. Peter Jackson reports that the mean number of offspring surviving to dispersal is only 4.54 per tigress (with an average of only 2 animals per tigress eventually incorporated into the breeding population).

Tigers normally go out of their way to avoid contact with human beings. Of course, tigers do occasionally attack and kill people, and some animals consume human flesh. In various areas of India, such as the Kumaon hills of Uttar Pradesh and the mangrove swamps of the Sunderbans, casualties have been especially high over the years (although elephants and snakes have been responsible for far more injuries and fatalities than tigers have caused). Jim Corbett, who probably knew more about man-eaters than anyone else before or since, pronounced the tiger "a large-hearted gentleman" and diagnosed man-eaters as aberrations owing to injury, starvation, or unusual provocation (most often the threat from intrusion that a mother may sense to her cubs). Very little has been discovered in the half century since Corbett's books appeared that would alter his opinion. Tourists in a national park like Kanha, however, need to bear in mind that the park is a *tiger reserve*. Never get out of your vehicle without the permission of the park guide!

And remember the fate of David Hunt, the British ornithologist who wandered off from his group one day in the 1980s in the cause of science at Corbett National Park. While he was foot trekking (strictly forbidden in Kanha), Hunt unwittingly disturbed a tigress, who killed him and partially consumed the body. Tiger Steering Committee member Brijendra Singh, who resides for part of the year in the park, was called on to intervene. Brij captured the tigress, but not before his servant had suffered terrible head injuries, from which the man barely recovered. He wears a turban to this day, which he unwraps proudly to show visitors what the

Barasingha are renowned for their majestic antlers

Sambar does

Chital Stag

Barking Deer female near Minkur Nallah Road

Sloth Bear in Royal Chitwan National Park, Nepal

Gaur Female

Blackwinged Kite

Indian Roller

Blackheaded Oriole

Racket-tailed Drongo

Sister Anita Horsey with Ahmet Sabir and Shivaji

Jungle Cat in Keoladeo National Park, Bharatpur

Tribal
woman
in Kanha

Munglu Baiga, Kanha's premier tracker

Forest Guard B. S. Maravi

Ernie Hulsey
with Ashok Kumar
and Rehman Khan

effects look like when you have had your head in a tiger's mouth and lived to tell the tale.

Occasionally, aberrations of another sort occur. White tigers are the result of a recessive gene, rather than of true albinism: white tigers, for example, have blue rather than pink eyes. All white tigers are reputed to be the descendants of Mohan, a tiger captured in the early 1950s by the Maharajah of Rewa. During·the 1970s in the USA, these animals rivalled the giant panda as the focus of blockbuster zoo publicity and exhibits. Unfortunately, they also became a fetish for individual and institutional collecting: witness the menagerie of white tigers maintained by the American entertainers Siegfried and Roy, or the collection of animals kept in suboptimal conditions at Nandankanan in Bhubaneshwar. Occasionally, black tigers have been reported, but the only concrete evidence of this colour phase (which does not seem to be true melanism) is a skin that was seized from illegal traders in Delhi in 1992.

As we have seen, the Indian (or "Royal Bengal") tiger is just one of five surviving subspecies. Tigers in India, however, probably account for over half of the world's total figure. How many tigers there really are in India is an intensely controversial subject, with fur flying constantly among government authorities, NGO's, and field biologists (see Chapter 1, page 22). As researcher K. Ullas Karanth has pointed out, however, the priorities of park managers ought to focus on 1) determining a reliable *range* of numbers for the top predators, especially tigers; and 2) determining upward or downward trends in the census for both predators and prey in the protected area.

In the India of old, tigers co-existed with two other species of large cat besides the leopard: the Asiatic lion *(Panthera leo persica)* and the cheetah *(Acinonyx jubatus)*. In the huge subcontinent, each felid had its ecological niche, with lions favouring more open, drier forest areas and cheetahs preferring the level plains that would afford scope for their dazzling bursts of speed to bring down prey. Now these two co-predators of the tiger are reduced to slender relics. The Asiatic lion exists only in the Gir Forest in Gujarat, with a population of some 250-300 animals. The prowess of the cheetah—celebrated in the hunting expeditions of Mughal emperors like Akbar the Great—is no more than a memory's wisp, evoked by the grace and speed of this cat's principal prey, the blackbuck *(Antilope cervicapra)* and the Indian gazelle *(Gazella*

gazella). The tiger's co-existence with the lion, an animal so commensurate in size and power but so different in social organization, would be an especially interesting facet of Indian natural history for further research—particularly since India was the only place in recent historical times where the two top predators were both present. In 1972, as part of the public relations effort in behalf of Project Tiger, the tiger displaced the lion of the Ashoka Column as India's national animal.

Field biology (sometimes called ethology) is a relatively young scientific discipline, having its origins in the 1940s with the work of a trio of brilliant Nobel Prize winners: Niko Tinbergen, Karl von Frisch, and Konrad Lorenz. (All three shared the prize in 1973 for their contributions to the study of animal behaviour.) Modern research on *P. tigris tigris* may be said to have begun in 1963-65— only slightly more than a generation ago—with George Schaller's studies in Kanha, which Schaller published in a landmark book entitled *The Deer and the Tiger* (1967). Schaller's base-line research convincingly established the ecosystem approach for the analysis of predator-prey relations. He reported on numerous aspects of the natural history of tigers, including population dynamics, ranges, social organization, communication, reproduction, hunting and killing, and feeding ecology.

It is interesting that subsequent tiger research in the subcontinent has moved forward in tandem with technological innovation. Schaller used fœcal analysis in the laboratory to acquire important information about the tiger's diet and feeding ecology. In the 1970s, Mel Sunquist pioneered the technique of radio telemetry at Royal Chitwan National Park in Nepal in order to determine the movements and associations of tigers. This method involves using a dart gun to tranquilize a carefully selected portion of a tiger population and then attaching a light-weight radio collar to each cat. The signals emitted by the collar are then monitored on a continuing basis with a receiver, and the data are plotted on charts. This information is supplemented by eyewitness observations. Over time (and with luck), a detailed picture of various aspects of the tiger's life emerges. Radio telemetry has done much, for example, to elucidate territoriality, associations with other tigers, and "activity budgets" (the different ways in which tigers expend their energy).

While radio collaring continues as one of the most productive technologies in the study of animal behaviour, an even more recent innovation appeared in the 1990s: the use of camera traps to aid identification of individual tigers and to refine census efforts. Camera-trap analyses have been carried out in Nagarahole National Park, as well as in a number of other parks (including Kanha), by K. Ullas Karanth. The technique actually has its roots in the 1920s, when the hunter-conservationist F. W. Champion placed trip wires at strategic points on Indian forest roads so that nocturnally prowling tigers would take their own pictures.

Although much has been learned about the tiger's natural history and ecology over the past thirty-five years, it would be foolish to assume that we have anything like an adequate picture of behaviour for this species. Descriptions of tiger behaviour containing the words *always* or *never* are thus especially worthy of skepticism, since orthodoxy is regularly overthrown by new discoveries. Only recently, for example, it was taken as gospel that male tigers "never" participate in the rearing of cubs. Observations by Valmik Thapar and Fateh Singh Rathore in Ranthambhore have persuaded scientists and tiger-wallahs to replace that adverb with "seldom" or "infrequently." In the literature, rearing of cubs was not viewed as a collaborative enterprise (in contrast to lions); yet in 1992 we observed two tiger families (females with two cubs each) feeding communally at a sambar kill in Kanha. One more example: conventional wisdom holds that you will never sight leopards or wild dogs anywhere near the areas where tigers are operating, but we have found numerous exceptions to this "rule" in Kanha. In the continuing effort to learn more about tigers, professional researchers and amateur observers alike need to keep an open mind.

In the troubled interaction of human beings with tigers, two major threats to the big cat have dominated the human side of the equation. The first was trophy hunting, which assumed the proportions of a slaughter in the 1950s and 1960s, thus provoking the "first tiger crisis", the passage of the Wildlife Protection Act in 1972, and the inauguration of Project Tiger in 1973. The second threat has been (and continues to be) poaching, the impetus for which has substantially increased by the large prices paid for tiger bone, which is used in traditional Chinese medicine (TCM). In TCM, no part of a tiger goes to waste. The animal's bones are ground up and made into preparations for rheumatism; the eyeballs are used to counteract epilepsy; the whiskers are reputed to alleviate toothaches; the skin is employed to treat mental illness; the teeth are said to remedy rabies and asthma; stomach parts may relieve stomach upsets; the tail is used for various skin diseases; the brain cures laziness (and pimples); the fat battles vomiting and dog bites; the blood is held to strengthen the constitution and to fortify human will power; and the testes are used for tuberculosis of the lymph nodes. Last but not least, tiger penis soup is a famed aphrodisiac.

Although the above catalogue may seem eccentric or fanciful to many readers, the fact that a substantial fraction of China's population of one billion people—not to speak of the large Chinese communities in North America—believe in the efficacy of TCM must be taken seriously. Furthermore, several meticulous surveys, notably by the international wildlife monitoring organization TRAFFIC (the acronym stands for Trade Record Analysis of Flora and Fauna in Commerce), have established that the trade in tiger parts is a worldwide problem, involving communities in New York City, San Francisco, Toronto, and Vancouver, as well as markets in Taiwan and Hong Kong.

Kanha National Park, currently known as Kanha Tiger Reserve, is probably the premier venue in the world today in which to view free-living tigers. In many other protected areas of the subcontinent, the chances for sighting a wild tiger are reasonably good: for example, Bandhavgarh, Corbett, Nagarahole, and Ranthambhore in India, as well as Royal Chitwan in Nepal. Over the past decade, however, our own experience, together with that of tourists whom we have informally surveyed, points to Kanha as the top tiger park in India—and, indeed, in the whole of Asia. In the past ten years, the Kanha authorities have steadily claimed a census count of approximately 100 adult tigers within the park. Extrapolation from our own observations of tigers and tiger sign in Kanha's tourist zone accords with this figure.

Good tiger habitat within Kanha is unevenly distributed, as is shown by the maps on pages 36-37. It is thus not surprising that the density of tiger territories largely coincides with the suitability of various regions within the park for chital. Even though the sambar, as a considerably larger ungulate, is the tiger's preferred prey (see above), chital are by far the most numerous prey species in Kanha for the major carnivores, outnumbering sambar by a factor of at least 6:1. In Kanha, chital straddle the forest edge or ecotone, the dividing line between two habitat types (for example, meadow and sal forest). This feature adds to their attractiveness as a prey species for the tiger.

Pinpointing the location of tigers within the park on any given day is, of course, the aim of 95% of the local punditry. In addition to direct observations, the evidence consists of pug marks, scats, signs of kills, and alarm calls. Practically anyone can be a source of useful information: park guides, naturalists, drivers, mahouts, and other tourists. Checking the tiger sighting books at Kisli and Mukki is worthwhile, as is planning one's daily routes through the park with attention to prime tiger sighting time—the hour after sunrise and the hour before sunset—as well as to the possibility of a tiger show.

We have sighted tigers in practically all parts of the tourist zone at Kanha. Certain areas have been more productive than others in various years. This makes generalization risky. Overall, though, it is fair to say that Kanha has a "core tiger viewing area" in the western sector of the tourist zone. This area includes the main Kisli-Kanha Road, Sal Ghat, Jamun Talao, the Kanha Meadow, Bari Chuhri Road, the Beniphat-Nakti Ghati connector, Lakara Gadhah Road up to Dhawa Dadar, Links 7 and 8, and Sijhora Road (see map facing page 16). Likely locations in the eastern sector of the park include Andhahari Jhap, Mahavir Road, Sondhar, Umer Jhula, and Minkur Nallah Road.

One of the principal attractions of Kanha, which helps to maximize the chances of a tiger sighting, is the tiger show (see Chapter 1, page 26). The fact that the view of a tiger that the show affords is somewhat artificial scarcely seems to bother most tourists, who may be subliminally aware that the entire experience of a national park is less than definitively "natural." Although the tiger show has been vehemently criticized by purists on a variety of grounds, we continue to believe that it is a valuable part of the Kanha experience. The show involves a restricted geographical area and a very small fraction of the park's tigers, who are arguably no more disturbed by it than by the peregrinations of filmmaking teams and road workers. In the course of tracking for the show, the park mahouts may amass important information about tiger movements and behaviour. Finally, the education and public relations value of the tiger show for an institution such as Kanha is significant, and the park's appreciation of this is evident in the staging of special tiger shows for VIPs on elephant back.

The tiger show is possible only because there is a delicate balance between tigers and elephants, with both species respecting limits and recognizing the danger if decorum is breached. This mutual respect carries a valuable lesson for humans. A tiger *darshan* is a rare privilege that depends on the skill of the mahouts, the training of the elephants, careful supervision by park authorities, and the forbearance of the tigers. Accordingly, human behaviour should be responsible and dignified. (See the boxed feature of **Do's and Dont's for the Tiger Show** on page 101.)

Photography: Everyone will have different objectives and approaches to tiger photography. George Schaller is said to have remarked once that there are probably more tiger experts than tigers left in India, and the same might be said of photography pundits. Some general advice follows.

If your camera is equipped with a telephoto lens (a basic necessity for decent wildlife photography), try to zoom in as close as you can. Tigers are large mammals, but they are nowhere near as large as elephants, or even gaur. If you are interested in making a positive identification of the animal on subsequent sightings, try to get the cheek and eyebrow markings.

Remember that a stationary animal's behaviour may change very rapidly. This is especially important for video enthusiasts. Like many big (and small) cats, tigers often stretch and/or yawn before they get up from a sitting or lying position to move.

Tiger sightings may occur in a wide variety of locales and lighting conditions. Hence, different lenses, film speeds, and aperture settings may be required. Even in the course of a single sighting, conditions may change appreciably. If you are using auto focus, keep in mind that even a single grass stem between you and the animal may distract the mechanism and result in a blurred image. It is far preferable to use manual focus.

During a tiger show, your mahout will turn the elephant so that the riders on both sides of the howdah will have equal time. Keep in mind that a tiger show may be unexpectedly extended if the tiger gets up and moves through the jungle. You cannot get a good still photograph if the elephant is moving. Therefore, if you are in a suitable position and close enough for a picture, ask the mahout to pause momentarily so that you can get your photo. Be aware that some tiger shows may involve more than one tiger: we have seen as many as six. Enjoy the experience!

Tigers: Facts vs. Fiction

The following are some common misconceptions about tigers:

1. **Wild tigers may be found in Africa.** Tigers are native to Asia, where they are presently found in 14 countries called the "tiger range states." Lions are now found almost solely in Africa; there is only one relict population in India, located in the Gir National Park and Lion Sanctuary in Gujarat.

2. **Tigers, like most cats, dislike water and carefully avoid it.** Actually, tigers take readily to water and are excellent swimmers, as is shown by the tigers of the Sunderbans, a vast area of mangrove swamps straddling the Indian border with Bangladesh. Tigers need to drink regularly, and they often slip into pools of water (hindquarters first) to cool off in the hot weather.

3. **Today's tigers are descendants of the prehistoric sabre-tooth tigers.** This is false. The sabre-tooth tiger *(Smilodon)* species that we know from fossil remains like those at the La Brea tar pits in southern California are not even close relatives of the modern tiger.

4. **Tigers will attack human beings every time they get a chance.** False. Tigers normally go out of their way to avoid human contact.

5. **Tigers roar when they attack their prey.** The tiger does not need to draw any more attention to its approach than is already the case in the Indian jungle, with many animals and birds issuing alarm calls that publicize the big cat's movements. Almost invariably, tigers are silent when they approach and attack their prey.

6. **Tigers prefer small prey to large prey.** If given a choice, tigers (like African lions) will go for large prey, since killing a "big-ticket item" is more energy-efficient.

7. **White tigers are albinos.** False. The colour of white tigers is due to a recessive gene. Unlike true albinos, white tigers have blue (rather than pink) eyes.

8. **All tigers are roughly the same size, with the exception that males are somewhat larger than females.** Depending on the subspecies and the habitat, tigers vary dramatically in size and weight. A Siberian male tiger, for example, may be four times heavier than a Sumatran female.

9. **The basic social unit in tigerland is a mating pair.** No: the basic social unit of this typically solitary species of big cat is a mother with her offspring.

10. **Tiger hunts have a high success rate.** The reputation of the tiger as a "killing machine" is greatly exaggerated. Only one in 10-20 tiger hunts is successful.

11. **Tigers are good tree climbers.** There are some famous tree-climbing African lions, notably in Lake Manyara National Park in Tanzania. Tigers, however, are not normally tree climbers, being too heavy. Tribals escape a charging tiger by climbing a tree, and for centuries hunters in India used to employ machans, or watch platforms in trees, to ambush tigers.

12. **A male tiger's territory measures about the same as a female's.** Typically, the territory of a male tiger is several times larger than that of a female. The reason seems to be that the primary cause of territoriality in males is not access to food, but rather access to females for breeding.

13. **Winter is the mating season for tigers.** This is an old dictum about tigers that one may see repeated in the *shikari* literature. However, while winter may be preferred in certain habitats, tigers in India may be conceived and born throughout the year.

14. **Every individual tiger can be identified by its pug marks, which are like fingerprints.** The battle over this one never ends. Suffice it to say that four eminent tiger authorities— George Schaller, Fateh Singh Rathore, Ullas Karanth and Billy Arjan Singh—are on record as puncturing the balloon of this myth. The best that can be hoped for (with practice and careful observation) is that pug marks may enable you to tell a female from a male, to verify the presence of cubs, or to learn of an unusual physical characteristic or an injury.

15. **Tigers never move around during the day.** Never say "never." Depending on temperature conditions, prey movements, and other factors, it is possible to see tigers moving in mid-morning and mid-afternoon, although sightings are generally unlikely during the middle of the day, when tigers prefer to rest.

DO'S AND DONT'S FOR THE TIGER SHOW

DO:

- Get film and lenses ready in advance while you are waiting to board the elephant. Take extra film: you may need it!
- Obey the mahout's instructions about where to sit on the howdah. It is important that the load be balanced.
- Appreciate the jungle as you ride to the location of the tiger. You are seeing the forest in a way that is quite unlike riding down a park road.
- Protect your eyes, spectacles, and equipment when you are riding through thick jungle. The bamboo can give you some nasty jabs if you're not careful.
- Be prepared for the tiger to move at any time. If it does, your elephant will probably stay with it. The tiger show will develop an entirely different rhythm, so hold on!
- Remain seated at all times, and make sure that small children are secure.

DON'T:

- Expect that there will be a tiger show every day. The mahouts are successful at their tracking only about 60% of the time.
- Try to get your vehicle driver to jump the queue.
- Try to persuade the mahout to disturb the tiger in any way.
- Stand on the howdah or unhook the bar.
- Make loud noise or use flash photography.

Wild Boar

The wild boar (*Sus scrofa*, Hindi *suar*) is one of the commonly sighted large mammals in Kanha. Wild boar's favoured habitats are grassland and lightly wooded jungle, and they especially like areas in the park that combine these two landscapes. Boar are gregarious, or group-living, animals; although you may occasionally glimpse a single aging male, it is far more common to see parties of boar, called sounders, consisting of 10-30 individuals or even more.

Wild boar are coloured dark brown to dark grey, with some black and white hairs mixed in. The coat is sparse, and the crest or ridge of bristles down the back is quite noticeable in adults. Males develop upper and lower tushes, or extended canine teeth, which project from the mouth and are used for sparring with other males and for defence. The lower tushes may be fully 30 cm (12 in.) long and are sharp enough to inflict fatal slashes on an opponent. A well-built male boar stands about 1 m (3 ft.) at the shoulder and may weigh up to 225 kg (500 lb.).

Like sloth bears (see page 82), wild boar are omnivorous, with a diet that ranges from roots and tubers to insects, flowers, fruits, vines, and shrubs. They are prolific breeders, producing litters of 4-6 young after a relatively short gestation period of 4 months. The sows raise their litters in specially constructed nurseries, which consist of holes dug out of the ground and then covered by grass and twigs for camouflage.

Wild boar are preyed on by tigers, leopards, and wild dogs, and young piglets are especially vulnerable. The razor-sharp tushes of adult males, however, offer a formidable defence against predation. This species is proverbial for its intelligence and its courage in the face of danger. On the other hand, when wild boar decide to give ground, they can be amazingly swift and agile.

Boar are fairly silent, except for the grunting noises commonly given out as they dig in the earth for food. We once heard a male boar scream when it was attacked by a male tiger just inside the forest on the Kanha-Kisli road (the boar escaped).

Photography: During many of our sightings of wild boar in Kanha, the animals have been on their way from one place to another, giving us few chances to take good pictures. Boar have a very keen sense of smell and a comparatively long flight distance. It is not uncommon to see an entire sounder streak across the track in single file. On several occasions, however, we have seen a sounder linger close to the road, contentedly foraging while our camera shutters clicked.

Wild Dog (Dhole)

Like the sambar and the tiger, the Asiatic Wild Dog or dhole enjoys an extremely wide geographical distribution in the eastern half of Asia. This animal is one of the top three predators in Kanha, and certain marked characteristics—notably its fearless disposition, its endurance, and its highly collaborative social organization—make the wild dog a competitor with which even the mighty tiger must reckon.

The wild dog (*Cuon alpinus*, Hindi *dhole* or *jangli kutta*) is a medium-sized, reddish-tawny animal with a bushy, darker brown, black-tipped tail. This dog is distinguished from species of the genus *canis* such as wolves and jackals by having one fewer molar on each side of the lower jaw (for a total of 40 teeth vs. 42) and a larger number of teats (typically twelve to fourteen). The overall appearance is very similar to that of a domestic dog. Wild dogs weigh on average 14-18 kg (30-40 lb.), and head-body length is about 1 metre (3+ feet).

Exact census figures are difficult to come by, but there may be as many as 150 wild dogs in Kanha. Based on sighting frequencies and on the overlap with tiger territories in many areas of the park, we believe that the population of this species has been increasing over the past five years. If the trend continues, it will be interesting to watch the dynamics of predator interaction—since usually, the wild dog is avoided by both the leopard (whose typical prey is of the same size) and the tiger. It is noteworthy that the three predators all coexist with ample prey within the relatively small area of Nagarahole N. P. in southern India.

Two striking features of the wild dog have consistently impressed observers: their highly developed social organization and their method of making kills. At a wild dog sighting, you will probably first be struck by the frolicsome behaviour and close network of cooperation these animals display. Whether playing or hunting, they seem part of a well-coordinated, happy family. Typically, wild dogs move in packs ranging from 4 to over 30 animals; keep in mind during a sighting that a smaller group may be a fragment that has temporarily split off from a larger pack. Wild dogs may be encountered in every sort of habitat, ranging from open grasslands in the meadows to lightly covered jungle or bamboo thickets, but they are basically forest dwellers who sometimes venture into open areas. Like its severely endangered cousin, the African Wild Dog (*Lycaon pictus*), the dhole may cover dozens of square kilometres in a day's ranging; and the two species share a number of other similarities, including an uncannily soft contact call (rather like a whistle in the case of the dhole) and an elaborate social structure within the pack.

The wild dog's method of killing, however, has outweighed any other fact about the animal and has been responsible for a long history of persecution. Rudyard Kipling, in fact, branded dholes as the "red peril" of the jungle. Dholes tirelessly run down their prey—typically barking deer or chital—and disembowel them while they are still in flight. The sight can be gruesome, especially when the pack is small and the prey dies slowly. In February 1996, we were returning across Kanha Meadow to park headquarters at the end of a three-hour elephant trek around 10:30 in the morning. Right out in the open, two wild dogs had secured a chital doe and were pulling at the animal with their powerful jaws from each end. The chital desperately rose to her feet twice. The rest of the herd of chital stood about 15 metres (50 ft.) away as if transfixed, shrieking alarm calls helplessly. We could only hope that the doe was in shock and could not feel the pain.

Such scenes are often contrasted unfavourably to the sudden severing of the spine or the choking bite of the big cats. But enough scenes of tiger and lion kills have now been filmed in Africa and India to show that the notion of "clean kills" for these powerful predators is largely a myth. Prey the size of zebra, buffalo, and sambar are often not easy to bring down, and the struggle continues for many minutes. Objections to the wild dog's way of killing will never disappear, but they are largely based on human sensibilities, rather than on the realities of the natural world.

We have seen wild dogs in many parts of the park, ranging from the Paparphat area in the west to the Kanha Meadow, Sijhora Road, the four-way crossing at Beniphat, the small waterholes on the western side of Bishanpura Meadow, and Mukki in the east. The area round Sondhar Camp and Sondhar Tank is especially good for wild dog sightings.

At the start of a wild dog sighting, you should observe the animals to determine how they are likely to behave. In our experience, wild dogs are usually on the hunt, moving in a rather determined fashion from one place to another with only minor deviations or delay. Only once have we seen them lying down to rest, gathered around a waterhole, where we were able to watch them for over an hour. In jungle terrain, they may exhibit extraordinary grace, with long, fluid leaps. Since a pack will often use the park roads to travel, it is possible that you will be able to follow the dogs in your vehicle for some time. A lead dog (or "alpha male," as he is called by biologists), can often be seen directing the pace and direction of the others, who may fan out in a "sweep" operation on either side of the road, cutting a swath through the jungle to pick up scent, and then returning to the track. Vehicles rarely seem to bother these animals, but you should keep a decent distance away from them nevertheless. You will often be rewarded: we once had wild dogs approach the Gypsy some thirty minutes after the beginning of a sighting and mate very close to the vehicle!

The nucleus of wild dog packs is often a dominant breeding pair and their pups. After a gestation period of a mere 2 months, the dominant female may give birth to as many as a dozen offspring, and both she and her mate share the duties of rearing them. For two to three months after the pups are born, they seldom leave the den. The parents feed them—in the manner of many species in the dog family—by regurgitating half-chewed meat. At five months of age, pups are able to follow the pack, and at eight months they can participate in kills, even of large prey. According to Rehman Khan, one of Kanha's most experienced drivers, a tiger killed one of a pair of wild dogs when the unwary dogs passed too close to the tiger, who was lying in the grass. The carcass was left uneaten. Belinda Wright, another experienced observer who filmed much of her film *The Land of the Tiger* in Kanha for National Geographic, reported that during the early 1980s at least one tiger was surrounded and killed by a large pack of dholes; several of the dogs perished in the encounter. Clearly the strength and courage of this predator make it a formidable inhabitant of the forest, and the dhole's increasing presence in Kanha should offer the visitor some chances for memorable sightings.

Photography: Since wild dogs may be seen at any time of day from dawn to dusk, you should be prepared with all-purpose film (for example 200 ASA) to photograph them in a wide range of lighting conditions. Keep in mind that the dogs are usually on the move and that they are essentially forest animals. This means that, in focusing, you may need to compensate for shrubs and other vegetation lying between you and your subject. On the other hand, the dhole's marked preference for moving along roads may help you, giving you a clear field for the shot. Best of all, of course, are lighting conditions about one hour after sunrise and one hour before sunset, when the sun's slanting rays light up the dhole's lustrous, dark red coat.

Other Mammals

The following mammals of Kanha are rarely sighted, and we therefore offer only brief discussion of them here. Most of them are either strictly nocturnal (like the porcupine, the pangolin, and the ratel) or crepuscular (visible at dawn or just before sunset, as well as at night).

The **Small Indian Civet** *(Viverricula indica,* Hindi *kasturi)* is grayish brown, with body features that are typically civet-like: short limbs, an elongated head, and a pointed muzzle. This animal, which may be distinguished from the Large Indian Civet *(Viverra zibetha)* by its smaller size and its lack of a dorsal crest, is lined and streaked along the back and possesses a handsome, ringed tail. A full-grown male weighs about 4 kg (close to 9 lb.) and measures about 90 cm (3 ft.), of which one-third is accounted for by the tail. The Small Indian Civet prefers a habitat of grassland or long scrub vegetation. Omnivorous, it hunts by night, preying on rats, lizards, squirrels, small birds, and insects. Civets also eat berries and fruits, and they have been known to take poultry.

The **Common Palm Civet** or **Toddy Cat** *(Paradoxurus hermaphroditus,* Hindi *lakhati, khatas)* presents a monochromatic appearance when compared to the Small Indian Civet, which it otherwise resembles in body structure and weight. In its long winter coat of coarse hair, this animal is uniformly blackish-brown; traces of spots and stripes may be seen while the new coat is growing after the animal sheds. Compared to the tail of the Small Indian Civet, that of the Palm Civet is noticeably longer, measuring about 60 cm (2 ft.). This animal is semi-arboreal, often spending the day curled up in the branches of a tree or in a hole in the trunk. The Palm Civet's diet consists of birds and small mammals such as rats and mice, as well as fruit. The nickname "toddy cat" does not signify any connection with the cat family, but springs rather from the Palm Civet's fondness for stealing the sweet juice when palms are tapped for toddy.

The **Common (Gray) Mongoose** *(Herpestes edwardsi,* Hindi *mangus, newala)* is almost certainly seen more often outside Kanha than inside the park. Monochromatic in appearance, this mongoose is tawny gray and grizzled-looking. It weighs about 1.5 kg (a little more than 3 lb.) and measures 90 cm (nearly 3 ft.), of which half is tail. The Common Mongoose hunts both by day and by night, and you may sometimes see one streaking across the road as you travel through the park. Mongooses do not linger long in the open, and photography is difficult. The diet consists of rats, mice, insects, frogs, snakes, and fruits. The gestation period is about 2 months, and 3 litters may be born in a single year.

The **Indian Wolf** *(Canis lupus,* Hindi *bheriya)* was not seen at Kanha for many seasons until quite recently (November 1995), when there were some sightings in the buffer zone on the western edge of the park, near the village of Mocha. Likewise, in Bandhavgarh N.P. about 230 km northeast of Kanha, two wolves were seen just inside Tala Gate early in the morning during March 1996. Like hyenas and foxes, wolves seem to flourish best when they are not in direct competition with the other large carnivores inside the park: tigers, leopards, and wild dogs. The Indian Wolf, whose colour is variable from sandy fawn to gray, brown, and black, stands 65-75 cm (2-2½ ft.) at the shoulder and weighs 20-30 kg (44-66 lb.). The wolf's diet is variable, depending on the habitat. Wolves, like wild dogs and lions, are eminently social carnivores, who typically spend their lives in packs, or extended family units. As M. K. Ranjitsinh has pointed out, the depressed populations and altered natural conditions for this species in India make observations and conclusions about the wolf in the subcontinent tentative at best. Further complicating the picture have been recent reports (peaking in 1996) of attacks by wolves on children in villages in a region of Uttar Pradesh midway between Lucknow and Varanasi.

The **Indian Fox** (*Vulpes bengalensis*, Hindi *lomri*) is quite often seen at Kanha, especially in the early morning in the buffer zone. Head and body of a full-grown animal measure 60 cm (about 2 ft.). The weight averages 2-3 kg (4½-6½ lb.). The coat is sandy, brownish-gray and the tail has a black tip. In poor light, the fox may be easily confused with the jungle cat or the golden jackal, but if you can get a good look at the animal, the tail is a useful diagnostic feature, being far longer in relationship to the body than a jackal's tail and lacking the rings on the tail of a jungle cat. The diet of the fox consists of small mammals, reptiles, and insects.

One of the most intriguing nocturnal animals at Kanha is the **Ratel** or **Honey Badger** (*Mellivora capensis*, Hindi *bejoo, bajra*). This member of the weasel family has a striking, two-toned appearance. The crown of the head and the back are pale gray or white, while the facial underparts, the chest, and the belly are jet black. The head and body measure 60 cm (about 2 ft.), and the weight of an adult animal is 8-10 kg (18-22 lb.). Ratels have short tails (about 15 cm or 6 in.), stumpy legs, and a rather squat appearance. They are equipped with extremely long, powerful digging claws. Widely distributed throughout Africa and Asia, ratels enjoy a reputation as fearless fighters on both continents. In India, their diet consists of small mammals, birds, reptiles, fruit, honey, and insects. Animals living near human settlements will raid poultry. Little is known of the ratel's social organization, breeding habits, or longevity. Zoo specimens have been reported to live in excess of 25 years, suggesting that the species is relatively long-lived. In Africa, cooperative behaviour between ratels and the Greater Honeyguide (*Indicator indicator*) has often been noted, although, as with the "mutualism" between the chital and the langur (see page 70), this relationship between badger and bird seems somewhat one-sided, with most of the advantage accruing to the ratel.

The **Indian Porcupine** (*Hystrix indica*, Hindi *sayal*) is Kanha's largest rodent. Porcupines measure 70-90 cm (28-35 in.) and weigh 11-18 kg (25-40 lb.). The animal's spines or quills measure on average 18-20 cm (7-8 in.) but may reach a length of 30 cm (12 in.) on the neck and shoulders. Porcupines live in underground burrows, which usually have a number of separate entrances and may attain a very considerable size. They eat vegetables, grain, fruit, and roots. Porcupines defend themselves against predators with a quick backward rush, with the spines doing the work that most other animals would depend on from teeth and claws. Despite the evident dangers posed by their quills, porcupines are regularly hunted by tigers and leopards, whose quest for the porcupine's tender meat lays the cats open to severe, occasionally fatal injuries.

Like the fox, the **Indian Hare** (*Lepus nigricollis*, Hindi *khargosh*) is occasionally seen in Kanha's buffer zone, especially in the half hour just before and after sunrise. This hare, which weighs 2-3 ½ kg (4 ½-8 lb.), has a dark brown patch on the back of the neck from the ears to the shoulder (the species name *nigricollis* means "black-naped"), and the upper surface of the tail is black. Hares often live near human habitation in villages.

The **Nilgai** or **Blue Bull** (*Boselaphus tragocamelus*) is the largest Indian antelope. The literal meaning of the animal's scientific name suggests, perhaps, a certain bemusement at its ungainly appearance: "cattle-deer goat-camel." Males and females are sexually dimorphic, with pronounced differences in physical appearance. Males may stand as high as 150 cm (5 ft.) at the shoulder, with a weight of 240 kg (525 lb.). The females are much smaller and weigh only about half as much as the males. Bulls are iron-gray in colour, while cows are tawny brown. Only the bulls have horns, which are disproportionately small for this large, horse-like animal: nilgai horns average 20 cm or 8 inches in length. Nilgai live in small aggregations that typically consist of cows, young bulls, and offspring. The species can flourish in a variety of habitats,

Barasingha at the Manhar Nallah anicut

Kans grasses in November

Striped Tiger *(Danaus genutia)*, Mundi Dadar Road

Common Jezebel *(Delias eucharis)*, Mundi Dadar Road

Park guides at Kisli Gate

Andha Kuan Forest Camp

Langurs and termite hill on Kanha Meadow

Nakti Ghati in early morning

The Chuhri Tigress grimacing

Female tiger cub on the move

The Digdola Tigress near
Bandari Bahara (November 2000)

Male tiger near Ganghar
Nallah in Paparphat

The Digdola Tigress near
Sonf Meadow (January 2000)

ranging from fairly dry scrubland to wetlands, such as in the bird sanctuary at Keoladeo National Park, Bharatpur, where it is quite delightful to see them galumphing through the marshes. In drier conditions, the animal has the ability to subsist for long periods without water. The gestation period is 8+ months. In Kanha, nilgai are rarely seen, being mainly confined to the extreme northwestern part of the park, which is normally off-limits to visitors.

The **Chowsingha** or **Four-horned Antelope** *(Tetracerus quadricornis)* is at the other end of the spectrum from the ungainly nilgai: slight, graceful, and capersome. These two species, however, are quite closely related: both are members of the tribe Boselaphini, belonging to the subfamily Bovinae. The chowsingha's common name, as well as both parts of its scientific designation, underlines a unique peculiarity: it is the only species of antelope with four horns in the male (as in nilgai, female chowsingha are hornless). The horns consist of a front (anterior) set, which is always the smaller pair, measuring a diminutive 1-2½ cm, or ½-1 inch, and a back (posterior) pair, which measures 8-10 cm (3-4 in.). The front pair of horns is often very inconspicuous, amounting to mere knobs. Observing captive male chowsingha in the Parc zoologique de Vincennes in Paris, we found it difficult to discern the anterior horns even at a distance of 3 m, or less than 10 ft. A dark stripe extends down the front of each leg. This antelope favours hilly terrain and, unlike the nilgai, is quite dependent on water. Also in contrast to nilgai, chowsingha are usually seen alone or in pairs. The gestation period has been reported as 8+ months. We have never had the luck to sight this antelope in Kanha, but many reliable witnesses indicate that the best place to look for it is the plateau at Bamhni Dadar shortly after sunrise.

The **Indian Pangolin** *(Manis crassicaudata,* Hindi *bajra kit)* is one of the most distinctive of all the inhabitants of the forest. Pangolins, which are related to the sloths and armadillos of the New World, are edentates, a designation signifying "toothless." The pangolin's body is covered with horny, overlapping scales, which extend to the entire tail. To defend itself, a pangolin curls into a tightly wound ball, a formation that makes it virtually impregnable. Pangolins feed on ants and termites, profiting from their long, sticky tongues to probe the insects' nests. They live in underground burrows that may be as far as 6 m (20 ft.) below the surface, but they are able to climb trees with ease. The pangolin's head and body measure 60-75 cm (2-2½ ft.), with a tail of 45 cm (1½ ft.) and

11-13 rows of scales around the middle of the animal's body. Males are far larger than females.

Bats at Kanha

According to a recent survey by Paul J. J. Bates and David L. Harrison (1997), 119 species of bats are resident in the Indian subcontinent, representing about 12% of the world's total of 950+ species. This percentage is comparable to the disproportionately large representation in India (given the subcontinent's land area) of the world's bird species (see page 112).

Bats comprise nearly one-fourth of the total number of mammal species on earth. They are classified in two principal divisions or suborders: the Megachiroptera (literally meaning, from the Greek, "big hand-wingers") and the Microchiroptera ("little hand-wingers"). The diet of the Megachiroptera is primarily composed of fruits, flowers, and nectar, while the Microchiroptera are mostly insect-eaters. With rare exceptions, Megachiroptera lack the remarkable navigational technique of echolocation that gives the smaller bats the ability to literally "see in the dark."

In Kanha, the Old World Fruit Bats (Family Pteropodidae) of the Megachiroptera are represented by two species. The larger of these is *Pteropus giganteus*, the **Indian Flying Fox** (Hindi *gadal, badur*), which is one of the most widespread and familiar bats in India. The Indian Flying Fox is the second-largest bat of the subcontinent, yielding only to *Pteropus vampyrus*, the Large Flying Fox of the Andaman and Nicobar islands. The Indian Flying Fox has an average forearm length of 168 mm (6-7 inches) and a wingspread of 3+ m (4 ft.). The head and body together measure about 230 mm (9 in.), and the animal has an average weight of 600 grams (21 oz.). The head of this bat is reddish brown, with the neck and shoulders a somewhat lighter shade of brownish yellow. The rest of the body is dark brown or black.

Flying foxes roost in colonies that may consist of hundreds or even thousands of individuals. These roosts are usually located in well-established trees, and the bats are known to favour certain species such as tamarind, peepal, and mango. When roosting, the colonies may be noisy and squabbling. They usually leave the roost within half an hour after sunset. The diet of flying foxes consists primarily of flowers and fruits: the bats discard the solid portions and swallow the soft pulp and juices. Long distances ranging up to 20 km (12½ miles) may be covered in a single night in search of food.

The gestation period of flying foxes is thought to be 4½ to 5 months. The species is not threatened worldwide but is listed in Appendix II of CITES. These bats are often found in close association with man, and the widespread perception of them as an agricultural pest has led to various control methods that may conceivably jeopardize their longterm future. In fact, the species is of incalculable benefit to human beings because of its service as a plant pollinator.

The other species of the Megachiroptera present at Kanha is the **Fulvous Fruit Bat** (*Rousettus leschenaulti*). On average, this bat is half the size of the flying fox, with a forearm length measuring 80 mm (3+ in.). Head and body together measure 127 mm (5 in.), with the tail accounting for a further 18 mm (0.7 in.). This bat is usually coloured dark brown, but is occasionally a lighter shade verging on yellowish brown. The eyes of this middle-sized bat are comparatively large.

The species is widely distributed throughout a broad variety of habitats in India, Nepal, and Sri Lanka. Like flying foxes, fulvous fruit bats roost in colonies that may attain a very large size (several thousand). These bats prefer caves, deserted buildings, and disused tunnels, rather than trees, for their diurnal roosts. As its name implies, the bat's diet consists of fruits, and it is especially attracted to mango orchards.

The gestation period is about 4 months, with females experiencing two pregnancies in swift succession in a single year. Strikingly for mammals, the early part of the second pregnancy overlaps with the lactation period of the first cycle. The fulvous fruit bat is not endangered, being abundant throughout much of its range.

Two families represent the suborder Microchiroptera at Kanha. The False Vampire Bats (Megadermatidae) are represented by the **Greater False Vampire** (*Megaderma lyra*). Widely distributed throughout the Indian subcontinent, this bat has an average forearm length of 66 mm (3.4 in.). It is coloured slaty or ashy gray, and one of its most distinctive features is its truncated nose-leaf. The roosting colonies, which are small by comparison with those of flying foxes and fulvous fruit bats, favour old buildings (for example, temples and forts), wells, and caves.

The diet may vary seasonally, ranging from beetles, moths, grasshoppers, and other insects to vertebrates, including wall lizards, birds, fish, and other small bats. The gestation period is about 145 days, with mothers occasionally giving birth to twins.

The smallest insectivorous bat at Kanha is the **Indian Pipistrelle** (*Pipistrellus coromandra*), which is sometimes called the Little Indian Bat. With a forearm of 30 mm (1+ in.) in length, this diminutive creature's head and body measure only 46 mm (1.8 in.). The Indian Pipistrelle is usually dark brown, with paler underparts.

The Indian Pipistrelle has a variety of diurnal roosts, including building roofs, fireplace chimneys, cracks between roof tiles, date and fig trees, and crevices between logs. The bat's flight is fast and especially unpredictable. It feeds on small flies and ants. Two young at birth are usual, and the females may give birth up to three times a year.

Bates and Harrison's survey, cited above, suggests that at least two more bat species are present in Kanha. Both of these, like the Indian Pipistrelle, are insectivorous and belong to the family Vespertilionidae (Evening Bats). **Horsfield's Bat** (*Myotis horsfieldi*) is a small bat (forearm length of 38 mm, or 1.5 in.) favouring wooded areas with a supply of fresh water. This bat has been observed occasionally to roost alone or in rather small colonies of two or three individuals. The **Javan Pipistrelle** (*Pipistrellus javanicus*), which is a slightly larger cousin of the Indian Pipistrelle, has a widespread distribution, having been recorded from Afghanistan and Pakistan all the way through India and Myanmar to Indonesia, the Philippines, New Guinea, and Japan, but little is known about the habits of this species in India.

4. BIRDS AND REPTILES

The Bird Life

There are an estimated 8,600 species of birds worldwide, and of these over 1,200, or about 14%, may be found in the Indian subcontinent. A visit to an Indian national park, therefore, may be unusually rewarding for the bird enthusiast. Checklists are available for several of the most popular national parks in India, including Corbett, Bandhavgarh, and Ranthambhore, as well as for Nepal's Royal Chitwan. Unfortunately, there is no current, official checklist of the birds of Kanha published by the park. However, during the 1980s Park Research Officer P. C. Kotwal compiled a list of 163 species together with rather scanty annotations. This document is available for public inspection at the Kanha Museum. Curiously, H. S. Panwar devoted only two pages to the bird life of Kanha in his *Kanha National Park: A Handbook* (1991).

In 1986, Paul Newton, Stanley Breeden, and Guy J. Norman published a more fully annotated listing: see "The Birds of Kanha Tiger Reserve, Madhya Pradesh, India" in *Journal of the Bombay Natural History Society* 83 (1986) 477-498. This list, based on observations made between January 1980 and July 1983, included 225 species, a total that the authors regarded as almost certainly an underestimate. This article still offers useful information.

The Kanha Museum contains a large wall display showing 64 "common birds of Kanha." Although the birds are generally well illustrated, some of them are sighted relatively rarely in the park: for example, the Nakta or Comb Duck *(Sarkidiornis melanotos)*, the Longbilled Vulture *(Gyps indicus)*, the Yellow-wattled Lapwing *(Vanellus malabaricus)*, and the Bluetailed Bee-eater *(Merops philippinus)*. Other species, which are relatively common and certainly notable for birdwatchers, are omitted on this list: for example, the Blackwinged Kite *(Elanus caeruleus)*, the Crested Hawk Eagle *(Spizaetus cirrhatus)*, and the Shikra *(Accipiter badius)*.

As of mid-1999, E. P. Eric D'Cunha and Rashid Ali are planning the publication of an updated, annotated list in the *Journal* of the BNHS, which will include in excess of 235 species for the core area of Kanha as well as the buffer zone.

As these numbers suggest, by the standards of Indian national parks Kanha offers a substantial range of avifauna: for example, at least 52 of the 77 families of Indian birds are represented here. Nevertheless, the park cannot match the riches of Corbett or Nepal's Royal Chitwan, each of which boasts well over 400 species. For the sake of a comparison closer to home, Hashim Tyabji's checklist for the birds in nearby Bandhavgarh National Park, published in 1994, totals 242 species.

The standard field guide for birders is now the twelfth edition of Sálim Ali's *The Book of Indian Birds* (1996). This classic reference work, which was first published in 1941, now includes illustrations and descriptions of 538 species (vs. only 296 species in the previous edition). Another helpful field guide is the *Collins Handguide to the Birds of the Indian Subcontinent* by Martin Woodcock (1980). Also useful for its illustrations is Sálim Ali and S. Dillon Ripley's *A Pictorial Guide to the Birds of the Indian Subcontinent* (second, updated edition, 1995). Specialists may consult the same authors' definitive ten-volume work, *Handbook of the Birds of India and Pakistan* (1968-74).

What can the birdwatcher expect at Kanha? Obviously, numbers and variety will differ with the time of year, but our experience suggests that a fortnight's visit should easily yield on the order of 100 species. For a comprehensive listing and detailed annotation, we eagerly await the reference work currently being prepared by D'Cunha and Ali. Meanwhile, we have selected forty species for brief treatment here. These "top 40" were chosen on the following criteria: the birds are sighted relatively frequently at Kanha; they represent a diversity of habitats within the park; and various features of their appearance, behaviour, and/or calls make them intrinsically interesting.

For the birds' common names, we have generally followed the nomenclature used in Ali's *The Book of Indian Birds,* and we have depended heavily on that work for physical descriptions and factual details concerning such matters as size, field characters, diet, and habitat. For ease of correlation, the list below also follows the order used in *The Book of Indian Birds.* For notes on birdwatching at Kanha and suggestions about the best birding spots, see Chapter 1, page 30, as well as the descriptions of individual species below.

The list below gives the common and scientific names of the 40 species chosen for discussion. An asterisk signifies that the species is illustrated.

THE TOP 40 BIRDS OF KANHA

1. Purple Heron   *Ardea purpurea*
2. Pond Heron (Paddy Bird) *Ardeola grayii*
3. Whitenecked Stork   *Ciconia episcopus*
4. Common Teal   *Anas crecca*
5. Blackwinged Kite*   *Elanus caeruleus*
6. Shikra   *Accipiter badius*
7. White-eyed Buzzard   *Butastur teesa*
8. Crested Hawk Eagle   *Spizaetus cirrhatus*
9. Whitebacked Vulture   *Gyps bengalensis*
10. Pied Harrier   *Circus melanoleucos*
11. Crested Serpent Eagle   *Spilornis cheela*
12. Red Junglefowl   *Gallus gallus*
13. Common Peafowl   *Pavo cristatus*
14. Bronzewinged Jacana   *Metopidius indicus*
15. Redwattled Lapwing   *Vanellus indicus*

16. Common Green Pigeon	*Treron phoenicoptera*
17. Roseringed Parakeet	*Psittacula krameri*
18. Common Hawk-Cuckoo or Brainfever Bird	*Cuculus varius*
19. Indian Cuckoo	*Cuculus micropterus*
20. Crow-Pheasant or Coucal	*Centropus sinensis*
21. Barred Jungle Owlet	*Glaucidium radiatum*
22. Whitebreasted Kingfisher	*Halcyon smyrnensis*
23. Small Green Bee-eater	*Merops orientalis*
24. Indian Roller or Blue Jay*	*Coracias bengalensis*
25. Hoopoe	*Upupa epops*
26. Common Gray Hornbill	*Tockus birostris*
27. Large Green Barbet	*Megalaima zeylanica*
28. Crimsonbreasted Barbet or Coppersmith	*Megalaima haemacephala*
29. Lesser Goldenbacked Woodpecker	*Dinopium bengalense*
30. Rufousbacked Shrike	*Lanius schach*
31. Blackheaded Oriole*	*Oriolus xanthornus*
32. Racket-tailed Drongo*	*Dicrurus paradiseus*
33. Tree Pie	*Dendrocitta vagabunda*
34. Jungle Crow	*Corvus macrorhynchos*
35. Scarlet Minivet	*Pericrocutus flammeus*
36. Jungle Babbler	*Turdoides striatus*
37. Verditer Flycatcher	*Muscicapa thalassina*
38. Shama	*Copsychus malabaricus*
39. Indian Tree Pipit	*Anthus hodgsoni*
40. Red Munia or Avadavat	*Estrilda amandava*

1. **Purple Heron** (*Ardea purpurea*). This is a middle-sized heron, coloured blue-gray above with black and brown underparts. The head and neck are rufous, black, and white, and the bill is yellow. The bird's common name comes from its purple appearance in bright sunlight. The purple heron feeds on fish, frogs, and snakes; it is largely solitary. Shravan Tal and Sondhar Tank are good places to look for this species.

2. **Paddy Bird or Pond Heron** (*Ardeola grayii*). This heron, which approximates the size of the Little Egret, is one of the most common marsh species in Kanha. It is delightfully varied in appearance: rather drab and speckled brown when on the ground or at rest, but flashing white when in flight. This heron feeds on

frogs, crabs, fish, and insects, which it finds either while waiting patiently at the edge of the shallows or by wading slowly through the water and keenly watching for the slightest movement. Nakti Ghati, Shravan Tal, and Sondhar Tank are all good places for sightings. These herons are sometimes seen singly, sometimes in pairs or small groups of 3-5.

3. **Whitenecked Stork** (*Ciconia episcopus*). The most graceful of the 5 stork species in Kanha, this bird stands 85-100 cm (33-40 in.) tall. It is, in fact, mostly black, with the neck and the crown of the head white. This stork has long red legs and a gray-to-black bill. It feeds on fish, frogs, large insects, and reptiles. Waterlogged areas of any of the large meadows in Kanha may offer a sighting of this species. As with vultures, the flight is often high and soaring.

4. **Common Teal** (*Anas crecca*). This is one of the most attractive duck species in Kanha. The head of the male is chestnut brown with a broad green band extending from the eye to the nape of the neck. When the drake flies, its three-coloured wing speculum (or iridescent patch)—black, green, and buff—is conspicuous. Sálim Ali observes that this species may be the commonest migratory duck in the Indian Union. It is largely vegetarian, subsisting on marsh plants and rice shoots. Look for flocks of Common Teal in the marshy areas opposite Sondhar Tank.

5. **Blackwinged Kite** (*Elanus caeruleus*). An elegant, nimble bird of prey, this is one of our favourite species in Kanha (see illustration). This kite is appreciably smaller than a House Crow, measuring 33 cm (13 in.). Predominantly white or ashy-gray, it has red eyes, a conspicuous black line (supercilium) above the eyes, and black patches on the shoulders. (In Africa, the bird is known as the Blackshouldered Kite.) It affects meadow habitat and feeds on mice, lizards, locusts, crickets, and other insects. Sálim Ali's observation that this species favours habitual perches has been borne out at Kanha, where on several days in succession we have seen Blackwinged Kites in the hour after sunrise perching at the top of their favourite trees in Sonf Meadow and Kanha Meadow. In flight this bird has a specialized hovering ability (very similar to the hovering of the Pied Kingfisher, *Ceryle rudis*, and the Kestrel, *Falco tinnunculus*), which it uses in mid-air to look for prey on the ground. The plummeting descent on prey is spectacularly rapid, with the kite holding its wings motionless vertically above the body until it is only a few feet from the ground. At the last possible moment, the kite folds its wings and seizes the prey.

6. **Shikra** *(Accipiter badius)*. In contrast to the Blackwinged Kite, the Shikra prefers wooded habitat. About the size of a pigeon, the male Shikra is blue-gray above and white below, with brown cross-bars. The tail is barred with black. The female is browner in colour and larger in size, as is often the case with raptors. At Kanha, you may look for the Shikra in sal forest or mixed sal and bamboo habitat. This bird is quite commonly seen flying low across the road or perched sufficiently low that photography is possible despite the Shikra's small size.

7. **White-eyed Buzzard** *(Butastur teesa)*. This bird of prey, which is larger than the Blackwinged Kite, is about the size of a Jungle Crow. It is much darker in colour and significantly smaller than the other commonly seen buzzard of Kanha, the Honey Buzzard *(Pernis ptilorhyncus)*. The White-eyed Buzzard has a conspicuous white throat patch and prominent white or yellowish-white eyes. Like the Blackwinged Kite, it favours dry, open areas and competes for the same prey, including lizards, locusts, grasshoppers, crickets, and mice. Places to look for the White-eyed Buzzard include Kanha Meadow and the open areas south of the Sulcum bridge on Sijhora Road. The species is sometimes attracted to areas where controlled grass burning is in progress because large numbers of insects are flushed out.

8. **Crested Hawk Eagle** *(Spizaetus cirrhatus)*. Sightings of this eagle, which is one of the handsomest birds of prey in Kanha, are relatively common. A bit larger than a Pariah Kite, the Crested Hawk Eagle may be seen in meadow habitat as well as in sal forest. On at least half a dozen occasions we have been able to approach a perching bird close enough for good photography. This eagle is brown above and white below, with brown-to-black streaks on the throat and breast. A conspicuous crest projects behind the head. In flight, the bird is pale, in contrast to the similarly-sized Crested Serpent Eagle (see #11 below). The typical call, frequently heard at Kanha, is a shrill, staccato series of 6-10 whistles, which grow in intensity and culminate in a scream. The call of the Crested Serpent Eagle is quite similar, but it is usually confined to 3-4 notes. The Crested Hawk Eagle's diet includes pheasants, squirrels, jungle fowl, and hares.

9. **Whitebacked Vulture** *(Gyps bengalensis)*. Although vultures are not everybody's cup of tea, this is one of the most important bird species at Kanha. It is by far the most common of the 4 species of vulture in the park. This is a large bird, about the size of a

peacock (without the tail). This vulture's common name points to its most prominent physical feature. The head and neck are naked, giving the bird a rather ghoulish appearance. In flight, the species may be identified by a conspicuous white band on the undersurface of the wings. As a scavenger with a diet of carrion, this vulture's eating habits are as useful in the park as they are in towns and villages. Like crows and various other birds, vultures may also be of great help to the tiger tracker by indicating the presence of kills. Aggregations of vultures in a single tree or in a group of trees in the same small area are a reliable indication of the presence of a kill. Jackals in association with vultures offer even stronger confirmation that a kill is nearby. If the birds have not yet ventured onto the ground, the predator is probably still in the immediate area. The sight of vultures actually on a kill is not likely to appeal to most observers: the birds are ungainly, voracious, and brusquely competitive. They occasionally express their aggression with loud squawks and hisses. As Sálim Ali observes, however, vultures riding the thermals (warm air currents) high in the mid-morning sky are the embodiment of grace on the wing. Vultures hunt by sight, and this feature is directly related to the tiger's habit of dragging its kill into close cover. At Kanha, whitebacked vultures may use the same tree for nesting year after year; we have spotted such nests near the Kanha Village anicut and in Bhapsa Bahara.

10. **Pied Harrier** (*Circus melanoleucos*). This elegant bird of prey favours the grasslands, and sightings are not uncommon at Bamhni Dadar. The male's plumage is black and white—the literal meaning of the species name is "black-white"—while that of the female is brownish. The Pied Harrier's diet consists of lizards, mice, grasshoppers, and frogs. The similarly-sized Pale Harrier (*Circus macrourus*), which is also present at Kanha, may be distinguished from the Pied Harrier by its whitish head and (in flight) by the ashy-gray wings, tipped with black at their extremities. The flying pattern of harriers, which so often involves repeated circuits as they comb their territory for prey, is doubtless responsible for the genus name (*Circus* = circle).

11. **Crested Serpent Eagle** (*Spilornis cheela*). This eagle is the same size as the Crested Hawk Eagle (see #8 above). It is coloured dark brown and displays a prominent crest on the nape of the neck. The underparts have black and white bars, and there is a white bar on the underside of the tail. The diet includes rats, frogs, lizards, and snakes, as well as the occasional junglefowl and peafowl. This

eagle favours wooded country. We have occasionally seen it on the ground at Kanha, especially after the monsoon in November.

12. **Red Junglefowl** *(Gallus gallus)*. This bird, the size of a domestic hen, is the ancestor of all domesticated fowl. Over a century ago, Forsyth observed that the distribution of the Red Junglefowl almost exactly coincides with that of the sal tree *(Shorea robusta)* and the Swamp Deer *(Cervus duvauceli)*. The striking colours of the male make it an attractive subject for photography, but the Junglefowl is a shy, skittish bird, and the dense habitat it favours makes photography difficult. This bird feeds on vegetable shoots, lizards, and insects. The Junglefowl's calls resemble those of its domesticated relatives. The bird's blaring, two-note alarm call may signal that a tiger or other predator is in the vicinity.

13. **Common Peafowl** *(Pavo cristatus)*. The peacock is the Indian national bird. For centuries it has played an important role in art and religion throughout the subcontinent: for example, it is associated with no fewer than three Hindu divinities (Kartikeya, Kama, and Saraswati), and the shape and pattern of its tail have acquired many symbolic levels of meaning. Males measure 92-122 cm (3-4 ft.) with a further 100+ cm (3+ ft.) of train, which is in fact an extension of the upper tail coverts. Females average 86 cm in length (34 in.). Hens are mottled brown, presenting a rather drab contrast to the cock's glorious combination of green and blue, and they lack the train. Both sexes are crested. Peafowl may live in both moist and dry forest, as well as in cultivated areas and villages. They are often seen in small parties that range from 3 to 8-10. Sometimes these groups comprise a single cock together with 3-4 hens; sometimes the sexes are seen separately. The diet consists of vegetable shoots, insects, lizards, and snakes. In Kanha the cocks shed their tails during the rains. These splendid appendages look short and scanty in November, but they are usually in fine shape by February-March. The sight of a peacock "dancing" (displaying his tail feathers) is among the highlights of any game drive in the park.

This species has a variety of calls. The most commonly heard vocalization is a piercingly loud, long-drawn-out *may-yow*, which may be repeated four or five times. The call, which suggests the sound of a cat in pain, has a melancholy, haunting quality. By contrast, the peacock alarm call is a loud, honking single note. Keep in mind that peacocks are wary and shy birds, and they may be spooked by your vehicle, so the alarm call is not an infallible indication of a predator. Peafowl may be taken by tigers, especially cubs: see the account of one such attempt in Chapter 3, page 146.

Peafowl are common throughout the park and are seen most often on the ground, although occasionally you may spot one roosting in a tree around sunrise or sunset, or in low flight if the bird has been suddenly disturbed. For such a frequently sighted bird, the peacock is surprisingly difficult to photograph. Sunlight is essential for a proper photo of the male's deep blue neck and ocellated train, but peacocks have a distressing tendency to scuttle away into shade just as you make your approach. Getting the more ornamental side of the tailfeathers when a peacock is dancing is even more difficult. Probably the best places for photo opportunities are the broad, open areas of Kanha Meadow.

14.   **Bronzewinged Jacana** *(Metopidius indicus)*. This marsh bird, which is about the size of a partridge, has a black head, greenish-bronze wings, and a short chestnut or red tail. Aside from its elegant plumage, the bird's most prominent characteristic is its enormous but dainty feet, with their thin, widely splayed toes—an adaptation to watery habitat that permits the jacana to negotiate the flotsam of vegetation in the marshes with relative ease. This species also exhibits a white stripe running from behind the eye to the nape of the neck. The diet is insects, mollusks, crustacea, and the seeds and roots of aquatic plants. At Kanha, the bird may be sighted near the Kanha anicut and on the marshes opposite Sondhar Tank.

15.   **Redwattled Lapwing** *(Vanellus indicus)*. This is one of the two lapwing species at Kanha; it is far more common here than its cousin, the Yellow-wattled Lapwing *(Vanellus malabaricus)*. The bird is a little larger than a partridge, with jet-black head, neck, and breast, and a crimson-coloured facial wattle positioned in front of each eye. This handsome, vocal member of the plover family has prominent yellow legs. Lapwings are often seen on the ground, where they deposit their superbly camouflaged eggs in the open. The adults noisily protest any hint of a disturbance with a loud, familiar call *(Did he do' it?)*. Distraction ("broken-wing") displays intended to sidetrack predators may escalate occasionally to dive-bombing when the birds feel panicked. Lapwings are most frequently spotted in meadow habitat and at the edge of tanks and waterholes.

16.   **Common Green Pigeon** *(Treron phoenicoptera)*. This is a yellowish-green and ashy-gray arboreal bird that lives in flocks. The diet is fruits and berries, and the Green Pigeon especially

favours the figs of banyan and peepal trees. Their coloration gives these birds very effective camouflage, and a sighting may take you by surprise when you are scanning the foliage of a tall tree with your binoculars in the early morning. Flocks on the wing overhead are a relatively common sight in Kanha.

17. **Roseringed Parakeet** *(Psittacula krameri).* A little larger than a myna, this is the middle-sized parakeet of the 3 species at Kanha; the other two are the smaller Plumheaded Parakeet *(Psittacula cyanocephala)* and the larger Alexandrine or Large Indian Parakeet *(Psittacula eupatria).* The Roseringed Parakeet is the most commonly seen of the three. Its common name alludes to the black and rosy pink collar of the male, which is lacking in females. The short, hooked beak is red. Small flocks are commonly seen flying overhead in the park, and the birds' long pointed tails and screeching calls make identification easy. The diet is seeds and fruits. Throughout India, trappers remove many young of this species from their nests for sale as pets.

18. **Common Hawk-Cuckoo or Brainfever Bird** *(Cuculus varius).* The old Victorian adage that children should be seen and not heard has been reversed in the case of the Brainfever Bird, who is often heard but rarely seen in Kanha. This species is about the size of a pigeon: ashy-gray above, dull-white below, with brown cross-bars. The chest is rufous-tinged, while the moderately long tail is broadly barred. Sálim Ali notes the superficial resemblance to the Shikra in size and coloration (see #6 above). This bird, which is strictly arboreal and usually solitary, inhabits lightly wooded country. The diet consists of insects and berries. The bird parasitizes the nests of babblers, often substituting its own eggs for those of the original nest-builders. The Brainfever Bird is mostly silent during the winter, but from the end of February onward, with the advance of the hot weather, it calls with increasing frequency, both by day and at night. The call consists of a series of 3-note groups *(Brain fe'-ver),* repeated from 4 to 10 times in an insistent crescendo. The accent within each group falls monotonously on the second note.

19. **Indian Cuckoo** *(Cuculus micropterus).* Like the Brainfever Bird, the Indian Cuckoo is about the size of a pigeon. This species is slaty-gray coloured, brown above and white below, with black cross-bars. There is a broad black band toward the end of the tail. The bird is arboreal and solitary, with a diet consisting mainly of caterpillars. Like its relative the Brainfever Bird, the Indian Cuckoo

is heard far more often than it is sighted. Its distinctive, four-note call (or'-ange pe'-koe) coincides with the advent of the hot weather and with the cuckoo's breeding season. The call may be monotonously repeated for several minutes on end.

20. **Crow-Pheasant or Coucal** (Centropus sinensis). One of the most distinctive ground-dwelling birds at Kanha, the coucal favours dense undergrowth. The coucal is about the size of a jungle crow, measuring 50 cm (20 in.) including the long, broad tail. The body and tail are glossy-black, and the wings are chestnut brown. The bird's gait suggests an ungainly combination of a stalk, a clamber, and a flutter. The diet consists of lizards, frogs, snails, mice, and the eggs of other birds. The call is a cluster of rapidly repeated notes, low-pitched and resonant. Coucals are often flushed from the ground to a low shrub branch (or vice versa) by passing vehicles. At Kanha they are seldom seen in open areas.

21. **Barred Jungle Owlet** (Glaucidium radiatum). This small owl is about the size of a myna. It is dark brown above, with a pale breast and conspicuous, rufous-hued bars. It lacks ear tufts. The Jungle Owlet is one of two small owls regularly seen in Kanha: the other is the Spotted Owlet (Athene brama), which is the same size but significantly paler in coloration. The Jungle Owlet favours forest areas, such as mixed sal and bamboo, and you may often sight it by day, even though it is predominantly crepuscular and nocturnal. Sálim Ali points out that this owl's habitat is much the same as that of the Racket-tailed Drongo (see #32 below).

22. **Whitebreasted Kingfisher** (Halcyon smyrnensis). This kingfisher is a little larger than a myna, measuring 28 cm (11 in.). No matter how often this bird is sighted, it affords inexhaustible pleasure. The Whitebreasted Kingfisher's appearance packs a series of dramatic contrasts into a relatively small frame: the head is chocolate-brown; the body is turquoise-blue; the throat and breast are white; and the prominent, heavy bill is crimson-red. Together with the Small Blue Kingfisher (Alcedo atthis), this is the most commonly sighted of the 4 species of kingfisher in the park. The smaller kingfisher lacks the white breast of its cousin and is only slightly more than half the size. The diet of the Whitebreasted Kingfisher consists of fish, tadpoles, insects, mice, and young birds. The call is a liquid series of rapidly descending notes. Although this species may be sighted at some distance from water, the best places in Kanha to look for it are nallah crossings, where you may often spot a kingfisher perched on an overhanging tree limb or standing

on a rock, patiently waiting for prey to appear. The flashing blue of the bird in flight is a joy to behold.

23. **Small Green Bee-eater** *(Merops orientalis)*. The size of a sparrow, this small gem of a bird is brilliant green, with a reddish-brown tinge on the head and neck, a blue chin patch, a black necklace, and distinctively elongated central tailfeathers. The wings extended in flight show a rufous-bronze semi-translucence. The bird favours open areas, catching bees, dragonflies, butterflies, moths, and other insects on the wing and returning to a perch to kill and devour them. The call is a dainty, high-pitched trill, often repeated. At Kanha, one of the best places to observe this species is the intersection of Desi Nallah with Manhar Nallah Road in Kanha Meadow.

24. **Indian Roller or Blue Jay** *(Coracias bengalensis)* (see illustration). With wings extended in flight, the two shades of blue (identified with the colours of Oxford and Cambridge) on this bird's plumage make it one of the most striking residents of the park. The Indian Roller, which is pigeon-sized, has a mottled, rufous-brown breast and a black bill. A resident of open areas, no species has a better claim than the Roller to being the signature bird of the Kanha Meadow, where it is often found on the ground or perching on the fence posts of the grass enclosures. The diet consists of insects, frogs, and lizards. The Roller has a variety of calls, none of which (cackles, clucks, croaks, and screams) can be regarded as musical. In this species, it is definitely the plumage that provides the melody.

25. **Hoopoe** *(Upupa epops)*. The size of a myna, the hoopoe is coloured brown, black, and white in a vivid and unique pattern of markings. The bird's head is surmounted by a prominent, fan-shaped crest; the bill, which visually offsets the crest with a certain pleasing symmetry, is long, thin, and slightly curved. This bird lives in open country and is frequently to be seen on the ground, pursuing insects and grubs. Hoopoes are normally seen singly or in pairs, occasionally in groups of three or four. As with peacocks, there is often a note of the comic about them. Perhaps this is due to the outsized crest, which injects an amusing dose of pomposity into their otherwise stylishly elegant image. Kanha Meadow is a good place to look for this species.

26. **Common Gray Hornbill** *(Tockus birostris)*. This is a substantially-sized, gray-brown bird measuring 60 cm (24 in.), with a long tail tipped black and white and a large bill surmounted by a

casque or protuberance, which is a diagnostic feature of the hornbill family. This species is arboreal, favouring open country and feeding on fruits, lizards, mice, and young insects. Small groups of these birds may often be seen in flight over Kanha Meadow, especially in early morning or late afternoon. Single-file flight formation is common, with a few wing strokes alternating with long glides. Occasionally you may hear a high-pitched, squealing call as the birds pass overhead.

27. **Large Green Barbet** (*Megalaima zeylanica*). Like the Brainfever Bird, the Large Green Barbet is heard far more than it is seen. A little larger than a myna, this barbet is brown above and green below, with a bare orange patch around the eye that runs to the base of the bill. This species is arboreal and subsists on a diet of fruits; it especially favours the figs of banyan and peepal trees. This bird also eats the petals and nectar of flowers. The Green Barbet has a monotonous, two-note call which it repeats for minutes (occasionally hours) on end. The call is sometimes answered by one or more barbets in the vicinity. The Green Barbet's plumage affords excellent camouflage. A good place to look for this bird is Kanha Meadow: for example, high up in the silk cotton trees at Schaller Hide.

28. **Crimsonbreasted Barbet or Coppersmith** (*Megalaima haemacephala*). This is a sparrow-sized bird, considerably smaller than the Large Green Barbet. It has a green-to-brown body; the forehead and breast are a brilliant crimson red; and the throat is yellow. This species is arboreal. Coppersmiths are frugivorous, especially favouring wild figs, and males have been observed gallantly offering food to females. Like the Green Barbet and the Brainfever Bird, the Coppersmith is heard much more often than it is seen. The nickname derives from the bird's monotonous, one-note call (*tuk-tuk-tuk*), which resembles the sound, heard from a distance, of a smith methodically hammering on metal.

29. **Lesser Goldenbacked Woodpecker** (*Dinopium bengalense*). This is the most commonly seen of the 6 woodpecker species at Kanha and is somewhat larger than a myna, measuring 29 cm (11½ in.). The upper parts are a dramatic combination of golden yellow, black, and white; underneath, the bird is whitish with black streaks. The head is crowned with a prominent red crest. This species favours lightly wooded jungle. At Kanha, you may see it singly, in pairs, or in small parties of 3-5. The diet consists largely of beetles and other insects, which the bird finds by chiseling away the rotten

wood of tree bark. This species may be seen throughout the forested areas of the park. We have had particularly good sightings near the waterhole on Bari Chuhri Road.

30. **Rufousbacked Shrike** *(Lanius schach)*. This is one of the most commonly seen and attractively marked meadow species in Kanha. A bit smaller than a myna, this bird has a gray head and a black forehead and eye band, with lower back and rump rufous-coloured. As with shrikes generally, the bill is sturdy and hooked. This shrike lives in open country or the scrub vegetation of lightly wooded areas, with a diet consisting of insects, lizards, and young mice. You may frequently see it clinging to a long reed or blade of grass 30-60 cm (12-24 in.) above the ground or perched on fence posts of the grass enclosures in Kanha Meadow. The whole genus of shrikes has acquired an unsavoury reputation as "butchers" for killing to excess and then storing the surplus victims by impaling them on thorns. More attractive is the Rufousbacked Shrike's renown as a mimic (see below on the Racket-tailed Drongo, #32). Two other shrikes are relatively common in Kanha: the Gray *(Lanius excubitor)* and the Baybacked *(Lanius vittatus)*.

31. **Blackheaded Oriole** *(Oriolus xanthornus)* (see illustration). One of the most spectacular birds at Kanha. The golden yellow body is offset by a jet-black head and throat, as well as by conspicuous black markings on the wings and tail. The head and throat of the female are ashy to dark gray rather than black. The Blackheaded Oriole is a little larger than a myna. It favours lightly wooded country, and the diet is insects, fruits, and berries. The calls range from extremely liquid to quite harsh. In Kanha, look for this species high up in leafy trees during the hour after sunrise. The similarly-sized Golden Oriole *(Oriolus oriolus)* also frequents the park but is more seldom seen. It is readily differentiated from its relative by its golden head, marked only by a prominent black streak through the eye.

32. **Racket-tailed Drongo** *(Dicrurus paradiseus)* (see illustration). For many hunters, naturalists, and ornithologists, this is the king of the birds. Glossy black, it is the size of a myna but looks considerably larger because of the two long streamers of the tail, each of which is tipped with a spatula or racket. The forehead has a prominent tuft. This drongo—in contrast to its meadow-dwelling cousin, the Black Drongo or King Crow *(Dicrurus adsimilis)*—favours forest habitat. Its diet consists of moths and large insects, and it may pirate the food of other birds. The Racket-

tail's ability to mimic other birds and animals is semi-legendary. Species whose calls it is said to imitate include Crested Serpent Eagle, Crested Hark Eagle, Shikra, Gray Junglefowl, Barred Jungle Owlet, Indian Cuckoo, Koel, Goldenbacked Woodpecker, Gray Hornbill, Pitta, Jungle Babbler, Scimitar Babbler, Blackheaded Oriole, Magpie-Robin, and Shama.

Racket-tails are virtually never seen on the open meadows in Kanha, but they are common in sal and mixed forest. These birds are seldom spotted at rest but rather sighted flying low across the road or through the jungle. Shady conditions and the bird's black colour make the Racket-tail generally difficult to photograph. In fact, a tape recorder with a sensitive microphone would probably be a better tool than a camera with which to get a good souvenir of the Racket-tail, given the complexity and variety of the bird's calls. Racket-tailed Drongos are early risers, and you may hear them soon after you enter the park in the morning, even before sun-up.

33. **Tree Pie** (*Dendrocitta vagabunda*). The Tree Pie is the size of a myna but looks significantly larger because of its long tail, which measures 20 cm (12 in.). The body is chestnut brown; the head is black; the tail is gray with a black tip; and white patches on the wings are prominent in flight. Tree Pies affect the same wooded habitat as Racket-tailed Drongos and Jungle Babblers, and they are often seen in association with these species. Tree Pies are omnivorous, eating insects, frogs, lizards, fruits, and carrion. The Tree Pie has a great variety of calls, ranging from a pleasantly liquid, flute-like *bo-bo-link* to loud, raspy chattering. The bird's squawking alarm call may signal the movement of a major predator such as a tiger or a leopard.

34. **Jungle Crow** (*Corvus macrorhynchos*). The Jungle Crow is smaller than a kite but appreciably larger than the House Crow (*Corvus splendens*), lacking the gray neck of the latter. Glossy and jet-black, with a stout, black bill, this crow is omnivorous. At Kanha, the mainstay of its diet is carrion furnished by the kills of tigers, leopards, and wild dogs. Thus, close attention to any unusual aggregations or movements of crows may help you to discover the whereabouts of a kill and, possibly, of the predator that made it. Crows in association with vultures and jackals are an even stronger confirmation of a kill nearby. Although the best-known vocalization of Jungle Crows is their hoarse caw, these birds actually possess an extensive communications repertory. It is entertaining and also instructive to observe the crows in the

morning at Kanha Village, where several dozen are attracted daily by breakfasting tourists.

35. **Scarlet Minivet** *(Pericrocutus flammeus)*. A little smaller than a bulbul, the Scarlet Minivet measures 20 cm (12 in.), including the tail. The species is a striking example of sexual dimorphism, with the males coloured scarlet and black and the females gray and olive (yellow below) with yellow-barred black wings. An insect eater, the Scarlet Minivet is strictly arboreal, favouring the tops of tall trees. The call is a high-pitched, gentle-sounding *tweet-weet*. The best time to look for this species at Kanha is the hour after sunrise. It is a favourite bird for many of the park guides, drivers, and mahouts, who justifiably admire the diminutive scarlet flash of the male on the wing, seen against blue sky and surf-green foliage in brilliant early-morning sunshine.

36. **Jungle Babbler** *(Turdoides striatus)*. This is a rather drab-looking brown bird, a little smaller than a myna. The gregarious lifestyle of these babblers is responsible for their popular nickname of "seven sisters" (Hindi *saat bhai*). Jungle Babblers favour well-wooded habitat. They are usually to be found on the ground, foraging for insects and moths. After your first few game drives, you will learn to differentiate the incessant chattering of babblers from more meaningful jungle noises, such as alarm calls. In addition to insects, babblers will eat wild figs and berries, grain, and the nectar of flowers. The nests of babblers, which are usually built 2-3 m above the ground, are often parasitized by the Brainfever Bird (see #18 above).

37. **Verditer Flycatcher** *(Muscicapa thalassina)*. This bird is a little larger than a sparrow. The male is coloured blue-green, while the plumage of the female is a somewhat duller shade of blue tinged with gray. The Verditer Flycatcher favours wooded country. Typically, it launches its aerial sorties in quest of dipterous insects (flies, mosquitoes, and gnats) from the exposed top of a tree. Like other flycatchers, this species captures its food in mid-air. Although this is not an especially common bird at Kanha, its striking coloration makes a sighting extremely rewarding. Look for the Verditer Flycatcher in early to mid-morning near the waterhole on Bari Chuhri Road.

38. **Shama** *(Copsychus malabaricus)*. This elegant bird, coloured black above and chestnut below, is the size of a bulbul. The Shama has a long tail, black above and white on the underside, with a white patch at the base. It favours moist, deciduous forest.

Belonging to the same genus as the Magpie-Robin (*Copsychus saularis*), the Shama is if anything an even more accomplished songster and mimic. Its diet is primarily insects, supplemented occasionally by the nectar from flowers. The Shama is mainly arboreal and quite shy, rarely emerging into the open. The musical virtuosity of the Shama, the Magpie-Robin, and the Racket-tailed Drongo often makes it difficult to tell which bird one is actually hearing, or who may be imitating whom.

39. **Indian Tree Pipit** (*Anthus hodgsoni*). This diminutive meadow bird is a little larger than a sparrow. It is greenish-brown, streaked with darker brown, and has a prominent white streak (supercilium) above the eye and a white double wingbar. The diet is insects and grass. You may often see the Pipit on the ground or on a blade of grass in Kanha Meadow. The call is a faint *tseep*.

40. **Red Munia or Avadavat** (*Estrilda amandava*). This bird, which is smaller than a sparrow, measures only 10 cm (4 in.). In non-breeding plumage, both sexes are brown spotted with white, with a red bill and crimson rump. When breeding, the male is largely red dotted with white. The Red Munia lives in swampy grassland and reedbeds, feeding on grass seeds. The call is a soft chirping note. In Kanha, look for this diminutive species at the dip on Manhar Nallah Road where the track intersects Desi Nallah. (On this bird, see also Chapter 3, page 147.)

Reptiles

Far more is known about the birds of Kanha than about the park's reptiles, which are not easy to locate or observe. In *Kanha National Park: A Handbook*, former Field Director H. S. Panwar lists the following species of snakes:

Common Name	Scientific Name
Indian Python	*Python molurus*
Cobra	*Naja naja*
Saw-scaled Viper	*Echis carinatus*
Common Wolf Snake	*Lycodon aulicus*
Rat Snake	*Ptyas mucosus*
Indian Egg-eater	*Elachistodon westermanni*

Of the snakes listed above, only the Cobra and the Saw-scaled Viper are poisonous. In November 1996, as we approached Kisli early in the morning, we saw a Common Krait *(Bungarus caeruleus)* lying dead in the road, barely thirty metres from the gate. Although both this species and its more colourful relative the Banded Krait *(Bungarus fasciatus)* are highly venomous, P. G. Deoras reports in *Snakes of India* (1990, fourth edition) that many villagers in Madhya Pradesh do not drive kraits away from their farms because they help to keep rats and other snakes under control.

Panwar also lists the following species of lizards in Kanha:

Common Name	Scientific Name
Common Indian Monitor	*Varanus bengalensis*
Garden Lizard	*Calotes versicolor*
Fan-throated Lizard	*Sitana ponticeriana*
Flying Lizard	*Draco dussumieri*
Chameleon	*Chamaeleon zeylanicus*

We recommend the following reference books on reptiles: J. C. Daniel, *The Book of Indian Reptiles* (1983); P. J. Deoras, *Snakes of India* (fourth edition, 1990); and Romulus Whitaker, *Common Indian Snakes: A Field Guide* (1978).

CHAPTER 3

KANHA'S PEOPLE

EVERY DAY OF the week from 1 November until 30 June or the coming of the monsoon, Kanha plays host to visitors from all over India and from around the world. Every week of the year, the monsoon months included, a dedicated staff monitors the park to make sure that the regulations governing protected areas are observed. The tasks of education and ecodevelopment in the buffer zone around the park are ongoing necessities; new staff must be attracted and retained to fill vacancies; forest blocks have to be patrolled; and interventions must be planned, implemented, and evaluated. Kanha is, in short, a complex institution which is always in flux, just like the plant and animal populations it conserves. Making this organization run is an endeavour that depends on the professional skill and dedication of a large team of individuals. The park, in a vital sense, depends on all its people.

In this chapter, we take a look at Kanha's people and their varied responsibilities. How are they trained, and for what duties? How do they feel about their jobs? What kinds of satisfaction, as well as stresses and frustrations, result from working at a place like Kanha? In Section 1, we discuss the organization of the park staff. Section 2 consists of a series of brief anecdotes and vignettes. In these portraits and sketches, we give our impressions of a wide spectrum of people whom we have met and learned from in the course of a decade at Kanha.

1. STAFF ORGANIZATION

An Overview

Staff organization at a national park such as Kanha somewhat resembles a military structure, in that it is essentially hierarchical.

At the top of the chain of command is the Field Director. For several years now, this post has had the additional title of Conservator of Forests. The current Field Director has been in office since 1991. Dr. Rajesh Gopal is a distinguished scholar as well as an administrator with extensive field experience. Gopal, who studied zoology at Delhi University and was a C.S.I.R. junior fellow, joined the Indian Forest Service (I.F.S.) in 1978. He completed diploma courses in administration and wildlife management in Mussoorie and Dehra Dun, and he has served in various positions both at the Centre and at the state level in Madhya Pradesh, including the posts of Deputy Director of Project Tiger, Director of Bhopal Zoo, and Field Director of Bandhavgarh National Park. Gopal has published numerous scholarly papers, as well as a hefty textbook entitled *Fundamentals of Wildlife Management* (Allahabad: Justice Home, 1992). He recently earned his doctorate with a dissertation on the social behaviour and feeding ecology of the barasingha. The majority of the research for this project was carried out at Kanha.

Assisting the Field Director at the top staff level are four other officers: Deputy Director J. S. Chauhan, Park Interpretation Officer H. S. Negi, Assistant Director R. K. Sharma, and Park Superintendent Tiwari. Although the principal offices of the top staff members are in the town of Mandla, located about 65 km from Kisli Gate, the Assistant Director and the Park Superintendent spend a great deal of their time in the field. The Field Director and the Deputy Director are both allocated official residences inside the park; these houses are located at Kanha Village.

The core area of Kanha, consisting of 940 km², is divided for monitoring and administration purposes into five ranges. In charge of each sector is a Range Officer. The diagram below shows the hierarchy serving in each range, as well as the uniform insignia at each rank (where applicable):

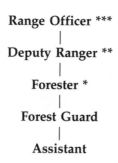

Range Officer ***
|
Deputy Ranger **
|
Forester *
|
Forest Guard
|
Assistant

The staff at Range Officer rank and below comprises the operational core of Kanha. Although the senior managers participate in setting policy and are ultimately accountable for park maintenance, it is the front-line troops in the field who are most important for the success or failure of any protected area in India—or, for that matter, of any wildlife sanctuary throughout the world. The tourist zone at Kanha consists of part of three ranges in the park's western sector: Kisli, Kanha, and Mukki. Except for the forest guards and their assistants (see below), the staff of each range normally lives and works at range headquarters. Also based at each of these three villages (Kisli and Mukki at the edges of the park's core area, Kanha in the middle) are teams of mahouts with their elephants. The mahouts are vital auxiliaries in a wide range of park activities that would not be possible without their participation and assistance.

Despite the vertical pattern of the diagram above, the notion of Kanha as a purely up-and-down command structure is somewhat misleading. Members of the top management level, for example, have a government grade and salary level as a result of their rank in the I.F.S. Lower-ranking staff, however, are Madhya Pradesh Forest Department personnel. There are checks and balances (and, some might say, spanners and monkey wrenches) in this system. As the head of a tiger reserve under the aegis of Project Tiger in Delhi, for example, Rajesh Gopal implements the policies framed at the Centre with regard to conservation of India's national animal. These policies emanate from several committee structures—notably the Indian Board for Wildlife and the Project Tiger Steering Committee—as well as from the Office of the Director of Project Tiger, which is part of the Union Ministry of Environment and Forests. On the other hand, Gopal is also accountable to the Chief Conservator of Forests in Bhopal, since the state of Madhya Pradesh, in which Kanha is located, is assigned the responsibility of implementing national park policy within state borders. The Chief Wildlife Warden in Bhopal is another official who has important authority in unusual cases: for example, in any decision taken to destroy a "problem tiger" (such as a man-eater) within the state. Such interlocking and overlapping spheres of authority suggest a mosaic or a grid-like network, rather than a ladder, as a visual metaphor for Kanha's administrative system. As in many governmental bureaucracies, authority and execution constitute a two-way street. Getting rid of an incompetent subordinate, even down to the level of Forest Guard, is not an easy task for a manager.

Although exact figures are not available, the full-time employees of Kanha Tiger Reserve comprise a staff of about 500. These are not the only people who play an important role in the life of the park, however. Freelancers with a semi-official capacity include the tourist guides stationed at Kisli and Mukki, as well as the regular drivers. The park takes an active hand in training and accrediting the guides, and Kanha management entrusts them with the responsibility of insuring that tourists and their drivers obey the park regulations. At various times of the year, moreover, the park's payroll increases very substantially with the hiring of casual labour for such tasks as road maintenance, weed eradication, fence-building, firefighting, and controlled grass-burning (see the section on management interventions, below). Villagers living around the park, most of whom are at a depressed socioeconomic standard, depend on this day-labour to supplement their meagre income.

This overview of the Kanha scene would not be complete without mentioning the tourist lodges and other facilities for the accommodation of visitors (see Chapter 1). Kanha is distinctive among Indian national parks for its tourist infrastructure: visitors may choose from a wide range of amenities and prices. As of mid-1999, the number of lodges is growing briskly, and there is every reason to believe that visitorship to the park will increase. The staff at some lodges includes amateur naturalists who possess a good working knowledge of Kanha's wildlife and who often function as ambassadors of Kanha to the public. Their expertise also contributes to the smooth running of the park.

Management Interventions

As noted above, it is the resident staff of each park "range" that is the heart of Kanha's day-to-day management. Many of these officials have routine duties or speciality areas. In Kisli Range, for example, Deputy Ranger Nagpure has the supervision of the twenty regular park guides at Kisli Gate among his areas of responsibility. Forester B. L. Sen is in charge of vehicle entry and the payment of park and guide fees at Kisli Gate. In Kanha Range, walkie-talkie in hand, Forester N. S. Maravi tracks every morning with the mahouts, and, if a tiger is located, supervises the tiger show.* Forester N. K. Bisen is an anaesthesiology specialist. A graduate of a wildlife institute in Maharashtra, he has

---

* See note on page 169.

anaesthetized dozens of animals from many different species who required medical treatment.

The range staff also spends a substantial portion of its time carrying out management interventions. Paradoxically, national parks throughout the world, which we are tempted to think of as pristine islands of nature, are seldom allowed to exist in a purely "natural" condition, even in the core area. Interventions are projects undertaken by park management in order to correct perceived short-term imbalances in the environment or in order to further special objectives, such as the protection or rehabilitation of a species. We discuss some of these interventions at Kanha in the paragraphs below.

From the tourist's point of view, probably the most important management activity is the yearly maintenance of Kanha's roads. The park network of roads measures 716 km, of which about 275 km are in the tourist zone. During the annual closure from 1 July to 31 October, the monsoon insures that the park will have to undertake substantial **road work**. The tracks must be in drivable condition for the opening of the season, and this project alone accounts for a hefty portion of the casual day-labour budget every year. In November, shortly after the park's opening for the season, it is common to see teams of Baiga and Gond workers, the men with their axes on shoulder and the women dressed in bright colours, moving throughout Kanha.

In addition to road maintenance, labour crews are also regularly called on to construct or maintain the small bridges over the nallahs and to work on the anicuts, or artificial ponds made by damming a water source. Park employees may also be occasionally ordered to close certain roads or areas, owing to special conditions such as flooding, fires, road blockage from fallen trees, the requirements of visiting film-makers, or unusual developments with wildlife such as a search for an injured tiger.

Visitors to Kanha seldom miss seeing the great Kanha Meadow in the centre of the park's tourist zone. In the past few years, **grass enclosures** there have been another prominent management intervention. These fenced areas look somewhat unsightly, but they serve the important function of allowing overgrazed areas to recover. To take only one example: Kanha's population of chital was estimated by George Schaller in the mid-1960s to number 900-1000. Over thirty years later, a conservative estimate of chital in the park would be 25,000—a quasi-exponential increase of 2500%.

When I met Schaller in late 1997, one of his first comments about Kanha "then and now" was on the way the grass had changed. Kanha is an ecosystem, a chain of life in which carnivores depend on herbivores, and herbivores depend on grass and other plants to survive. Allowing the grass to regenerate is an important management project, and one that will apparently be ongoing, unless there is an unexpected relaxation of the grazing pressures on meadow habitat in Kanha.

When you visit Kanha, your guide may occasionally point out one of the park's **firelines.** Some of these are marked with the number 8 on a low tree-stump-like post: this number is part of the roadside system of numerical indicators on features of the park (see page 15). The Chimta fireline, for example, intersects the road from Kope Dabri to Bnadar Bahara. You can see another fireline on the left as you travel southeast on the Kanha-Mukki main road just before you get to the open clearing called Junakhet (see map facing page 16). The largest fireline in the park's tourist zone is the one marking the boundary between Mandla and Balaghat districts: this is located a bit to the north of Chatta Pattar (Umbrella Rock) on the main Mukki-Kanha road between Bishanpura and Nakti Ghati.

Why does the park management create and maintain firelines? Fires in a dense forest can be extremely destructive, both to the habitat and to wildlife. Illegally set fires have a major impact on Kanha, and the park management must make strenuous efforts to combat them. As the park's Road Guide pamphlet points out, firelines act as insulators, which divide various blocks of jungle by means of a clear strip measuring 12-24 metres wide. Every year, all combustible material on these strips is burned, so that fires may be more easily contained, even in windy conditions. The park roads on which visitors and personnel travel, of course, also function as firelines. Firewatchers and firefighting squads go on special alert during the hot, dry months of April, May, and June, with several teams of 10-15 persons in each range.

Another category of management intervention concerns **species rehabilitation or maintenance.** Just outside Kanha Village on the way to the great meadow, for example, you can see a fenced enclosure that was originally built for barasingha. Kanha's crucial role in saving this species from extinction is one of the brightest and tallest feathers in the park's cap. After part of the barasingha population was gradually relocated to other suitable habitat around the park (for example, Bishanpura and Sonf), the enclosure near Kanha Village was used for blackbuck. This intervention, however, was less successful: ironically, although blackbuck are fleet enough to outrun any predator in Kanha, a number of them fell prey to the ambush of slow-moving pythons.

Grass burning is another management intervention that you may notice in Kanha, especially in the months of February and March. Among wildlife specialists, this activity has long been controversial, with the experts divided on whether or not burning the old grass helps to facilitate new growth. The balance of the evidence, as currently perceived, is that it does, if the timing and the temperature of the burn are right: hence, many work crews may be seen in the early spring at the edge of the park roads in Kanha, carrying out a programme of controlled burning. Although the smoke from burning may cause mammals to avoid such areas temporarily, you may wish to observe how this intervention affects other wildlife. For example, birds such as White-eyed Buzzards and Crested Serpent Eagles may be especially attracted to such areas because of readily available prey emerging from the grass.

Because of Kanha's climate, **water availability** is another critical factor in the yearly wildlife cycle. There are about 25 anicuts in the park, as well as over 50 ponds or small tanks. These water sources, together with the small springs called jhirias, yield an average of one waterhole for every 8 km². Starting in April, however, temperatures begin a relentless upward climb before the rains arrive, peaking in June and July at more than 45° Celsius, and many water sources dry up. The Banjar River shrinks in some places to isolated pools; depending on the particular conditions of any individual year, by June the park's wildlife may be parched with thirst. Park management tries to alleviate these conditions by filling specially constructed water saucers. Some of these are visible on the Kisli-Kanha main road between Kanha Village and Kanha Ghat. A new waterhole was completed on Link 7 near Mundi Dadar Road in 1997. Chital, who need to drink every day, must be especially appreciative of these efforts.

Finally, **special circumstances** may call for management interventions on an emergency basis. Although the general policy with regard to injured animals is to let nature take its course, Kanha officials will sometimes try to give an injured tiger emergency medical aid. Regular preventive inoculation against animal diseases is carried out annually around the periphery of the park; memories are still fresh of the devastating rinderpest epidemic of 1976, when Kanha lost more than 100 gaur. (In the authors' opinion, however, the park's veterinary arrangements need improvement: see page 194). Poaching incursions are always a potential concern, as are mishaps resulting from aberrant tourist behaviour or problems with the elephants.

Most unusual, perhaps, was the storm of controversy resulting in 1997 from an insect, the sal borer, which affected many of the trees in Madhya Pradesh's protected areas. Sal is, of course, the backbone of Kanha's flora, with over half the trees in the park belonging to this species alone. At the outset of an election campaign, politicians were quick to enter the fray, and at one point it was feared that hundreds of thousands of trees would be cut—many of them illegally—with a tiny beetle *(Hoplocerambyx spinicornis)* serving as an excuse for the rape of protected forests. Kanha's officials judiciously refused to panic or to bow to the pressures of alarmists/ exploiters. They recognized, and patiently explained, that the sal borer is one of those balance mechanisms in nature that periodically resurface to prevent unhealthy spikes of growth. Happily, the tempest subsided into the teapot. This was a case, then, when management's timely *refusal* to intervene served the park's, and the country's, best interests.

The Forest Guards

No one is more important to the success of a protected area than its staff of forest guards. In all of India's national parks and sanctuaries, the forest guards are the footsoldiers, the first line of defence, in the effort to conserve several endangered species, including the tiger, the great one-horned rhinoceros, and the Asian elephant. Kanha's forest guards, like those of every Project Tiger reserve, are especially concerned with the tigers. It is no exaggeration to say that the fate of *Panthera tigris tigris* in the subcontinent critically depends on the dedication and professionalism of these officials. Their job is one of the most challenging of all in the park.

Kanha is divided into 118 blocks or sectors, each of which is patrolled and monitored by a forest guard. Forest guards live in small, relatively unobtrusive structures, called camps, which serve as their base for weeks, and occasionally months, at a time. You can see some of these forest camps from the tourist tracks: for example, Kope Dabri, Chimta, Alegi Dadar, Parsatola, and

Andha Kuan. Some of the camps are relatively large, especially those that serve as regional wireless stations or elephant bases: for instance, Sondhar, Bamhni Dadar, and Gorhela. Most forest camps, however, are tucked away in the jungle and are quite small, affording just enough room for the forest guard and his two assistants.

The condition of some forest camps is poor, and Kanha has recently embarked on a programme of upgrading the camp facilities, as well as of building new camps in especially sensitive areas that are vulnerable to intrusion. On balance, we think it is fair to say that life for the park's forest guards is quiet, perhaps even monotonous. There are virtually no amenities, and most forest guards must put up with being separated from their families for extended periods.

To find out exactly what the guards do, we interviewed a number of them in different sections of the park. Nandu Das Sharve is the forest guard at Moala Camp, located to the west of the Kanha-Mukki main road between Minkur Nallah and Sondhar. Nandu is a Gond who has worked for the park for 17 years. As a relatively senior forest guard, he has been given a sensitive assignment at Moala: the camp is located only 100 m from the Banjar River, which is the park boundary on the southwestern side of Kanha (see map facing page 16). In the buffer zone nearby, resentment against the park still smoulders from the relocation of villages that was implemented a quarter of a century ago; and the terrain makes incursions into the park quite feasible, especially in summer, when a dry riverbed is dotted with only a few scattered pools.

Nandu tells us that he patrols regularly, both on foot and on bicycle, twice a day. His area measures about 8 km². Typically, he will complete one round in mid-morning and another in the late afternoon. I ask what he is looking for on these excursions. He answers that anything unusual—above all, with a tiger—has to be reported. Making a report involves bicycling to the nearest camp equipped with a wireless. In Nandu's case, this is Sondhar Camp, which is about a 15-minute trip.

I want to know how Nandu likes working here. He smiles broadly, as if to indicate pride in his position of trust, and he gestures proudly to the small, well-kept garden inside the camp's bamboo enclosure. Our driver translates his answer as a salutation: "You are most welcome, sir!" Suddenly, Nandu's facial features and his surname resonate with a note in my diary. I ask through our interpreter, "Don't you have a relative at Kisli?" It turns out that Nandu is the father of Suresh, one of the regular Kisli park guides. In this, he is typical at Kanha, where many park employees are related, by blood or by marriage. The ability of the park to attract and retain successive generations of personnel within the same families is an encouraging sign, since a tradition of park loyalty and dedication has been the outcome.

Very near the northeast corner of Kanha Meadow lies Phuta Talao Forest Camp, recently constructed in 1997. Forest Guard B. S. Maravi, also a veteran on the Kanha staff, is in charge here. Maravi enjoys an idyllic view of the Sulcum River, which wends its way about 30 m to the rear of the camp enclosure. Unlike Nandu Das Sharve, Maravi is posted near the nerve centre of the park. For news and companionship, he has only to bicycle across the great meadow to Kanha Village, a 10-minute trip. From there, it is easy to get a ride to the market on Wednesdays at Mocha, where he can buy the food he needs for the week.

I ask Maravi to describe his routine. He pursues much the same schedule as Nandu Das Sharve down at Moala, but he also adds that any barasingha death must be immediately reported to the Range Officer, who transmits the information to Rajesh Gopal's office in Mandla. Maravi's territory includes some of Link 7, which has always been a productive road for tigers, and he smiles broadly when talking about frequent tiger sightings on his beat. Disappearing for a moment inside the camp, he brings out a large register. Opening it, he displays the entries that he makes on a daily basis to record his observations. Maravi presents the register regularly to the Kanha Range Officer, who signs off on it after examining the entries.

Although the patrolling routine of Kanha forest guards might seem enviably placid to nature lovers, all is not sweetness and light. Deputy Director J. S. Chauhan told us of angry confrontations between villagers and forest guards in the 1996-97 season, some of which escalated to the level of physical assault. In these cases, the root cause seems to have been anxiety on the part of people in the buffer zone that the park was preparing to expand its core area, thus threatening once again to displace its neighbours. According to the Deputy Director, this concern, whipped up by some outside agitators, was baseless: what was worrisome was that his forest guards were being beaten up by local women!

Recently, owing to the initiative of such organizations as Valmik Thapar's Tiger Link, recognition schemes have been established for forest guards and other front-line personnel in India's national parks, and annual cash awards have been established. The ceremonies and publicity that accompany such awards are worth their cost many times over if they serve to reinforce the idealism and dedication of India's forest guards. The guards are, in truth, the chief conservators of forests.

The Elephant Men

An old saying has it that, whereas only 10% of Asian elephants can be well trained, only 1% of human trainees are suited to become successful elephant men. Certainly, the job of mahout demands special physical and emotional qualities—including strength, patience, endurance, unshakable confidence, and a capacity for backbreaking labour. Mahouts serve a lengthy and challenging apprenticeship, moving up from the lowly job of grass cutter to the post of assistant and then finally to full mahout over a period of six or seven years. In the course of this training, they amass a formidable pool of knowledge about the individual temperament and the physical requirements of their animals. Oral tradition and a healthy respect for the supernatural are prominent features in the world of the elephant men, which somewhat resembles a fraternity or secret society. Not surprisingly, about half of Kanha's 26 mahouts are tribals, whose intuitive knowledge of the jungle serves them well in their jobs.

Mahouts must also master an extensive repertory of between 50 and 100 commands. It has occurred to me, while on elephant back in Kanha, that this communications system is considerably more flexible and efficient than the park's wireless network. The British travel writer Mark Shand lists some of the commands he learned while being trained by Parbati Barua, the remarkable mahout revered as "queen of the elephants" in Assam. In addition to such practical words as "slow," "push," "step over," and "lower knees for dismounting," Shand mentions the following: "lift tail," "hold breath," "keep tail still," and "open ears."

Collectively, the mahouts and their elephants comprise a vital support group for the park. Probably their most important task in Kanha is to facilitate off-the-road access for monitoring the habitat, censusing species populations, and checking on the animals. For example, elephants are sometimes assigned to follow up sightings of an injured tiger (see page 194), and the mahouts will also investigate unusual behaviour, such as evidence of the infanticide of tiger cubs by adult male tigers. Elephants are assigned to help in various construction and maintenance tasks throughout the park, and they are used, with special permission, by wildlife photographers and film crews. From the tourist's point of view, the mahouts and their elephants are most visible for their role in the tiger show (see page 26).

Elephants are based at the headquarters of each range in the tourist zone: Kisli, Kanha, and Mukki—although the Mukki elephants, in fact, spend most of their time at Gorhela Forest Camp, about 7 km from Mukki Gate. Each contingent of mahouts has a chief: for example, Ahmet Sabir at Kisli or Saur Singh at Kanha. Like the forest guards and various other employees, Kanha mahouts sometimes have a family tradition of park service: for example, Saur Singh's older son Dharam Singh is also a Kanha Range mahout, and his younger son Nain Singh is a Kisli Gate park guide. Another park guide, Harishchandra Rajurkar, is the grandson of a mahout; Ahmet Sabir has a brother-in-law who is a mahout in Bandhavgarh.

The elephant men are probably better acquainted with the terrain of Kanha than anyone else in the park, with the exception of the forest guards. Although most of the mahouts speak very little English, it is always fun to prick their brains about their latest sightings and observations in the park. Since tiger tracking occupies so much of their time, the mahouts have a sharp eye for pug marks. Men like Ahmet Sabir, Saur Singh, and Lakhan Singh can tell you from the look of the grass where a tiger bedded down, and how long ago the cat-nap took place. The complex task of figuring out the travel direction of a moving predator from alarm call sources is second-nature for the elephant men. Their observations of very young tiger cubs, who are normally hidden by their mothers for at least the first three months of life, are especially valuable to the park's management.

It is impossible to overestimate such jungle craft. At the same time, it is well to bear in mind that the mahouts' ways are not necessarily those of modern science. For example, we failed for several years to understand the strange proliferation in Kanha of tigers named Chhoti Mada, or "Little Female." We assumed at first that this was the tigress we had followed on Kanha Meadow during a memorable series of sightings in February 1993 (she is pictured on the cover of this book). But if she were a single individual, the accounts of the mahouts implied that her territory was unusually large: in fact, she appeared to roam throughout the entire core area of Kanha. It finally dawned on us, after a study of the photographs of different tigresses over several seasons, that the mahouts are in the habit of using this name for any small-to-medium-size tigress with cubs! Raman Sukumar, who has spent years in southern India researching the behaviour of wild elephants, points out in his memoir *Elephant Days and Nights* that, ideally, the indisputable talents of trackers and scouts should complement or mesh with the methods of scientific researchers. At work in Kanha with the mahouts, we have often experienced the same kind of synergy.

India is a land of many wonders, and among these is its seemingly bottomless treasury of elephant lore. For an entertaining introduction, the Kanha visitor can do no better than dip into two books by the British travel writer Mark Shand. In Shand's award-winning *Travels on My Elephant* (1991), he recounts his own apprenticeship as a mahout and his trek across Orissa and Bihar with Tara, the elephant who now resides at Kipling Camp near Mocha Village. In *Queen of the Elephants* (1995), Shand discovers a new elephant guru, the mysterious Parbati Barua, daughter of Prince Prakitish Chandra Barua of Gauripur in Assam, who inherited her father's mantle as an expert with a quasi-mystical affinity for elephants. *Queen of the Elephants* was also a "Discovery" feature-length television film.

2. AROUND THE PARK

Good Guidance (As You Like It)

Mid-February, 1994. It is just after 5 PM and we are on Link 7, a few kilometres north of Kanha Meadow. The sky is the colour of a blue topaz, and there is very little breeze. It is the time of year when the late afternoon sun is strong enough to burnish your cheek, yet the shade is deep enough to cool you within seconds.

Once again, Ashok Kumar is our guide. After dozens of park rounds with Ashok, we have evolved an easy, informal relationship, and we appreciate his impish sense of humour and his infectious laugh. Ashok's English is better than that of most of the Kanha park guides, and he is long-suffering at teaching us Hindi. At thirty, he is handsome enough to take a stab at "Bollywood."

Like most of the guides, he is an information broker. Whenever we meet another vehicle on the park roads or stop in at Kanha Village for news, he is quick to learn the latest.

When he is perched on the back of a Land Rover or a Gypsy, however, Ashok seems transported to another world. His copper-flecked green eyes rake the landscape continually. His ears are even more finally honed than his eyes, if we may judge from dozens of cases when Ashok has heard a langur alarm call above the noise of a clattering Land Rover.

Now we are sitting in partial shade, our attention fixed on a small meadow of short to medium-length grass. About five minutes ago, while stopping to photograph a striking group of chalky-barked kulu trees nearly half a kilometre from our present position, we heard a tiger calling up the road and off to the right. After two or three minutes, more roars split the air, and we suspected that there was more than one tiger in the vicinity. Could they be fighting, or are they possibly mating? Among tigers, the latter commonly involves elements of the former. We have edged northward about 500 metres and stopped again to listen. A sambar issues a single alarm call somewhere in the jungle, and in the middle of the road a peacock freezes, staring intently in the direction of the roars. At Ashok's suggestion, we have been sitting at a crest in the road so that we can see the maximum distance in each direction. Now he has the driver reverse a little in order to give us a view of the open clearing on the western side of the road. An extra-loud chorus of roars follows almost immediately, together with some blaring peacock alarm calls. It is getting late, but we can't possibly leave now. We have never prayed so hard for a tiger to materialize. Scanning the tree line, some 150 yards away almost due west, is difficult, even with binoculars, because of the sun glare.

Our prayers are answered. At 5:45 PM, not one but two tigers suddenly emerge from the forest edge. In less than a minute, the male mounts the female, and we hear her snarl ferociously. I pick some of the action up on the video, but the lowering sun and the distance make the tigers indistinct in the tiny viewfinder, even after I zoom in on them. I switch the camera off and snatch up the binoculars to take mental pictures of a sight that we have never witnessed before. The male has another go, biting the back of his partner's neck. This time both tigers roar. The male throws his head back as he dismounts, and the female rolls on the ground luxuriantly. After a few minutes, both tigers amble back placidly into the jungle.

The sun will be down in a few minutes. We must rush to get back to Kisli Gate so that Mr. Sen will not fine us for being late. The euphoria lasts all the way there. Ashok says that, in nearly a decade now as a guide, he has seen mating tigers only four or five times before. Crossing Kanha Meadow, we see an enormous sambar stag, a frozen statue in the dusk. Standing up for a few moments in the Land Rover, I feel the cool twilight air whip my face and I take deep, exhilarating breaths. Our red-letter day ends with a fluke: a Spotted Owlet flounders somehow into the vehicle, and for a brief moment lies cradled in a fold of my jacket before it escapes.

Like the good drivers in Kanha (see below), park guides strive to be at the right place at the right time. Achieving this goal requires finely tuned senses, a willingness of the guide and the driver to work together, and quick-witted presence of mind. Within the park, the guide is the boss of the vehicle—responsible for making sure that the park rules are obeyed and that the safety of visitors and animals alike is not jeopardized. One measure of good drivers and guides is how smoothly they interact with each other.

Over the years in Kanha, few people have done as much as Ashok Kumar to help us understand the park and its ecosystem. He is a born teacher, and we were not surprised to learn that he teaches English to village children.

Ashok's ability as a mimic is almost as impressive as that of the Racket-tailed Drongo (for this bird, see page 125). One afternoon in March 1996, on the same road (Link 7) about two kilometres from where we had seen the mating tigers, this talent stood us in very good stead. Sometimes tiger sightings occur completely without warning: there are no alarm calls or pug marks. Just a tiger, suddenly. Such was the case that afternoon at Nang Bahara, when Ashok tensely alerted us, "Tiger!"

A tigress sat in medium-length grass about fifty feet in from the right-hand side of the road, with only her head and upper forequarters visible, staring straight at us. Biru, a young freelancer behind the wheel of our white Gypsy, braked sharply, and we scooped up our cameras, despite the indifferent quality of the light. After a few shots, we decided to exchange cameras for binoculars. But just as I focused mine, the tigress decided she didn't care for our curiosity. With a sharp cough, she charged directly at us.

Fire on four legs: there have been few more vivid descriptions of a charging tiger. We had never dealt with a charge on a vehicle before, although we had been charged several times on elephant-back. Biru hugged the wheel in terror, and all of us behind him shrank into a crouch in the open Gypsy—not a posture that would have been likely to do any good whatever if the tigress had serious designs on our vehicle. Ashok, too, recoiled, but with a difference. Out of his mouth came an ear-splitting roar. I will never know if the tigress registered a signal, but she braked and turned aside with five metres to go.

Like many other Kanha people, Ashok comes from a park family. His father has served as a forest guard for a quarter of a century, patrolling a beat and helping to build the Gorhela anicut. Ashok's concentration in the field is balanced by an easy-going amiability when he's not on duty, and every year his jet-black hair boasts one of the loudest symphony of colours at the spring festival of Holi. His favourite expression when we offer him tea or coffee at breakfast on the vehicle, with or without milk and sugar, is "As you like!" Whenever I show him wildlife photographs or books, however, Ashok displays a keen interest, and I am often aware that beneath his nonchalance lie a passionate devotion to nature and an unshakable loyalty to the park. In 1997, Ashok was able to buy a second-hand Gypsy of his own, and he now doubles as a freelance driver and guide.

In the Nick of Time

Being first at the gate in the morning does not guarantee that you will see a tiger in Kanha, but it gives you a leg up. There are several reasons. First, tigers are often active on roads in the hours just before and after sunrise, and the first vehicle into the park may sight an animal which then, if it is shy, will quickly move off into the jungle. Second, a prompt start will insure priority in the queue if there is to be a tiger show by elephant later in the morning (see page 25). Finally, being in the first vehicle assures you a dust-free excursion in the early morning and allows you to listen better for alarm calls and the wake-up songs of the birds.

Every time we get a late start for the park, we know that at least one of the vehicles ahead of us—usually the Number 1 vehicle—will be the blue Gypsy driven by Rehman Khan. Now a freelancer, Rehman was the premier driver at Indian Adventures Wild Chalet. Before that he worked for Bob Wright at Kipling Camp. Married with four children, he lives where he was born, in Mocha Village. Handsome, well-spoken, and quintessentially professional, Rehman is the best driver in Kanha. Not only is he never late, he has the gift of being in the nick of time.

On the dozens of occasions he has driven us in the park, I have never failed to be aware of Rehman's acute senses. He adds something extra, moreover, to a set of finely tuned eyes and ears: an intuitive ability to arrive at the timely moment. This is, of course, a valuable asset when you are driving tourists in a wildlife park.

It is a warm afternoon in March 1997. For some days now, one park road has been uppermost on every vehicle's PM agenda. Two male tiger cubs, who were born and raised in the Bari Chuhri area, are just about a year old. They still remain close to their mother, of course, and will for some time. Sightings of the tigress have confirmed that she is the same female whom we found early last May on Kodai Dadar road, barely a kilometre away. We photographed her then with her udders distended: she was suckling these cubs, who lay concealed in the dense bamboo brakes. Now they are bolder, and their curiosity brings them out nearly every afternoon, so that they and Kanha visitors may take each other's measure. Rehman, who often branches out on his own to "take a chance" for a sighting, sees every reason this afternoon to go with the flow.

Sure enough, shortly after 5 PM on 12 March, we sight the young tigers. They are about 75 metres north of the Bari Chuhri waterhole. For twenty minutes or so, while several more vehicles arrive, we watch them play. Wrestling, nuzzling, and nipping, the cubs captivate the photographers among us, for whom the golden, late-afternoon light streams from the other side of Bari Chuhri Road. The cubs must weigh nearly 90 kg (200 lb.), but they are behaving like schoolchildren on a playground.

A peacock saunters by. Something in one cub's reaction registers on Rehman's face, and he promptly sits down and starts the Gypsy's engine. "Just one second, sir," he murmurs. The Gypsy coughs, then purrs, and Rehman makes his move. As he reverses toward the waterhole, his strategy is clear. The bolder of the two cubs is going for the peacock!

It all happens so fast that the national animal and the national bird beat us to the waterhole. Lunging for the peacock, the young and inexperienced tiger seizes the bird's tail in its mouth but fumbles. Like a street-smart target of a mugging, the bird wriggles free, minus a clump of tail feathers. In shock and confusion, the peacock tumbles into the water. After a moment's mystified stare, the tiger rushes into the pool, but once again the peacock proves elusive. Scrambling back up the side, it makes the road, and the tiger gives up. The peacock walks away crying, straight down the middle of the road, with only one tail feather remaining. The tiger cub shakes himself, returns to the pile of feathers, and sits down to gloat over his trophy. Soon, the cub's sibling appears, and they take turns licking the nutrients from the quills of the feathers.

Ninety per cent of the action is on video, thanks to Rehman. He has insured that we have the best seat in the house for this drama. Our only regret is that his seven-year-old son Usman, who accompanied us yesterday, did not get to witness the excitement.

It is 5:55, and the shadows are lengthening. We can be next-to-last at Kisli, but being dead last will make Mr. Sen frown. Rehman looks up with one hand on the steering wheel and the other on the ignition key. "OK, sir?" It is his signal to call it a day. We nod, smiling broadly.

The Bird Man of Kanha

Some people think that waiting to get into the park in the morning is a chore. I think of it as a chance to exchange one of Kanha's crucial commodities: information. This morning, with twenty minutes to go before Mr. Sen gives us the nod at Kisli Gate, I am standing with Bafati Khan. Thin to the point of emaciation, Bafati's bright eyes and lively conversation remind me of the birds that he loves so well. Bafati, who is now a freelancer, used to drive for Kipling Camp. He bears a distinct facial resemblance to the American entertainer Sammy Davis, Jr., and the likeness is accentuated by Bafati's fondness for wearing hats at rakish angles. His skills as a mechanic are really those of a magician: I recall his fifteen-minute repair of a Land Rover gear shift that broke off at the base while we were on the Sondhar causeway. But Bafati's heart is in ornithology, not auto mechanics. One tourist at Kipling was so impressed by Bafati's avian expertise that he went home to England and promptly shipped, as a token of his appreciation, the unabridged edition (in 10 volumes) of Sálim Ali and S. Dillon Ripley's definitive work, the *Handbook of the Birds of India and Pakistan*.

This morning, knowing that Bafati will have exchanged stories with the other drivers last night at Kisli and Khatia, I start out with the standard questions. Who sighted what, and where, during yesterday's afternoon drive? Are the elephants tracking today? If so, in what area? Does Bafati have a strategy for this morning's round? Then I get down to brass tacks.

"Bafati, be honest with me. In the whole park, what is your very favourite bird?"

"Of all the birds? My favourite of all?" He smiles beatifically, and considers long and hard.

I am expecting him to name something dramatic, like the Blackwinged Kite or the Crested Hawk Eagle. Or maybe he will go for a rare passage migrant, such as the Peregrine Falcon. I know he is fond of Scarlet Minivets and their glinting flashes of colour and high-pitched calls. But Bafati surprises me.

"I think I would have to choose the Avadavat."

"The Ava—," I stammer, out of my depth.

"Red Munia is other name. You will find, I think, on Plate 98 in the *Pictorial Guide*, sir." Bafati's combination of punctilious courtesy and mind-boggling accuracy never ceases to amaze me.

"Well, that's very good, but where will I find in Kanha?"

"Try the grass in the dip on Manhar Nallah Road, just as Desi Nallah crosses."

There is a sudden commotion. The bar at the gate is being raised, and we scurry back to our vehicles, eager to maintain our place in the queue. I wave good-bye to Bafati and wish him a good round.

We happen to have a copy of *A Pictorial Guide to the Birds of the Indian Subcontinent* (another, somewhat more portable work by Ali and Ripley) on board this morning, and as soon as it gets light enough, I look up the Avadavat (alias the Red Munia, *Estrilda amandava*). It is tiny (a bit smaller than a sparrow) and beautifully marked. About 7:15, in the middle of prime birding time (the hour after sunrise), we find ourselves on Manhar Nallah Road in Kanha Meadow. Sure enough, it is less than a minute before we sight a pair of Red Munias. We take turns looking at them through the binoculars, although the diminutive birds are only 40 feet away. Bafati is right. The Avadavat is a small gem.

A Mahout and his Elephant

Kanha's tourist zone extends over three of the park's ranges, or geographical divisions: Kisli, Kanha, and Mukki (see map facing page 16). Each range has its contingent of elephants and its chief mahout, or elephant driver. The chief of Kisli Range is Ahmet Sabir.

Although Sabir has the enviable capacity to look younger with every passing year, he is one of the most experienced mahouts in the park. It is fitting that he sits astride the park's most majestic elephant, the great tusker Shivaji. These two go way back together, both in good times and in bad. In 1983, they appeared on the front page of *The Times* of London, on the occasion of a visit to Kanha by Prince Philip, the Duke of Edinburgh. Another souvenir of that occasion is the name of the small, looping track off Bishanpura Meadow, which was christened the Duke's Road in honour of the royal visitor. Sabir and Shivaji have worked with numerous researchers and filmmakers in Kanha, including Belinda Wright, and Sabir has seen many moments in the private life of tigers—including mothers suckling tiny cubs—that are denied to most lovers of wildlife. His elephant and the forest are his world; like his brother-in-law, who is a senior mahout in Bandhavgarh Tiger Reserve, a five hours' drive from Kanha, Sabir is a keen nature photographer.

A little more than ten years after Prince Philip's visit, however, New Year's Eve 1993 was a night of horror rather than celebration at Kanha. Shivaji had gone into musth, a condition experienced periodically by bull elephants (both Asian and African) in which secretions flow copiously from their temporal glands and the animals may become dangerously unpredictable. Shivaji was more than unpredictable during this onset of musth; he ran amok. Sabir, unfortunately, had been sent away from Kanha on another assignment in northern Madhya Pradesh, where wild elephants were rampaging through villages, and no one else was able to control Shivaji. That New Year's Eve, the tusker attacked the forest camp at Kope Dabri. The three men inside ran, but only two made it to safety. Pinned against a great sal tree at the side of the road, a forester named Bhagwan Das Patel lost his life, torn limb from limb.

Was this tragedy avoidable? We shall never know. Unlike the unfortunate pachyderm in George Orwell's famous essay "Shooting an Elephant," Shivaji was judged not guilty by reason of insanity. At the very least, the incident points up the vital importance of insuring adequate supervision at all times for park elephants.

Now it is 7:15 on a March morning in 1996, and we are not far from Kope Dabri in the Paparphat area. Ashok Kumar is our park guide, and we have a rendezvous with Sabir for a three-hour tracking expedition on elephant-back. We board Shivaji, and two tourists from Holland clamber onto Chankal Kali, a female elephant who is a veteran of many tiger shows. This is the period, however, in which the tiger show has been suspended. The Flying Dutchmen are spending only three nights at Kanha. Dripping with cameras, they are hedging their bets that an elephant ride will yield a tiger.

There is nothing quite like seeing the park by elephant. The pace, the silence, the details in nature that you can observe: it is almost as if you are part of a different landscape from the one you traverse so rapidly in a vehicle. During the first hour with Sabir, we sight a fine pair of Crested Serpent Eagles, followed by a big sambar stag and a Jungle Cat. Sabir instructs Shivaji to pick up with his trunk an old fragment of sambar antler, and he hands it to us so that we may feel the texture and the weight.

At 8:45, near the road called Bandari Chappar (meaning literally "monkey salt lick"), we hear a series of sharp, barking alarm calls: a langur somewhere overhead has sighted a predator. Sabir is convinced that we have either a tiger or a leopard close by, and he urges Shivaji on to a faster pace. We cross the road and plunge into the jungle on the other side. The vegetation is dense, and we shield our faces from tall, sharp stalks of bamboo. Sabir uses a wide range of verbal commands, in addition to his bare feet pumping behind the ears of our mount. With uncanny precision, driver and elephant derive a series of fixes from the monkey's calls, whose intensity and shifting direction suggest that our quarry is a moving target. The calls are punctuated by the bird-like sounds of an infant langur.

At 8:50, only five minutes after the adrenaline has started to pump, we have her: it is a female leopard, or rather a darkly spotted sliver of gold that streaks through the undergrowth in dappled light. Sabir chuckles with satisfaction. He says that he thinks the leopard, whom he has seen quite often in this area with two small cubs, has just killed. During the next few minutes, we lose the leopard twice and then recover her. Sabir points out the fresh remains of a langur carcass, consisting principally of skin, fur, and intestines. Ironically, however, this superb game run is treated with indifference by the Dutch tourists. They wanted to see a tiger, not a leopard, and above all they wanted photographs, which the leopardess inconsiderately refused to permit. After the excursion is over, we thank Sabir and politely bid the tourists farewell.

Perhaps they will see a tiger in Bandhavgarh, which is the next stop on their itinerary.

The Managing Member

Bob Wright is not easily forgettable. Tall, stout, and stentorian-voiced, with a crisp slash of a mustache, he seems a throwback to the days of the Raj, and in many ways he is. In Calcutta, Bob presided for decades over the Tollygunge Club, a mecca for that city's sports- and social-minded, whose grounds offer an island of serenity in the middle of a sea of grime. Resident guru, doyen, arbitrator, host, and broker, Bob was officially accorded the only title that could aptly describe his role at Tolly with the evocativeness of British understatement: Managing Member.

9 February 1990. It is our first visit to Kanha, and we are in awe. Three days ago, we sighted a tiger by vehicle. Each succeeding day has brought a viewing by elephant. It all seems too good to be true. The previous winter at Ranthambhore, we drove around the dusty tracks for three days before we finally sighted a tiger. Maybe it's a case of "beginner's luck," but we are sold on Kanha as a place to see the big cat.

Just after 9:00 AM, our young British escort from Kipling Camp tells us that the mahouts at Kisli have located a tiger. Tall, angular, and passionately devoted to wildlife, Katie has worked hard to answer our questions about the park and smooth out the rough edges of a Kanha visit: the amenities of an Indian wildlife excursion, we have noticed, are not yet comparable to East African standards. But all will be forgiven if we can make the acquaintance of a few tigers, and our batting average so far here in India's Central Highlands is very promising.

A certain amount of confusion is inevitable at any tiger show in Kanha. This will be only our third *darshan* by elephant, and we don't really know the system yet. (For what we hope is a current and reasonably accurate description, see page 26.) Providentially, shortly after 9:15, Bob Wright appears at Kisli Gate, where we are cooling our heels. Clad in military-looking shorts and black knee socks, with a broad-brimmed hat and a kerchief around his neck, he strides purposefully toward our Land Rover, waving to the park employees and dragging on a cigarette. Even as he explains the token system for waiting vehicles, the waters magically part, and we are suddenly rolling down the Kanha-Kisli main road. Bob tells us that we will be two on a side on the howdah and cautions us to get cameras and film ready.

The Land Rover brakes to a halt on the northern side of the road. An elephant is waiting, and a forest official quickly beckons us to ascend the ladder to the howdah. Bob and I sit on one side, with Ernie and my aunt, Sister Anita Horsey, on the other. Aunt Anita is a Roman Catholic nun of the Society of the Sacred Heart. She has been in India since 1946, the year before independence. She has spent most of her years in India as a professor at a college in Bombay and as a builder of schools for the Warli tribals of northwestern Maharashtra. Although Anita has never before seen a wild tiger during all these years in India, she explains to Bob Wright that the tiger-god is an important deity in the Warli pantheon. I can tell that this veteran of royal visits, diplomatic bashes, and charitable benefits is somewhat intrigued. After all, Calcutta is also the city of Mother Teresa.

Our mahout checks to see that the bar is secure on each side of the howdah, and we glide into the forest. Our mount is named Sita, after the heroine of the *Ramayana*, one of the two great Sanskrit epics. Bob is a great lover of elephants. He and his wife Anne Wright, in fact, acquired Tara, the Kipling Camp elephant, from Mark Shand, the British travel writer whose memoir, *Travels on My Elephant*, is wonderfully entertaining. Tara has become the Kipling Camp mascot, and Bob never tires in his efforts to get her a mate. Now he exchanges a few words in Hindi with our mahout: I wonder if they are talking about marriage brokers.

Three hundred yards into the jungle, at 9:50 AM, we find our tiger. It is a young adult male, who is lying in brightly dappled light, paws extended, beside a pool of water. Commenting in an undertone while I have the video rolling, Bob estimates his size as just short of 3 metres (9½ ft.) from nose to tail-tip, and his weight at 190 kg (425 lb.). When the tiger drinks with surprising delicacy from the waterhole, Anita is entranced. We can hear the sounds of the long pink tongue lapping. Then the harshly booming rasp of a barking deer alarm call breaks the serenity of the scene.

We will later learn in Kanha that every tiger show is unpredictable. Tigers may snooze or pose placidly, or they may charge the elephant. If they want to disappear into the forest, nothing will prevent them, and they will be invisible within seconds. Sometimes, however, a tiger will simply want to move. On many such occasions, the mahouts will follow. This is what happens now, as our young male decides he will take a promenade through the jungle. There is no show of aggression, and we certainly do not have the impression he is trying to lose us. He simply wants to go his way.

We shadow him for twenty minutes. The barking deer continues to call. Bob estimates that the deer is barely 30 metres away, but the tiger ignores the alarms. The tiger's stripes and colours continuously merge with grass blades and bamboo stalks in the dappled light, and I get my first vivid impression of how subtly evolution has arranged the counterbalances between predator and prey in this habitat: the barking deer is like a radar detector whose pinpoint fixes are frustrated by the ghostly, disruptive outline of the tiger's coloration. A little after 10 o'clock, our mahout decides that our presence may be intrusive. We give up the pursuit and return to the road.

We are in high good humour on the way back to Kisli. Bob stops to give a lift to some Baiga tribals. It is Wednesday, and they are wending their way to the Mocha Village market. For many of them, the weekly shopping excursion entails a 20-kilometre round trip on foot. Unbelievably, nineteen Baiga women and children are able to crowd into the back of the Land Rover. Aunt Anita, who has earlier been invited to visit a Baiga tribal village, cheerfully remarks, "Now the village has come to us!"

"A Special Intimacy"

"There is a special intimacy between the Baiga and all wild animals." So wrote the anthropologist Verrier Elwin sixty years ago in *The Baiga* (1939), his groundbreaking ethnography of the Baiga tribals of the Central Provinces. Elwin's informants recalled tales about a powerful magician named Dugru Baiga of Barangi, who used to spend nights alone in the forest. Tigers would come to lick his hands and his feet and stroke him with their paws. Another magician, Balli Bhumia, was said to have been accosted by a tiger in the middle of a jungle road. When the tiger rushed at him, roaring, Balli Bhumia caught it by the ear, slapped its face, and remonstrated, "Am I not your guru?" The tiger crouched to the ground and licked Balli Bhumia's feet, waiting until it received permission to return into the jungle. Elwin reported that such tales were "constantly repeated and firmly believed by everyone." In 1982 at Kanha, Mohan Baiga told Belinda Wright and Stanley Breeden that there is no fear between tigers and the Baiga. "Tigers will never harm us," said Mohan, "even though we spend all our lives in the jungle."

There are, of course, apparent exceptions. Several years ago in Bandhavgarh, for example, we met up with a Baiga mahout who was traveling on foot through the forest in the early morning. Hitching a ride, he climbed into our vehicle, explaining that he had just been charged by a male tiger. This male was notoriously aggressive: the mahouts had, in fact, named him "Charger." We asked Ramchal, our new Baiga acquaintance, how he had dealt with the problem. "I climbed a tree—very fast!" he replied.

Tigers like "Charger" may be no respecters of persons, but it is indisputable that the tribals who live in and around India's protected areas are profoundly sensitive to the jungle and to the ways of its creatures. Moreover, the idea that certain privileged individuals enjoy a special relationship with tigers is widespread in India. From the Warli *bhagats* (priests) of northwestern Maharashtra to the *gunins*, or shamans, of the Sunderbans, these special intermediaries function as propitiators, diviners, and interpreters. The word among Kanha tribal Baigas and Gonds for such a person, borrowed from orthodox Hinduism, is *pujari*.

It is February 1995. Tiger sightings have been poor during our visit this year—only three in two weeks—and we have devoted much time to speculating about the reasons. Most obviously, there is no tiger show this season; it was suspended in May 1994, following a complaint from Bittu Sahgal, editor of *Sanctuary* magazine and a member of the Tiger Steering Committee. There is also an unusual amount of water in the park for this time of year, so that tigers do not have to travel far in order to drink. A third, more sinister reason suggests itself: perhaps we are seeing fewer tigers because there are fewer in Kanha as a result of poaching. Ashok Kumar, our regular guide, assures us that there have been no poaching incidents, at least none of which he is aware.

Two days before our visit is to come to an end, Ashok takes us into his confidence. If we would like to have a tiger *darshan*, he suggests, we might request a *puja* from one of his Baiga friends. We know of several tribal *pujaris*, and without being too inquisitive about our intercessor's identity, we gladly agree, promising a handsome fee of Rs. 100 for a successful outcome.

On 15 February, the morning drive begins well. Just before 7 o'clock, we spot some interesting pug marks at Partak Puliya, the small bridge at the nallah that marks the entrance to Kanha

Meadow. Although distinguishing individual tigers from their pug marks is highly controversial among tiger watchers (see page 22), there are two inferences that can readily be made, even by amateurs: male vs. female, and healthy vs. injured. In this case, the irregularly deep imprint of one mark shows that a male tiger has something wrong with its right hind leg. We learn that the elephant men are trying to track the injured animal.

During a break in the morning drive, arrangements are duly made for the *puja*. We ask Ashok where and when he thinks we will see the tiger.

"This afternoon," he smiles. "On Sal Ghat. It will be a male tiger. He will cross the road, either in front of you or behind."

We are dubious. The three sightings we have had so far this season have all been on or near Sal Ghat, and Ashok knows this very well. At least we have not paid any money in advance.

During the latter part of the morning, we explore a newly re-opened road leading down from Bamhni Dadar to Gorhela. It is a steep descent, and I would not like to do it in wet weather in a heavy Land Rover. Half way down, as I smell the brakes burning a bit, we level out and pass Alegi Dadar Forest Camp, which is painted a beautiful shade of aqua. The place seems lonely; perhaps that is the reason that the forest guard and his helpers have used this colour to brighten it up.

At Gorhela we spend half an hour photographing the elephants. One young male has a cut trunk, the result of an accident in infancy. I wonder how serious a disability this is for him. We give a ride to one of the mahouts from Gorhela to Sondhar Camp. After leaving him off there, we pass Sondhar Tank, three kilometres from the camp, where we photograph some excellent female barasingha. Graceful for their size and honey-coloured, they are as stunning in their way as barasingha males, although the racks of branching antlers on the latter are the most famous feature of this species.

It is business as usual in the afternoon. We have to skirt the Kanha Ghat, which is closed to eastbound vehicles. At 3:35, half way to Nakti Ghati from Kope Dabri, we spot a baby sambar on the right about six metres in from the road. The mother must be nearby, but we can't see her. Nearer to Nakti Ghati, a painted spurfowl scuttles into the undergrowth. As so often this year, in contrast to past seasons, Kanha Meadow fails to yield any alarm calls. Since we have taken the Nakti Ghati route at the beginning of the drive, it is only natural that we should start home from the Meadow by way of

Sonf Road, which will lead us to Sal Ghat. As we travel northward with the shadows lengthening, we look meaningfully at Ashok, who only smiles.

At 5:50, just before the left turn onto Sal Ghat, the tempo changes. We see the very fresh pug marks of a tigress. A minute later, after we make the turn, a sambar blurts its deep, bell-like call, and we stop the vehicle. The sambar calls a dozen times in succession, once every 30 seconds or so, and the tension rises. Another vehicle approaches from behind. Ashok signals Patel, who is guiding the other party of tourists, to keep his distance, and they halt about 30 metres away. There are some heavy, thudding sounds in the jungle.

At 5:59 a large male tiger appears on the left hand side of the road. He is lame, with an injury to the right hind leg, and he limps badly, twitching his tail with every movement. We watch for twelve minutes as he crosses and re-crosses the road five times. He is plainly hungry, and we observe him trying to eat bamboo as well as grass. Perhaps he has been injured in a fight with another male. We saw a female in estrus on Sal Ghat last week, and we know that there is at least one other male in the vicinity. We can only speculate that several males may be competing to consort with her. Two conclusions are clear, however: we have found the animal that left the peculiar pug marks overnight at Partak Puliya, some three to four kilometres away; and we owe the *pujari* Rs. 100.

At Kisli Gate, Ashok immediately reports the sighting, and a message is sent to Mandla by wireless. We hope that action can be taken promptly. With clear weather and a brilliant full moon just rising, perhaps the Kisli elephants can keep an eye on the tiger until morning.

In the event, no action was taken, and the mahouts were unable to locate the tiger for several more days. On the morning after the sighting, however, we ran into Deputy Director Jagdish Chandra on Kanha Meadow. We told him the story, and that evening he dropped by our camp in order to watch the video footage. Jagdish assured us that the mahouts would make every effort to find the lame tiger and that the animal would receive medical attention.

And what of the *pujari*? Ashok, of course, was vindicated. He had intuited that we were skeptical, and we humbly apologized for our lack of faith. I reflected again on the "special intimacy" between Kanha's tribals and their jungle. Only the next morning did it occur to me that the circumstances of this unusual sighting on Sal Ghat had left us with another, unanswered question. For whose benefit was the *puja*, really: ours, or the tiger's?

The Deputy Director

J. S. Chauhan became Kanha's Deputy Director in 1995. The post of "D.D." ranks just below that of Field Director, so the Deputy Director is the park's second-ranking official. Stocky, plain-spoken, in his late thirties, Chauhan is an I.F.S. officer, with a government rank grade. He has the use of a special car and driver. Even better, he is allocated a house in Kanha Village with a verandah commanding a view of Desi Nallah. It is one of the prettiest views in the park.

On an early May evening in 1996, we sit on this verandah with our friend Jane Swamy from Mumbai, sipping tea and trying to think cool thoughts. Sundown is approaching, but the temperature is still 45° Celsius. Chauhan tells us how impressed he has been, during his relatively short time in Kanha, by the knowledge and dedication of the staff. He singles out Munglu Baiga, a man in his late fifties who was born in Kanha and has lived his whole life here. Munglu, says Chauhan, has never received any formal training in anatomy or veterinary science. Yet he can autopsy a wild animal with the accuracy of the best post mortem specialists. (Two years later, in fact, we learned that Munglu's skills are in wide demand outside the park as well: he was sent to help round up a man-eating leopard in another part of Madhya Pradesh.)

Like most of the park's senior managers, Chauhan has his main office and his family home in Mandla, some 65 km away. He comes to the park several days a week to supervise training courses, solve personnel problems, investigate needs for management interventions (see page 133), and entertain VIPs. The trip to Kisli takes slightly over an hour each way, with another half hour's drive through the core area to Kanha Village. If Chauhan has to go to Supkhar, which is the administrative centre of the park's eastern zone, the journey time will double.

For a government servant, Chauhan is unusually forthcoming. He is willing to discuss controversial issues, such as the methods for censusing tigers and the occasionally strained relations between forest guards and villagers. Like many Forest Department senior staff, Chauhan views his job with mixed feelings. He appreciates the importance of public relations, but he does not want Kanha to be overrun with busloads of tourists. He admits candidly that he does not know whether national parks like Kanha can succeed in saving the tiger in India in the long run.

On another occasion, when we have got to know him better, he ruefully tells us that NGOs and researchers are doing less than they might to support the park's efforts. I ask for an example, and Chauhan answers by mentioning a prominent south Indian scientist who has sharply criticized the Forest Department's census methods.

"This researcher was in Kanha for three months," Chauhan asserted. "He was testing new census techniques. But he left without sharing any of his results with us.

"Another tiger man, one from the Steering Committee in Delhi, came on a VIP visit for two days," the D. D. continued. "All he did was to criticize us for maintaining our vehicle tracks in good condition. He also didn't like us spending money to improve our forest camps. You've seen the appalling state of some of these camps. How can I ask my forest guards and their assistants to spend months at a time in firetraps?"

We get the sense from several interviews that the new D.D. of Kanha will be good at defending his staff and building morale. As I write these pages, a little more than two years after that evening on his verandah, Chauhan's horizons are most surely expanding. He is in rural Idaho—his first trip to the United States—completing a special three-month course at the University of Idaho's College of Forestry and the Hornocker Wildlife Institute.*

The Captain and his Lady

Captain Navneet Singh (Indian Army, Ret.) strides up the gravel path of Royal Tiger Resort in the village of Mukki on Kanha's eastern edge. Even in the dim, pre-dawn light of mid-November, Navneet cuts an impressive figure. Although he is a retired army officer, he is still on the good side of forty. Six-foot-two, with a soft but firm voice, he exudes authority, and his commanding presence is amply reinforced by the enormous German shepherd ambling at his side. Fittingly, the dog's name is Tiger.

After a quick, early-morning salutation, we board a gleaming black Gypsy under a brilliant moon, three days past full, and set out for the Mukki Gate. Navneet sits in the front, with his right-

---

* See note on page 169.

hand man, Associate Manager Raj Singh, behind the wheel. It is 5:50 AM.

Navneet Singh and his wife Deepika first fell under Kanha's spell nearly a decade ago. The park is now their permanent address. Together with a group of partners, they are the proprietors of the Royal Tiger Resort. This lodge has brought a new standard to Kanha, not only with its superb design and the comfortable amenities, but through the personal touch of the Singhs as resident owner-managers.

This morning we decide to head for gaur, the wild cattle that are Kanha's largest mammals (see page 60). At Mukki Gate, we give a lift to Lakhan Singh. Just after we leave the elephant man off at Gorhela Camp, we sight a herd of eight adult female gaur at the beginning of Mahavir Road. Three calves suckle at their mothers' teats. Navneet explains that all-female herds are the norm; males will not join up with them until the onset of the rut, which is still a month off. It is only 6:20, and the light is too poor for photography. Navneet quietly comments on the condition of the animals' horns, which is often an indicator of their age. Many gaur are shy, but this herd seems habituated to vehicles, and they even drift closer to the Gypsy. We linger, enjoying the sight. Then, as we roll on into Sondhar Maidan, fluffy pink clouds herald the dawn. We reach Sondhar Tank in time for the sunrise; here are lots of Common Teal in the marshy patch opposite the tank, as well as some female barasingha.

Our next stop is the network of narrow, twisting roads to the west of Bishanpura Meadow. The mixed forest habitat here, dotted with dense bamboo stands, is also an excellent place to look for gaur. We arrive at prime birding time, shortly after 7:00, and we are rewarded with a pair of Blackheaded Orioles, wings flashing. Slowly we make the circuit by the two small *talaos*, Bauatinga and Sengarpur. But there are no gaur, and, rather surprisingly, there is a complete absence of deer. Sambar, chital, and barking deer are all familiar denizens of this wooded section of the park, but they seem to have taken the morning off. Still, there is a profusion of wildflowers and colourful flowering grasses, particularly lovely at this time of year after the monsoon. Huge spider webs sparkle in the slanting sunshine, and every so often a tall spike of wild ginger adds a deep red exclamation point to the roadside landscape.

At 7:35 Navneet touches Raj Singh's arm, and Raj smoothly brakes to a halt. "Langur alarm," Navneet murmurs. We back up about a hundred feet, stationing ourselves near a cluster of tall sal trees. The langur's calls are frequent and intense. The complex, staccato pattern and the pitch indicate that the caller is a male. Scanning the tree branches, however, we cannot pick out the monkey in the foliage. Although this is frustrating, we continue to wait as the minutes tick by. After all, steady langur calls are an almost failsafe sign of the presence of a major predator.

Suddenly, at 7:45, Navneet points wordlessly to the trijunction ahead of us. Two wild dogs have appeared, their ruddy coats resplendent in the morning light. After the briefest of notice, they pay us no further attention, but rather comb the trijunction with their noses to the ground. Their businesslike pace and the pattern of their movements suggest that they are hunting. Although it is possible that there are only two, the odds favour a larger pack, and we wait quietly to see how many more dogs may emerge. In less than half a minute, six more issue forth from the jungle. By this time, the two leaders have crossed the trijunction toward Bishanpura and are out of sight. Of course the pack could be even larger: this may be a fragment of a bigger group that has split off for several hours, or even days. Navneet decides to move, not only to see what this group of eight may be up to, but also because the light is perfect for photography. Both he and Raj are skilled drivers as well as knowledgeable hosts, and they want to put us in the best position for pictures, if the dogs will permit.

We glide down to the trijunction and bear left. Three dogs are sitting in the road, and we can see two more, one on each side of the track. Like tigers, wild dogs often use the park roads as the easiest travel routes when they are hunting, although in other respects the two species could not be more different. Tigers are largely solitary, while dholes are gregarious animals. Since the dogs rely on long-range chases to bring down prey, they seldom bother to conceal themselves in the first stages of a hunt; in contrast, concealment is a basic strategy for the tiger.

Photography of wild dogs is tricky, because at the majority of sightings the creatures are on the move, and they seldom stop to pose for the camera. This time we are lucky, however. The dogs decide to take a short intermission, and four of them trot close to the vehicle, seemingly curious about their mid-morning visitors. Whenever I see wild dogs, I am struck by how utterly fearless they are. Tigers, quite often, are more shy. Raj expertly adjusts our position, and we get some good shots at a distance of only ten metres. After three or four minutes, the lead dog (who is often the dominant or so-called "alpha male") decides that the photo opportunity is over. He branches off into the jungle at an angle. Within twenty seconds, all the other dogs have followed. They are not intimidated in the least; they have simply decided to continue with their morning programme. The entire sighting has lasted ten minutes. We adjourn to Sondhar Camp, where we enjoy a hearty breakfast of sandwiches and fruit under the great kanji tree.

On another drive a few months later, we also find ourselves at Sondhar Camp for breakfast. Navneet fills us in on the history of forest villages. The origin of many villages around Kanha like Mukki, he explains, is intertwined with the management policy of the British. During the latter half of the nineteenth century, as timber extraction and sport hunting became more subject to regulation, forest villages were organized to provide a pool of labour for certain basic tasks: for example, logging and firefighting. Villagers received housing and the right to work the land, but they did not own the plots where they lived. In emergencies, they were expected to pitch in on a volunteer basis. This system is the ancestor of today's setup, but with the significant difference that villagers now own their land and supplement their meager income with casual day-labour for the park, for which they are paid at the rate of about Rs. 50 per day.

The potential for conflict and exploitation, it occurs to me, seems clear, both then and now. Today, the presence of villages inside protected areas in India is an ongoing bone of contention—not so much at Kanha, where there are only three villages left inside the park, but elsewhere across the country. It is ironic to learn that many of the villages which conservationists and Forest Department managers want to see relocated were deliberately created a century ago in the cause of forest management.

As we finish our tea and coffee, Navneet checks with the wireless operator at Sondhar to see if the elephants are tracking this morning. We learn that the elephant men from Gorhela Camp are working, but there is no news of a tiger sighting. Navneet decides to return to Mukki at a leisurely pace on a route that will take us by Gorhela. Like Bishanpura and Sondhar, Gorhela was a forest village that was relocated in the 1970s to the buffer zone. The forest camp at Gorhela is one of the oldest buildings in the park, dating from 1930, and its dilapidated condition supports Deputy Director Chauhan's contention that Kanha needs to upgrade its facilities for forest guards. Fronted by a tall eucalyptus tree, the camp is located at the edge of Kudh Maidan, one of Kanha's great meadows. As we arrive there, a little after 9:30, we see the elephants striding back to base. We enjoy the fragrance of the eucalyptus as we wait for Lakhan Singh to see to his mount, Pawan Kali.

When Lakhnu appears, we greet him affectionately. His experience and skills are comparable to those of Sabir on the Kisli side of the park. Indeed, Lakhnu was the recipient of a special award for dedicated service to Project Tiger, and the government flew him to Delhi for a ceremony marking the twentieth anniversary of the project in 1993. We chat with him about his family and recall some of our tracking experiences.

The previous November, Lakhnu had taken us on an enchanting afternoon elephant ride. Navneet had to drive other guests in the park, so we were joined on elephant back by his wife Deepika and their seven-year-old daughter Priyanka. Tall and slender, gracious and fun-loving, Deepika Singh makes running a resort look easy. The high standard of Royal Tiger Resort is largely due to Deepika's meticulous attention to detail, her artistic eye, and her congeniality with a wide range of people. Staff supervision, menu planning, financial accounting, entertaining, and parenting routinely occupy Deepika eighteen hours a day, but her energy seems boundless. A gifted artist and jewellery designer, Deepika has drawn and coloured the bird pictures that adorn the walls of the lodge's dining hall; these are so fine that they could be in a field guide. Ernie and I decide that hers is a thoroughly appropriate talent for the great-granddaughter of the former Maharajah of Bharatpur.

The afternoon of our elephant ride is brilliantly sunny. Priyanka has been on elephant back before, but nevertheless Lakhnu takes special care to see that she is comfortably seated on the howdah. We set off from Gorhela at 3:15 in the direction of Sondhar Tank. On the way we alternate between chatting with Lakhnu (it is mostly Deepika speaking with him in Hindi) and pointing out various sights to Priyanka. How lucky this little girl is, I think, to be growing up with the jungle so near! Will it be so available, or so unspoiled, in the time of her children a generation from now? Deepika entertains us with some family stories. The interaction between the British and the rulers of the Indian princely states was often worthy of a spy thriller, and the history of Bharatpur is no exception.

We reach Sondhar Tank around 4 o'clock. Lakhnu guides Pawan Kali through the marshy patches that border the road to the west of the tank. Here are three beautiful barasingha stags, their antlers showing reddish at this season, about a month before the rut, after they have shed their velvet. They move majestically through the shallow water, foraging for water plants. Pictures are tricky, however. Even though we are on elephant, the barasingha are shy, and their reflection in the water makes focusing difficult. It is enough just to appreciate them, as the sun sinks further and the shadows begin to lengthen. On the way back, Deepika helps Priyanka to put on her jacket.

We ask Deepika to consider drawing some birds for this book, and she readily agrees.

"Which ones do you think would go best?" I ask.

"You make up a list of your twenty favourites," she says merrily, "and I will do the same. Then we will compare lists and make the final choice!"

A Visit to Supkhar

Supkhar is the hub of Kanha's eastern zone. The word "hub" is something of a misnomer, since Supkhar seldom hosts visitors, and only a small contingent of park employees is posted there permanently. They are responsible for the overall integrity of the Supkhar and Baisanghat Ranges, an area of the park that is strictly off-limits to tourists. As in many other parks, Kanha's management has long been committed to a policy of safeguarding part of the ecosystem in as pristine a condition as possible. In Kanha's case, only 227 km^2 of the core area of 940 km^2 (or 24.1%) is utilized for tourism. It is possible, nonetheless, to travel to Supkhar if you stick to the main road, as we found out in April 1998.

We decided to make a long day of it: into the park at Kisli, across Kanha Meadow and a morning run down to Mukki, and then over to Supkhar by late morning, with a return to Mukki for lunch during the mid-day break when the park closes. You get to Supkhar from Mukki on State Highway 26, a route that leads you in and out of the park boundary several times and through the small town of Garhi, which is located outside the park. A sign-in system allows Kanha officials to keep track of the vehicles that ply this highway; the journey reminds you that national parks and other sanctuaries have grown up with complex boundaries, some of which are all too permeable.

Just as the western half of Kanha centers on the Banjar River valley, the spine of the eastern half is the valley of the Halon River.

The eastern half of Kanha, however, has had a rather more checkered history. In 1935, the Supkhar area, most of which is located in Balaghat District, was accorded the status of a sanctuary, less than two years after Kanha, in Mandla District, was removed from the shooting blocks. Several years later, however, this decision was reversed because of damage from the wild animals to the crops and livestock of local villagers. It was not until the mid-1970s, after Kanha had been brought under the umbrella of Project Tiger, that the Supkhar region was restored completely to the status of a protected area—this time as part of the national park.

But Supkhar has ghosts of its own that go back long before the era of national parks. These spirits reside in one of Kanha's most remarkable buildings, the Supkhar Forest Rest House. Built in 1910, the rest house is the twin of a venerable structure in Kanha Village, which was erected in the same year. The wayside marker at Kanha gives some idea of the ambience and lore that these structures conjure up:

Old Forest Rest House

This rest house, built in 1910, marked the beginning of scientific forestry operations in Kanha. Today it does not have the colonial decor of the past, when British sportsmen stayed here. They came on foot, on horseback, or on elephant. There were no roads to lead their way to this remote jungle, nor electricity connections. Yet they came, attracted by the pristine forest, in anticipation of what it had to offer.

Unfortunately, we had never been able to see the decor of the Kanha Forest Rest House, and so had no opportunity to evaluate it vis-à-vis any colonial antecedents. The building's exterior, moreover, had lately been repainted a rather unattractive colour. But the rest house at Supkhar, we were told, was quite a different matter, and well worth the detour. All you had to do to look around inside was to find the chowkidar, who would let you in with the key and serve you tea.

We set out from Mukki Gate a little after 8:15 AM, after a leisurely game drive across the park from Kisli. Before reaching Mukki, our route has taken us up to Bamhni Dadar, the highest point in the park, for the first time this season. There are lots of bauhinia in bloom on the ascent, and once we gain the plateau we see a Pale Harrier, wheeling beautifully over the grasslands. Our park guide is Pandey, one of the senior freelancers, who has a delightfully dry sense of humour. We pause for a snack at Bamhni Dadar, enjoying the spectacular view. Then it is down to Gorhela via Alegi Dadar Camp, and on to the Mukki Gate.

On the state highway heading east from Mukki, we have the park on our left and reserve forest on our right. Just after Lal Puliya Forest Camp, we pass a roadside shrine to Hanuman: an appropriate landmark for this excursion, since the only animals we see on the whole way to Supkhar are troops of langurs. Pandey, a Hindu, says that Hanuman is his special deity. At the Baisanghat Gate, about 9 km from Mukki, we stop to register, signing our names and vehicle number into a book. Then it is on through Garhi, located a further 10 km eastward, the half-way point to Supkhar. At the Supkhar Gate, about 5 km from the Forest Rest House, we must register again, since we are re-entering the park. A sign requests us not to disturb the wild animals, blow our horn, use any searchlight, or "during check-in feel otherwise but cooperate in law procedure."

Travelling on the main road, we parallel the Halon River soon after we enter the gate. The Halon, unlike the Banjar, is perennial for its length within the park. Pandey points out some pine trees—noteworthy because of their complete absence from the tourist zone on the park's western side. Once again, langurs scamper across the road, but we see no chital. Soon we reach a fair-sized meadow, with a row of small buildings flanking it at one end. On the left is a magnificent old bungalow, fronted by a broad verandah and sheltered by the largest thatched roof I have seen in India. We have arrived at the rest house.

Pandey asks a young boy to hunt up the chowkidar. As we wait for the rest house to be opened, we chat with a clerk about the Supkhar Range. He says that he is one of approximately 30 full-time park employees in this sector. There are perhaps ten or eleven resident tigers here, which would be 10% of the official total in Kanha. Having seen no prey at all, although the grasslands look suitable for chital, I am dubious. Clearly, the overall quality of the habitat—and the density of tiger territories—is poorer than on the western side of the park. In fact, according to the park's own census of 1988, 75% of Kanha's tiger population (70 out of 94 individuals) were in the 3 western ranges: Kisli, Kanha, and Mukki.

Inside the rest house, it is dark, cool, and a trifle musty. Relics of a bygone era abound. My favourite is the enormous overhead fan, which a servant, discreetly stationed outside the dining room, would have worked manually by means of a long rope (there was a very similar contraption in the courtroom scene of the Merchant-Ivory film of E. M. Forster's *A Passage to India*). We're also taken with the wall decorations, some of which consist of a series of sardonic send-ups of hunting stereotypes during the Raj. One cartoon shows a British hunter seated at a writing table. He is smoking a pipe and wearing a self-satisfied expression, despite a missing right leg. Behind him, mounted on the wall, is the head of a large tiger, with the hunter's leg in its mouth. With delightful ambiguity, the caption proclaims, "My trophy."

Also on the walls are framed photographs of some of the heroes of Indian independence, as well as some paintings on jungle themes by Manik, a contemporary artist who lives near Mukki in the town of Malanjkhand. One painting shows Pandit Nehru with his back to the viewer, staring out into an eerie, moonlit jungle. The final stanza of Robert Frost's poem "Stopping by Woods on a Snowy Evening," written in both English and Hindi, accompanies the image:

> The woods are lovely, dark and deep,
> But I have promises to keep,
> And miles to go before I sleep,
> And miles to go before I sleep.

We explore further. On each side of the living room and dining alcove are symmetrical bedrooms, both with attached dressing room and large, tiled bath. These rooms can be rented with the permission of the Field Director. Even with no animals in evidence at this hour of the morning, it occurs to us that it would be an adventure to spend the night here. Perhaps we may hear one of the Supkhar Range tigers calling in the darkness! Stepping out onto the back verandah, which is screened in, we see a large pantry. The kitchen is located in a small, separate building about 30 metres away.

After a bracing cup of tea, we take our leave, thanking the chowkidar. We retrace the same route to Mukki. Passing the gate, we must sign another register before we move on to Malanjkand for some shopping and then lunch at Royal Tiger with Navneet and

Deepika. We run into R. K. Sharma, the park's Assistant Director. He is glad we have been to Supkhar, and justly proud of Kanha's efforts to keep the old rest house in good condition. The roof must be re-thatched every three years, he says, at a cost of Rs. 50,000. Soon this may no longer be possible, adds Mr. Sharma, not because of the expense but because thatching is a dying art.

A Tiger for Joan Burtenshaw

Important as Kanha's employees are to the national park as an institution, the total Kanha experience also involves the other visitors you will meet while you are here. I often think that the people we have encountered in wildlife parks are some of the most lively and interesting it is possible to meet. Many of them are passionately devoted to nature and unusually well-travelled. Needless to say, they are often good storytellers and very useful sources of information. In fact, our first trip to Kanha was owing to a recommendation from a young English couple, Nick and Tracy Burdett, whom we met in Ranthambhore in 1989.

There are significantly more visitors to Kanha from the U.K. than from the U.S.A., and British tourists probably also outnumber those from any other European country. Perhaps this is natural, given the historical fact of the Raj. We ran into one particularly charming British lady, Mrs. Joan Burtenshaw of Peterborough in Cambridgeshire, on a visit to Kanha in March 1997. Travelling with her were her son Peter and his wife Helen. Peter is a retired British Army officer in his early fifties. His father was also an army officer, and Peter was born in India in the year before independence. It was also in that year that the senior Mrs. Burtenshaw had seen her last tiger. She described the scene vividly.

In those days Viscount Kerens, she told us, was fond of evening, open-air play readings. As the son of the viceroy, Field Marshal Archibald Wavell, the viscount had a large bungalow located in the hill station of Chaubattia, a stable full of elephants, and servants to spare. After his guests had finished their outdoor theatricals, there would be scrambled eggs and sausages *al fresco*, and then home to bed. On a warm evening, very late, one such party returned to the bungalow, only to find a large male tiger comfortably sprawled in a pool of moonlight on the front verandah. The servants raised a hue and cry, and the tiger peaceably moved off.

Now, in a very different India after more than half a century, would she see a tiger in Kanha, Mrs. Burtenshaw wondered? Not that she would *really* mind if she didn't, because returning to India was thrilling in so many other ways. But still . . . it would be exciting!

We tell the Burtenshaws that, since they are staying for four days, the chances are reasonably good. The sightings have been frequent around Schaller Hide in the late afternoon, and I have a word with their driver to make sure that he checks up that part of Kanha Meadow after 5 o'clock.

The following afternoon, we are at Schaller Hide at 5:35 PM, facing into brilliant sunshine. A single chital call leads to a whole series of alarms, punctuated by the blaring honks of peacocks. A small party of chital is visible to the left, strung out along the edge of Klingi Nallah, while the peacocks are concealed in medium-length grass to the right. Ernie predicts that the tiger will emerge and cross from right to left.

Indeed it does, within less than twenty seconds. With a road-cross at close range to a vehicle, it is usual for a tiger to hesitate, if only ever so slightly, in order to appraise the situation. But this tigress pays us no attention whatever. The hour of the day, the presence of the chital, her determined gait, and the configuration of the nallah give us every reason to think that she is hunting.

Ten metres in from the road on the other side, the tigress turns to the right, follows the curve of the nallah, and disappears. As quietly as possible, we advance half way up a moderate incline. As we station ourselves at the side of the road, we are just in time to see a chital stag, who is standing on the rim of the nallah, crumple down and disappear. An agonized chorus of alarm calls, a blur of motion: and the tigress rockets up from the nallah, this time with her jaws clamped in a strangulating bite on the chital's throat. She drags him back up to level ground.

It is at this point that Joan Burtenshaw and her family arrive. Rehman signals their driver, gesturing excitedly: "Tiger kill!" The tigress is now facing us at a distance of only twenty metres, but the view is partially obstructed by some low bushes. Her jaws are still locked on the stag's throat, choking off the airway. As she bends forward, I am struck by the splendid musculature of her back; we can clearly see the whiplash of her tail from side to side. There must be no relaxation of the tremendous effort now, in the face of flying hooves and stabbing antlers. With no hesitation, and agile for her seventy-five years, Joan Burtenshaw takes off her shoes and stands on the seat of the Gypsy for a better view.

The tigress holds on for a full four minutes. Then she drags the carcass for about twenty-five metres and conceals it in thick vegetation. It is not yet 5:45, and the spectacle is over. After seven years of visiting Kanha and over a thousand hours in the park, it is the first tiger kill we have seen from start to finish. Rehman moves us up parallel to the Burtenshaws' Gypsy.

"You waited fifty-one years to see another tiger," I joke. "You certainly got one this time!" Mrs. Burtenshaw is too excited to speak.

Note: Since this chapter was written, Deputy Director J. S. Chauhan has been transferred to the post of Field Director of the Palpur-Kuno Wildlife Sanctuary in northern Madhya Pradesh. Chauhan will thus be a key figure in overseeing one of the most important wildlife conservation projects in India during the next few years: the translocation of some of the Gir lions to a new home. H. S. Negi has become Kanha's new Deputy Director. Deputy Ranger Bastaram Nagpure has been promoted to Range Officer of Kanha Range. B. L. Sen and N. S. Maravi have both been promoted to the rank of Deputy Ranger.

Munglu Baiga was attacked by the man-eating leopard he had been sent to track in April 1998. Although the leopard seized him by the throat, Munglu managed somehow to throw the animal off. As of November 1998, he had recovered from serious injuries and returned to his home in Kanha Village, where he continues to work for the park.

CHAPTER 4

KANHA AND THE FUTURE

"To ESTABLISH A reserve is relatively easy," George Schaller has written, "but to maintain and manage it is a complex and difficult endeavour." Schaller was referring to the Chang Tang Reserve in Tibet, a new protected area in which he has played an instrumental role. His observation, if anything, is even more relevant to an established Indian national park like Kanha, where the shifting interplay of socioeconomic factors, an international tourist profile, and the emotionally charged battle to save the tiger from extinction perennially demand skillful, imaginative management.

In the last chapter of this book we look at Kanha's future, just as the park enters a new century and prepares to celebrate its fiftieth anniversary in the year 2005. We first examine the linkage between Kanha's destiny and the uncertain future of the tiger, a discussion that inevitably involves a look back at the two "tiger crises" of the past twenty-five years and at the uneven history of Project Tiger. Next we discuss the impact of ecotourism on Kanha, with particular attention to the role that visitors and the revenues from tourism can play in the conservation mix. Finally, we put forward a dozen practical suggestions for consolidation and improvement in the park's operations.

1.   THE PARK AND THE TIGER

Project Tiger and Madhya Pradesh

The future of Kanha is clearly linked to the future of the tiger. As if to underscore the importance of India's national animal (and one of the world's most charismatic large mammals), the official name of the park has been changed from Kanha National Park to the Kanha Tiger Reserve. Kanha was, in fact, one of the original nine protected areas of Project Tiger in 1973. As of 1998, this select group of reserves has now grown to 23. The Project Tiger reserves are listed by state below, together with figures for total area and core area.

Project Tiger Reserves

State	Tiger Reserve	Total Area (km²)	Core Area (km²)
Andhra Pradesh	Nagarjunasagar	3568	1200
Arunachal Pradesh	Namdapha	1985	1808
Assam	Manas	2837	470
Bihar	Palamau	1026	213
	Valmiki	840	336
Karnataka	Bandipur	866	523
Kerala	Periyar	777	350
Madhya Pradesh	Bandhavgarh	1162	625
	Indravati	2799	1258
	Kanha	1945	940
	Panna	542	542
	Pench	758	293
Maharashtra	Melghat	1597	308
	Tadoba Andheri	620	220
Mizoram	Dampa	500	340
Orissa	Simlipal	2750	846
Rajashthan	Ranthambhore	1334	392
	Sariska	800	492
Tamil Nadu	Kalakad-Mundanthurai	800	571
Uttar Pradesh	Corbett	1134	338
	Dudhwa	811	648
West Bengal	Buxa	759	315
	Sunderbans	2585	1330

As is easily seen from the list above, Madhya Pradesh has the largest number of tiger reserves (5) of any state in India, and indeed M.P. has officially adopted the nickname of "the Tiger State." The official census figures of 1993 showed a population of 912 tigers in Madhya Pradesh, 755 of which (or nearly 83%) lived outside tiger reserves. This population figure represented a decline of 73 tigers, or 7.4%, since the previous census of 1989. In 1995, no enumeration for tigers outside the protected areas was published. Official census figures in 1997 for the five M.P. tiger reserves are given below.

Madhya Pradesh Tiger Reserves: 1997 Census

Bandhavgarh	46
Indravati	15
Kanha	114
Panna	22
Pench	29
Total	**226**

At the time of writing (mid-1998), the Madhya Pradesh Forest Minister had announced a 1997 total for the state of 927 tigers, representing a modest increase of 15 animals over the 1993 total. Tigers within the five tiger reserves were also said to have increased, to a total of 226. Considerable doubt persists, however, concerning the methodology of the census (see page 22), and Kanha Field Director Rajesh Gopal, in forwarding results to officials in the state capital in Bhopal, referred to the tabulation as "a compilation only." Even if the current numbers are somewhat inaccurate, though, it is safe to conclude that Madhya Pradesh holds an impressive percentage of the surviving population of wild tigers: perhaps as much as 30% of India's total figure (about 2500-3000?) and upwards of 15% of tigers worldwide. This makes Madhya Pradesh of paramount importance, not only to the survival of the Indian tiger (*Panthera tigris tigris*) but to the future of the species on this planet.

For the past decade, Kanha's tiger population has been stable, hovering around 100 individuals. Clearly, the tiger is the park's star attraction. You have only to speak to a few of the tourists milling around Kanha Village as they wait for "tiger news" at 8 AM, hoping for a chance to see the magnificent cat from elephant-back. And when vehicles meet inside the park, one question is on the lips of drivers and guides alike: *mila*? "Did you meet up with a tiger?"

It is very hard to imagine people coming to Kanha, from all corners of India and from around the world, in anything like present numbers if there were no tigers here.

The Two Tiger Crises

Within the past quarter of a century, there have been two tiger crises. The *first tiger crisis* occurred in the early 1970s, when it was realized that the tiger population in India had sunk to alarmingly low levels. It has often been claimed that at the turn of the twentieth century in 1900 there were as many as 40,000 tigers in India. This figure is pure guesswork, since even the imperfect census machinery we have today was lacking a hundred years ago. But the 1972 estimate of approximately 1,800 tigers country-wide was shocking enough to propel action at the highest levels of government. Supported by Prime Minister Indira Gandhi, the political will and dedicated effort of hundreds of wildlife experts, scientists, and devoted footsoldiers within the national parks gave birth to Project Tiger in April 1973.

For its first dozen years or so, Project Tiger was an outstanding success story. The comeback of the tiger, like that of the alligator and the wild turkey in the United States, evoked admiration. Tiger numbers increased to above 3,000, reflecting the resilience of this species when it is adequately protected and its habitat and prey base remain intact. H. S. Panwar, possibly Kanha's most energetic and productive field director, published a paper in 1984 whose title reflected the general euphoria: "What to Do When You've Succeeded: Project Tiger, Ten Years Later."

Under the dynamic leadership of Field Director Fateh Singh Rathore, Ranthambhore National Park in Rajasthan became India's most famous tiger reserve during this period. The tigers there, which had become a great deal more active by day than they had ever been before, were photographed, filmed, and intensively monitored. Their names became famous: Lakshmi, Kublai, Padmini, Genghis, Noon, Nuri (or Nurjahan). Not only were the tourists thrilled, but a great deal of additional information was gathered about tiger behaviour. We learned, for example, that males sometimes associate with females and cubs and cooperate to some extent in bringing up a tiger family. This was an aspect of tiger behavior that flew in the face of the "traditional wisdom" about the species.

But despite the real evidence of progress, all was not well in tigerland, and the 1990s have been an increasingly troubled decade. The *second tiger crisis* erupted in 1992, with the shocking news that as many as 15 tigers had been slaughtered in Ranthambhore, or a third to a half of the park's population. Forest Department officials were lamentably slow to acknowledge the catastrophe. Even more seriously, over the next few years neither Project Tiger at the centre nor the bureaucracy in the states moved to address two insidious threats that were suddenly combining once again to put the tiger in danger of extinction in the wild: poaching and the loss of habitat.

Poaching

The first of these threats, and the most dramatic, was (and continues to be) poaching. The Ranthambhore tigers were killed for their bones, not their skins. Tiger bone is one of the most sought-after substances for the manufacture of medicinal products in Traditional Chinese Medicine (TCM). Used against a wide range of ailments, most commonly rheumatism, these products involve many different parts of the tiger, including the whiskers, the claws, the eyes, and the genitals. The bones, however, bring the highest prices. One tiger produces about 8-11 kg. of bone. In Taiwan, tiger bone may command as much as $3,000 (Rs. 1.2 lakh) per kilogram; this is roughly 30% of the price of gold. Poachers consider the humerus or upper bone of the front legs as the most valuable.

The tiger bone trade, like the TCM market that it supplies, is extremely complex. Trade in tiger bone and tiger bone derivatives (products made from tiger bone or claiming to be made from it) ranges across the world. It is common, for example, to see packages labelled as tiger derivative on store shelves in the Chinatowns of North American cities such as Vancouver, Toronto, San Francisco, and New York. The effectiveness of tiger products is also difficult to analyse, given such problematic factors as cultural conditioning and the psychosomatic dimensions of a traditional pharmacopoeia. The myth of the aphrodisiac effect of tiger parts was forcefully attacked in a recent series of print advertisements that appeared in Asian publications.

Further complicating the picture is the black-market trade in Shahtoosh, or the extremely fine wool of the chiru (*Pantholops hodgsoni*), a graceful antelope that lives on the Tibetan plateau. The name "Shahtoosh" means "King of Wool." The chiru's coat is even finer than that of the vicuña (*Vicugna vicugna*), a small camelid of the South American Andes that has faced similar problems, with relentless persecution for its wool and its meat. A chiru provides about 125-150 grams of wool, and Tibetan herdsman can sell it for up to $1,500 (Rs. 60,000) per kg, or twenty times the price for pashmina wool from goats. At the other end of the black market, Shahtoosh scarves and shawls may sell for $2000-$8500 each (Rs. 80,000 to 3.4 lakh), depending on size. Contrary to some rumours, the wool is not harvested from rocks or bushes where the antelope scratch, but rather directly from the chiru, which are invariably slaughtered for this purpose. Because the wool is warm and yet so fine that it can be pulled through a finger ring, Shahtoosh shawls are in great demand in Delhi, London, and New York. Yet these elegant mufflers have the blood of tigers on them, because Shahtoosh is the *quid pro quo* for tiger bone smuggled across international borders (often via Nepal) by poaching gangs. The bones continue on from Tibet into China, where they are ground up into TCM preparations. The Shahtoosh goes back into Kashmir, where it is prepared for sale to fashionable buyers, both in India and abroad. The linkage is so tight that Ashok Kumar and Belinda Wright of the Wildlife Protection Society of India (WPSI), based in New Delhi, concluded in a report in late 1997: "[We] have no doubt whatsoever that it will be impossible to control the tiger bone trade if the Shahtoosh trade is not brought to a halt."

On the first day of the "Tigers 2000" conference held in February 1997 in London, the international assemblage of tiger experts had an unexpected visitor: an inspector from the Metropolitan Police. Graphic evidence of the Shahtoosh-tiger connection lay inside two large shopping bags: a haul of 170 Shahtoosh shawls from a raid carried out the day before the conference began. Estimated value of the goods: 353,000 British pounds (or Rs. 2 crore).

Throughout the 1990s, the pressure on tigers from poaching has escalated at a sinister pace. In 1996, WPSI estimated that the country might be losing one tiger a day to poachers. Evaluations of the poaching threat in other tiger range countries differ widely, with some experts claiming that the tide may have turned in the Russian Far East (where Global Survival Network's no-nonsense anti-poaching program has made a substantial impact) and other observers reporting drastic inroads by poachers in Southeast Asia and Indonesia.

Belinda Wright, who is Executive Director of WPSI and has long been active in Kanha, reported in her book *Through the Tiger's Eyes:*

A Chronicle of India's Wildlife (1996) on seizures from poachers on the edge of the park's buffer zone. Wright was offered tiger skins in the town of Baihar in April 1994, and three tiger skeletons were discovered in a house in Mocha Village the following year. TRAFFIC International, the division of WWF and the International Union for the Conservation of Nature and Natural Resources (IUCN) that is responsible for monitoring illegal wildlife trade worldwide, reported that in April 1995 two tiger skins and two skeletons were seized in separate incidents in Mandla, the town where Kanha's administrative offices are located. Although Kanha, by comparison with other tiger reserves, is well monitored and protected, the poaching threat can be said to have reached the park's front door.

Habitat Loss

Although poaching is the most brutal frontal assault on the tiger's survival, it is far from the only one. As crucial in the long run, perhaps even more so, is habitat loss. Recall that tigers have three basic needs: food, water, and cover. They can survive in a remarkable diversity of habitats, ranging from the taiga of the Russian Far East to the steamy jungles of Indonesia. But they cannot survive if their habitat is seriously degraded. If forest cover is depleted, if the prey base diminishes, if roads or mines or fishing licenses or logging interests impinge on the tiger's habitat, not only will tiger numbers dwindle, but entire ecosystems will languish and die. Thus the tiger is not only a charismatic species; it is also a keystone species, since assuring its continuation at the apex of the food chain helps to insure the survival of numerous other animal and plant species as well.

Sadly, however, habitat loss proceeds in India at an alarming rate. In the "tiger state" of Madhya Pradesh alone during 1997, over 4000 km^2 of forest cover disappeared. We often lose sight of the fact that a high proportion of India's tigers, perhaps as many as two-thirds, live outside the tiger reserves. Many of these animals, in fact, live outside protected areas of any sort. Loss of habitat brings special pressure on these tigers, making conflicts with humans ever more likely.

Except in the Sunderbans (where tiger attacks on fishermen and on wood- and honey-gatherers continue to be a serious problem) and other isolated special cases, such conflicts need not take the form of injuries or deaths from tiger attacks. From the tiger's point of view, the more serious danger results from cattle lifting or other predation on domestic stock. The situation in Panna Tiger Reserve is an instructive example. Panna is a small park located near Khajuraho in Madhya Pradesh. Unlike Kanha or Bandhavgarh, Panna is an example of suboptimal habitat for tigers, where the low density of suitable prey is positively correlated with low tiger density. A recent nine-month study by Wildlife Institute of India scientist R. S. Chundavat at Panna revealed that 57% of the kills by one radio-collared male tiger were on local cattle. This finding clearly signals the potential for a high level of conflict with the human population living on the borders of the park. It should be noted that Panna is fully representative of 50% of the reserves in India, so the trends observed there are important in any overall picture of the status of Indian wildlife.

In late 1997 and early 1998, six to eight tigers were poisoned in Corbett and Dudhwa Tiger Reserves as a result of such incidents. The anger of local villagers at seeing their cattle killed or maimed by tigers (or other predators) is understandable. Such incidents commonly result in severe economic hardship. The villagers' revenge is often to poison the carcass of the prey; the predator's status as an endangered species matters little. The compensation schemes that have been organized in a number of areas to deal with such conflicts obviously need re-thinking and considerable improvement. It can be argued, in fact, that revenge poisoning is potentially more dangerous to tigers than is poaching for bones, since a single poisoned carcass may result in multiple tiger deaths, including mothers with cubs.

Ashok Kumar, Vice President of the Tiger Crisis Cell in New Delhi, has called for a comprehensive survey of cattle kill compensation schemes in all the tiger reserves. Kumar notes that the Corbett and Dudhwa tiger poisonings underscore the importance of prompt payment of compensation, and he contrasts the failure to pay compensation in Simlipal with Kanha's system of prompt payment (letter to *Sanctuary* XVIII. 2, April 1998, 88).

Rallying to Save the Tiger

It was the mid-1990s before the Government of India, the Forest Department, and many international conservation organizations woke up to the "second tiger crisis." The disregard of WWF, given its high profile and influential position throughout the world on conservation matters, is especially disturbing. Although WWF had used the tiger, along with other megafauna like the giant panda, as a fundraising gambit for years, they had put very little money into tiger conservation directly. After a thorough investigation, the American writer and tiger expert Richard Ives established that, during the period 1977-1997, WWF had in fact channelled only Rs. 54 lakh ($135,000) per year directly into tiger conservation activities in India—despite the fact that India is home to over half of the world's tigers. The imbalance with the organization's annual fundraising effort is glaring: WWF gets Rs. 1200 crore ($300 million) a year in donations worldwide. For the two most critical decades in the tiger's modern history, WWF's annual support for the species in India amounted to about two-thirds of the funds that Kanha receives yearly from Project Tiger in New Delhi.

Meanwhile, many of the Project Tiger reserves were in disarray. Gun battles plagued Kaziranga, with poachers firing at rangers. A forest official's house was burned down in Nagarahole. Mining interests encroached on Panna, fishing interests intruded on Pench, and 500 km^2 of Melghat were denotified.

According to some NGO sources, of the 23 Indian tiger reserves comprising approximately 33,000 km^2, only one-third had fairly assured future prospects; the outlook for another one-third was highly uncertain, while prospects for the remaining third were decidedly grim. The present Director of Project Tiger, P. K. Sen, is himself a field veteran, having served as Field Director of Palamau Tiger Reserve in Bihar before he arrived in New Delhi. In 1996, Sen went on record as saying that six tiger reserves were so subject to violence and encroachment that they were simply "not within government's control."

Administrative inefficiency and the lack of adequate resources made this bleak picture of tigerland even more distressing. In a survey he conducted in 1995 of sixteen Project Tiger reserves, Valmik Thapar found that 63% of these national parks did not receive their budget on time, 69% did not have a yearly awards scheme for their staff, 56% did not monitor daily movements of tigers, and 75% lacked a bilingual interpretation centre for local communities and tourists. Perhaps most seriously, 63% had no vehicle to transport anti-poaching teams.

It is to the credit of a small number of NGOs that they took arms against this sea of troubles. Largely due to their efforts, the picture in the summer of 1998 looks somewhat different than it did barely three years back. The plight of the tiger has been extensively publicized and analysed worldwide in a plethora of books, magazine articles, reports, and international conferences. In 1996, the Exxon Corporation announced a five-year $5 million campaign to save the tiger (increased by a further $1 million in 1998). WWF committed $1 million to tiger conservation in 1998. Information on tigers was rapidly accumulated and distributed on a World Wide Web site on the Internet (the address is www.5tigers.org). Taking a cue from the Ranthambhore Foundation, which was established in 1987, several foundations focused on individual parks, including Dudhwa, Corbett, and Bandhavgarh, were established. Kanha has yet to be targeted as a foundation effort.

The foundations are an interesting case study in themselves. They have all been established on the basic principle that people-park relations is a key factor in the success of a national park and in the protection of its wildlife from poaching. In the words of John Seidensticker, a big cat expert who currently serves as Curator of Mammals at the National Zoological Park in Washington, D.C., a basic challenge in the interface between any national park in the tiger range states and its neighbours is to make "a live tiger more valuable than a dead one."

The Ranthambhore Foundation addressed this problem with a multi-pronged strategy. Founded and administered from New Delhi by Valmik Thapar, who has authored five books on the tiger and has been associated with Ranthambhore for more than twenty years, the foundation focused on one of India's smallest but best-known national parks. The fundamental premise was that the people living in and around the park play a critical role in its survival. The foundation undertook initiatives in health, education, cattle management, crafts development, and the encouragement of local artists. It sponsored special awards to outstanding, dedicated forest guards and other staffers in national parks, reserves, and wildlife sanctuaries throughout the country. The foundation also established a clearing-house publication, *Tiger Link*, which continues to offer a valuable summary of developments in tigerland for concerned people and organizations around the globe.

The Ranthambhore Foundation registered some real successes, but not even this kind of innovative effort could foresee, much less prevent, the slaughter of the Ranthambhore tigers in 1992. The widespread belief that the poachers responsible for this tragedy had insider cooperation points up the fact that no private foundation, however well-intentioned, can substitute for solid links of trust and respect between park administrations and local villagers. In the last analysis, the Forest Department is in charge of making the rules for management of a protected area, and it is the department which the local residents often hold accountable for their quality of life. The travails of Indian national park foundations also point up one of the principal lessons learned by similar organizations in East Africa: the time lag between sowing the seeds and reaping the rewards is often discouragingly long.

Where We Stand (1999)

The rallying cries to save the tiger have been loud and strong. To the degree that these efforts have increased public awareness, they are certainly laudable. The bottom-line results to date, however, are not that encouraging. We are still losing tigers to poachers and habitat to encroachers at an alarming rate.

In July and October 1997, in two separate operations, tiger skins and skeletons were seized in Calcutta. The tigers had been poached in the Sunderbans Tiger Reserve, a region with the largest single tiger population in the country. Protection of the Sunderbans, both on the Indian and the Bangladeshi side of the border, is especially crucial because it may be the only population in the world that is large enough to insure genetic variability through the next century. The Sunderbans tigers—perhaps 250 on the Indian side of the border and as many as 500 in all—were thought to be relatively safe from poaching due to the inaccessibility of the swampy mangrove habitat and the reputation of the tigers for attacks on humans. But the Calcutta raids showed that not even the Sunderbans Tiger Reserve is immune to the poaching scourge.

As for habitat loss, a survey released by the Ministry of Environment and Forests in February 1998 revealed that in the space of two years since 1995 a total of 45,000 km^2 of forests in India had been either completely lost or substantially degraded. Every new issue of *Sanctuary* and *Tiger Link* brings fresh news of threats to protected areas. As we write these pages, the Buxa Tiger Reserve in West Bengal faces the threat of being sliced in two by the Sankosh canal project, while a 191 km steamship route is being planned for the state's other Project Tiger reserve, the Sunderbans. Meanwhile, in Orissa's Simlipal Tiger Reserve, thousands of Birhor tribals roam the park for their traditional six-week *akhand shikar*, a ritual hunt that threatens irreparable damage to Simlipal's biodiversity. "Many of the plants and animals here," says Field

Director S. S. Srivastava, "may be pushed to the brink of extinction if the practice continues, year after year."

It should be acknowledged that, to a certain extent, such conflicts are to be anticipated in a country that contains 15% of the world's population and 15% of its cattle. Since the inception of Project Tiger, the population of India has climbed by 50%, and early in the twenty-first century India will become the most populous nation on earth.

It is also important to bear in mind that the conflicts between development and conservation in India are scarcely unique. In the United States, for example, similar tensions are a continuing story, even for large, well-established national parks such as Yellowstone and the Everglades. Although these areas are comparatively well funded, people-park relations are often strained. The strident debate over the reintroduction of wolves to Yellowstone and the environmental threats posed by the citrus industry in south Florida are outstanding examples.

Paradoxically, even the euphoria from good news about the resurgence of an endangered species may swiftly dissolve into contention and rancour. In March 1996, for example, a jaguar (Panthera onca) was sighted in the San Bernadino Valley in Arizona. This was the first jaguar sighting in a decade in the southwestern United States. The sighting was documented with photographs, and five months later a second sighting of a jaguar was recorded in the Baboquivari Mountains in southern Arizona. Because biologists had believed jaguars to have vanished from the United States, the species is not covered by the Endangered Species Act, which became law in 1973. However, even though the jaguars were almost certainly stragglers from northern Mexico, United States officials were forced to list them as endangered after the 1996 sightings. This action, in turn, alarmed local ranchers, who feared the loss of their land rights and even began to worry about possible financial losses if the jaguars should start to prey on cattle.

In this context, M. K. Ranjitsinh, one of the most knowledgeable and eloquent authorities on Indian wildlife, has pointed out that we should have no illusions about the continuing battle to conserve nature. This struggle, especially in democratic countries, promises to be both lengthy and intensive for the foreseeable future. Protecting nature reserves, no matter how large or small, involves a direct competition for space, and insuring the survival of large carnivores inevitably runs the risk of incurring the bad will of those who must live nearby.

With reference to Kanha, it is important to note that depredations by large carnivores—that is to say, tigers and leopards—have been relatively infrequent. During the period 1980-1992, for example, loss of human life and human injuries by tigers and leopards amounted to 14 and 22 cases respectively, or a total of 36 serious incidents over a 13-year span. During the period 1977-1992, official park records list 824 cases of cattle killed by tigers and leopards, which resulted in a total compensation amount of Rs. 4.64 lakh. The average rate of cattle lifting in the Kanha area, therefore, was slightly in excess of 50 cases per year.

In April 1998, when we were taking questions after a slide lecture on tiger conservation in Mumbai, one well-meaning student asked, "What about captive breeding? Even if the battle to save the tiger in the wild is lost, can't we breed tigers in zoos and reintroduce them into the jungle?"

The question deserves careful attention, and there is no categorical answer. Yes, zoos now have the technology—and a few of them even have the space—to breed many species in captivity, and there have been some outstanding examples of carefully researched, successful reintroduction programs. The IUCN even established a Captive Breeding Specialist Group. Two notable and very expensive reintroduction campaigns in the past few decades involved the golden lion tamarin (*Leontopithecus rosalia rosalia*), a diminutive and stunningly beautiful primate, in the tropical forests of Brazil, and the Arabian oryx (*Oryx leucoryx*) in the desert kingdom of Oman on the Arabian peninsula.

On the other hand, every reintroduction faces a unique set of factors, depending on the requirements of the species, habitat conditions, local attitudes, and a host of other considerations. Tigers are large carnivores that require a lot of space to live in, and their interactions with an ecosystem are naturally quite different from those of tiny primates or desert-adapted antelopes. Reintroduction of a captive-born tiger into the wild has been accomplished only once to our knowledge, by Billy Arjan Singh at Dudhwa Tiger Reserve in the 1970s. The controversy that raged around Arjan Singh's tigress, whose name was Tara, made her one of the best-known members of her tribe in modern history. The case proved simultaneously that a tiger could be successfully returned to the wild, but at the considerable price of resentment and ill will on every side. We simply have no reliable data base to indicate how well captive-bred tigers will adjust to wild conditions, although there is some evidence that such tigers can be trained during a pre-release period to acquire the necessary hunting skills.

Other recent cat reintroductions have also run into problems. For example, the preliminary results of reintroductions of Eurasian lynx (*Lynx lynx*) in Switzerland and Poland appeared encouraging. However, the Swiss cats seem to be suffering from an imbalanced sex ratio, and with the lack of males the population has stopped expanding. Some of the Polish lynx fell victim to road kills and irate livestock owners.

The case of the critically endangered Florida Panther (*Felis concolor coryi*) in the United States is even more problematic. The small remaining population (probably fewer than 50 individuals) of this subspecies of puma is already genetically impaired by inbreeding depression. American wildlife authorities have attempted to address the panther's plight by translocating wild-caught Texas panthers, as well as by reintroducing captive-bred panthers from both Florida and Texas. Road kills, conflicts with humans, bureaucratic entanglements, and controversy over the "intercross breeding" policy (eerily reminiscent of Arjan Singh's situation with Tara) are continuing problems.

Peter Jackson, Chairman of the IUCN Cat Specialist Group, has well summed up one of the principal lessons of the last-ditch effort to save the panther: "The complexity, difficulty, and costs involved demonstrate the importance of taking action to conserve cat populations *before* they become seriously threatened" (emphasis added). Jackson joins George Schaller in pointing out that the captive breeding approach to the tiger crisis will mean very little in the future unless both habitat and prey base have been sustained at acceptable levels and the continuing threats to wild tigers have been successfully addressed.

In the light of these factors, what agenda should we realistically contemplate for the future of the tiger in India, and specifically for Kanha? The following is a brief list of five recommendations. (For a more detailed list of suggestions for improvement at Kanha, see page 191 below.)

(1) Although habitat loss will prove critical in the long run, tiger numbers are now so low that the most urgent priority for allocating resources should be anti-poaching programs. Effective anti-poaching measures are absolutely critical to any conservation effort. On a practical level, this means dedicated manpower and competent training, even more than money. It also requires

equipping men in the field with the most basic tools, such as communications equipment, transport, and the means to defend themselves if necessary. Finally, wildlife staff urgently need training in investigative techniques.

(2) No level of poaching is acceptable. Deterrents to poaching in India, however, are largely ineffective. Courts do not currently expedite wildlife cases, and penalties are ridiculously low. As of 1997, for example, the penalty for poaching a tiger was Rs. 5,000 ($125) and a jail term of 1-6 years. For the sake of comparison, Indonesian penalties for illegal trade or possession of protected animals include fines ranging up to Rs. 3.6 lakh ($9,000), and the Chinese have, upon occasion, sentenced panda poachers to life imprisonment. Penalties should be increased.

(3) Resources are limited. Our priority should be to strengthen smaller, well-protected areas as opposed to larger, poorly protected sanctuaries and reserves. Obviously, Kanha falls into the first category. But this status entails responsibilities as well as advantages. Kanha must try even harder to develop initiatives that can serve as models for other, less favoured areas.

(4) There must be even more attention than at present to people-park relations. In 1993, Kanha Field Director Rajesh Gopal, in collaboration with Khageshwar Nayak, outlined specific strategies in a well-reasoned paper entitled "Towards Eliciting Public Support: The Kanha Case Study." Gopal and Nayak correctly identified the buffer zone, consisting of 1005 km^2 and 145 villages around the park, as a critical focus for the park management in the coming years. Their report began with an analysis of the socioeconomic conditions in the buffer zone, and they included a cogent summary of people-park conflicts.

From the park's perspective, these sources of tension included illicit grazing, petty theft of fallen fuel wood and poles for house construction, fishing, honey collection, animal poaching, setting of fires to promote the new flush of tendu leaves (used in making *bidis*), and contamination of peripheral water holes by village cattle.

From the local villagers' perspective, the most urgent conflicts with the park included lack of grazing ground for cattle, loss of usual rights and concessions such as the collection of fuel and minor forest products (MFP), crop raiding by wild ungulates, loss of livestock to wild carnivores, and human injury and loss of life due to lethal encounters with carnivores.

Recognizing that Gond and Baiga tribals are the main inhabitants of the forest villages around the park and that the vast majority of local villagers are substantially below the poverty line, Gopal and Nayak envisioned creating a network of Village Forest Committees (VFC) that would serve at the grass-roots level to give villagers a more significant, participatory role.

But as of mid-1998, these micro-institutions have yet to be established. According to Kanha Deputy Director J. S. Chauhan, conflicts between forest guards and local villagers still regularly occur, with incidents reported of guards being beaten with sticks. Locals are still quite susceptible to inflammatory misinterpretation of the park's policies and intentions by outsiders, and resentment still smolders over the relocation of villages like Bishanpura, Gorhela, and Sondhar, although it is more than twenty years since the villagers were moved. An ecodevelopment centre has been constructed in Khatia Village, but our repeated visits there over the past year have revealed next to no activity. Clearly, efforts to improve people-park relations seem stalled at Kanha. The comments of journalist Neena Singh in a *Times of India* column entitled "Don't Exclude Local People from Ecodevelopment" (16 January 1997:11) are apposite:

> Local people will only come forward . . . if they are made equal partners in the management of these reserves and when they become the largest beneficiaries from the revenue coming into these protected areas. We have to go beyond seeing the participation of people just as an appeasement strategy. True participation can build and strengthen local institutions, empower communities to make rational decisions based on their own knowledge and traditional practices of conservation, and, most importantly, give them rights.

(5) We must devise ways to monitor management effectiveness objectively. Wildlife sanctuaries are no place for political hay, but the politics of conservation—sad to say—are not limited to the staffs of ministries and tiger reserves. For NGOs and Forest Department officials alike, there is a clear imperative: stop wrangling about "numbers game" issues such as the tiger census,

and adopt more constructive (dare we say imaginative?) ways of working together more cohesively. Give credit where it is due, and work to remedy deficiencies. Remember that, for the sake of the tiger, you are all on the same side, or at least you ought to be.

2.   THE IMPACT OF ECOTOURISM

A Glimpse into the Future

Ecotourism is a special kind of travel, usually involving a deliberate decision to make a long-distance journey into remote areas, to enjoy natural surroundings, and to put up with a relatively high level of material inconvenience (for example, spartan amenities, indifferent food, early wake-up calls, and frequent power outages). Jeffrey A. McNeely, who is Chief Scientist of the IUCN (International Union for Conservation of Nature and Natural Resources) has an extensive background in Asian conservation issues. On the growth of tourism worldwide, McNeely commented as follows in a 1997 IUCN report entitled *Conservation and the Future: Trends and Options Toward the Year 2025:*

> A decade from now, the tourism industry is expected to employ 338 million people and have revenues of $7.2 trillion. The overwhelming expansion will be in the middle class, and especially in the field of adventure tourism, or tourism to the very destinations that conservation organizations are often working to conserve.

As an ecotourism destination from abroad, India has yet to hit its stride. According to one analysis, India's share in the entire world tourism market is a mere 0.31 per cent. Yet the country has magnificent potential, and there is every reason to believe that ecotourist numbers will grow. As urbanization and industrialization increase within the country, growing numbers of Indians are seeking out the serenity and recreation opportunities afforded by nature sanctuaries.

Kanha now receives approximately 50,000 visitors a year; the vast majority (over 90%) are Indian citizens. This annual visitorship makes Kanha one of the most frequented parks in South Asia: others include Corbett Tiger Reserve, Royal Chitwan National Park in Nepal, and Yala National Park in Sri Lanka. For comparative purposes, when George Schaller did his landmark research on tigers at Kanha in the early 1960s, there were only a few hundred visitors to the park in the course of an entire season (November-June).

Tourism at Kanha in such numbers has a variety of important implications for the future of the park, some of which have yet to receive much attention or study. In the following sections, we will discuss some of the major factors.

Rupees, Dollars, and Sense

Revenues generated from ecotourism are substantial, but they might be even more so. Some recent lessons from Royal Chitwan National Park in Nepal could be considered with profit by those who care about Kanha's future. First, the current fee structure at Kanha should be revised. The park entry fee at Royal Chitwan National Park is Rs. 470, or the equivalent of approximately U.S. $12. The entry fee at Kanha is Rs. 10 for Indian nationals and Rs. 100 for foreigners. Raising the fee for both categories of visitor might generate some initial resistance. However, there is substantial reason to think that visitors will pay considerably higher fees in order to enjoy the park. Entry fees of Rs. 800-1,000 per day are common in East African parks, for example, and the relatively high entry fee at Chitwan has not prevented that park from becoming one of the most popular in South Asia. Tripling the entry fee for Indian nationals to Rs. 30 per day and the fee for foreigners to Rs. 300 per day would not impose undue hardship on either group. The increase could be phased in gradually over the next few years. The extra accrued revenue should be ploughed back directly into the park infrastructure and personnel salaries.

Kanha should also raise its tariff for the use of video and movie cameras by professional film-makers. As the premier place in the world for shooting tiger documentaries, Kanha can credibly require a daily fee far higher than the present Rs. 1,000 for a 35 mm camera. During 1996-1998, for the better part of two seasons, the BBC used the Kisli and Kanha ranges of the park extensively while making a documentary. Although the exact terms of their agreement were not made public, one hates to think that they paid on the order of $25 a day in exchange for the run of the park's tourist zone (as well as certain closed areas). Even the budgets of nature documentaries, especially programs produced in western countries, can afford far more than that. Film-makers should also not be allowed to interfere unduly with other visitors to the park (see page 195).

The second lesson from Chitwan that ought to be of interest here in Kanha concerns the relationship of tourist revenues to the local area. In the mid-1990s, a survey conducted by WWF of the villagers who live around Chitwan revealed that only 6% of them benefit directly from the revenues generated by ecotourism. Legislation in Nepal has recently required that 50% of all park revenues be ploughed back into the economy of the buffer zones. Such a policy in Kanha would obviously have to depend on action at the state level. But, closer to home, it is to be hoped that hotel and tourism operators, who reap the lion's (or tiger's) share of the profits from park visitorship, will carefully consider their obligation to nurture the village communities around the park, because without the active cooperation and support of these communities, the park itself will wither.

Too Many Tourists?

The Forest Department and conservation NGOs have agreed about very little lately, but one of their oddest points of concurrence has been that tourism in national parks is something of a nuisance. Valmik Thapar, for example, has objected to the "excessive tourism" in various tiger reserves, while park officials habitually sacrifice the interests of ordinary, garden-variety tourists for the special privileges accorded to VIP visitors (see page 193 for comments on this trend at Kanha). As long ago as 1989, the Kanha Management Plan (possibly taking a cue from the Steering Committee of Project Tiger) made somber reference to the "disquieting" interest of "private parties" in creating new tourist facilities around the park. Unaccountably, the plan characterized this rather hopeful interest in Kanha as a "malady." It has even been suggested that tourists make poaching easier—a ridiculous assertion that flies in the face of common sense. Ecotourists, if anything, are potentially a pool of highly effective partners in patrolling and monitoring protected areas.

Besides adding hundreds of extra pairs of eyes and ears in the cause of park security, tourists can provide valuable information in the ongoing process of documenting a park's flora and fauna. Although some field biologists may be tempted to denigrate tourists' reports as sketchy and anecdotal, others have cheerfully enlisted tourists' cooperation. We recall from 1990, for example, questionnaires on signboards at lodges in Tanzania's Serengeti

National Park calling for any information that tourists could provide about sightings of the African Wild Dog *(Lycaon pictus)*. These carnivores, which were in severe decline at the time, ranged over huge territories, and it was obviously difficult for a small research team to gather information on their movements.

In addition, it should be stressed that tourists are good-will ambassadors for the cause of conservation in an increasingly complex world, where conservation, however implicitly it is accepted by nature lovers, is often a hotly contested issue. Hotel owner Bob Wright, who presides over Kipling Camp on the western side of the park, believes that the single most important step the Kanha administration could take would be to increase efforts in behalf of ecotourists. Although Wright is obviously an interested party, his view makes sense from the standpoint of the park's longterm best interests.

But what about the effects of all those tourists on the environment? Won't masses of buses and hordes of picnic parties have a chilling impact on the serenity of the forest—not to speak of petrol fumes, litter, dust, and disturbance of the animals? Ranthambhore, whose core area is less than half the size of Kanha's, grew so crowded in the late 1980s that vehicle tracks had to be rationed on every game drive, morning and afternoon. In the United States, many parks are now so popular that the National Park Service has had to establish a reservations system for campers and other visitors. Back in 1989, the Kanha Management Plan floated a number of options for curtailing tourism: for example, contracting the tourist season from eight to seven months, closing the park entirely for one day per week, developing a fleet of special "excursion vehicles," and diversifying vehicle traffic by channelling tourists along specific routes. None of these measures has been implemented, as of mid-1999.

It was precisely to study the impact of ecotourism that Canadian field biologist Renata Jaremovic arrived in Kanha in 1993. Based in Mukki, Jaremovic spent eight months recording data concerning the *flight distance* of various species on roads open to the public within the tourism zone. A wild animal's flight distance is defined as the distance separating it from a human observer's approach before the animal will flee. The flight distance is generally considered to be an indicator of animals' level of habituation.

Jaremovic surveyed both the Kisli-Kanha and the Mukki sides of the park. Predictably, she found that animals on the Mukki side, who are less habituated to vehicles, had longer flight distances. This finding accords with visitorship statistics, which show two-thirds of the park's visitors entering by Kisli gate and only one-third from Mukki. Unfortunately, however, Jaremovic could not secure permission to travel in closed areas of the park in order to carry out comparable surveys. Thus what could have been one of the most valuable outcomes of her research was frustrated by bureaucratic delay and lack of interest. (By contrast, two years later Kanha park authorities readily accorded permission to the BBC to film in closed areas such as Sonf and Rondha.)

Jaremovic did, however, establish some important points, especially with regard to the tiger show (see page 26) and to the general level of tourist supervision in Kanha. Replying to criticisms of ecotourism by *Sanctuary* editor Bittu Sahgal, she pointed out that rules and regulations are stricter in Indian national parks than in many other parks worldwide. Jaremovic noted in particular the policy prohibiting vehicles from leaving designated roadways (still allowed in many East and South African parks); the prohibition against foot trekking by tourists; and the closure of the park at night. Jaremovic also pointed out that the 400-500 park labourers moving through Kanha each day on foot or by bicycle were a potential source of disturbance, every bit as much as the activities of tourists. She correctly noted that rowdy behavior and littering are park policing problems, rather than compelling reasons to curtail tourism.

Obviously, more research is needed into the effects of ecotourism on the environment, not only at Kanha but also at national parks worldwide. Just as obviously, however, there needs to be more of an acceptance on the part of Indian park officials and conservation advocates that tourists are a fundamental part of the equation—perhaps even the parks' primary reason for existence. Concern about overload in the years ahead is understandable, but the dismissal of tourists as an administrative bother or as an environmental threat in national parks is pure foolishness. To realize how silly and contemptuous this attitude is, imagine for a moment a national museum that is confined to art history experts, or a publicly funded library whose precincts are off-limits to everyone except bibliographers or professional scholars. National parks are institutions that must strive to mediate among a variety of competing interests, but their primary constituency should always be the people whose sovereignty has set aside protected areas in the first place for preservation and recreation. Just as forest guards are the front line in making the parks run, tourists are the end users of what the parks have to offer. They can also be the parks' best ambassadors to the rest of the country, and to the world.

3. AREAS FOR CONSOLIDATION AND IMPROVEMENT

The Kanha Record

As Kanha approaches its fiftieth anniversary as a national park in the year 2005, the park may fairly be proud of its record in Indian conservation. No park in the country is better monitored or protected. As we have pointed out, the Kanha success story includes groundbreaking research on several species of mammals, the rescue of the hard-ground barasingha from almost certain extinction, and the careful maintenance of an ecosystem that is now the premier location in the world for seeing tigers in the wild. These are very substantial achievements, and the park deserves to be saluted on them.

As M. K. Ranjitsinh has reminded us, however, we must expect that the struggle to conserve nature will be an ongoing effort, and as the second tiger crisis that erupted in the 1990s clearly shows, no one can afford to be complacent. When we asked Jagdish Chandra, former Deputy Director of Kanha, to identify top priorities for the park over the next decade, he answered without hesitation: (1) Protect the tigers; (2) Build up the barasingha population; (3) Improve people-park relations.

A Dozen Recommendations for Consideration

Chandra's list of priorities underscores the importance of consolidating prior achievements. In a spirit that combines admiration for a place we love, confidence for the park's future, and constructive criticism, we offer the following twelve recommendations for Kanha at the start of a new century.

(1)   Relations with the buffer zone villages need continuing effort. Activities such as the wildlife film programme at the Visitor's Centres should be expanded, with a wider variety of films on offer, including films that have been made in Kanha. Eric D'Cunha, the manager of Indian Adventures Wild Chalet in Mocha, gave us details about a cooperative

undertaking for an annual village children sports day, with prizes presented by park officials. Along these lines, perhaps the park can take a more active hand with environmental education in village schools. The assumption may well be that many forest children enjoy an instinctive knowledge and appreciation of wildlife, and this assumption is probably correct. The challenge is to build constructively on that base as the pace of modernization and the pressures of more tourism increase.

(2)   For locals and ecotourists alike, the park should consolidate its already considerable infrastructure, especially the Orientation (Visitor's) Centres and the Museum. The displays in these facilities are excellent educational resources (see Chapter 1), and a few modifications would enable visitors to get more out of them. For example, a signboard should be created at Kanha Village to indicate the presence of the Museum, and an expanded, more convenient schedule should be set up for the Orientation Centres (which currently open only after tourists start their park excursions and close before they return!) In fact, the park should consider renaming the Kanha Museum, which really functions as the major Orientation Centre.

(3)   The park should make every effort to create and distribute a reliable map of the western section (or tourist zone), highlighting the routes that are customarily open to tourists. Although the open areas change from time to time, there is enough continuity from year to year so that a map would remain current over a reasonably long period. In terms of tourists' orientation and enjoyment, we can think of few tools so important and so inexpensive as a good map. We created the map facing page 16 by painstakingly riding the park routes many times, measuring distances and taking compass bearings, and repeatedly interviewing drivers and guides over the course of a decade. Until the park publishes its own official map, readers are urged to communicate any errors they find to the authors so that we may incorporate revisions.

(4)   While we are on the subject of publications, the park should seek funding and/or cooperative assistance to reprint H. S. Panwar's excellent guide book in its English edition. (The Hindi version is still available at the time of this writing.)

(5) Kanha managers should take a firmer line on the vexed issue of VIP visits to the park. High court judges, police superintendents, district collectors, army officers, steel and oil executives, diplomats . . . the list is almost as long as the convoys of vehicles that typically accompany the exalted visitors and their families, and it even includes members of the Tiger Steering Committee. As A. S. Negi, former Field Director of Corbett Tiger Reserve, has dryly remarked, "Park managers are still waiting for the day when the eco-friendly concept is accepted by everyone, including VIPs." In our own experience, perhaps the nadir was reached in March 1997, when park opening in the morning was delayed so that the Bulgarian ambassador and his entourage from New Delhi could arrive in private—and by helicopter! Kanha officials point out that special treatment for VIPs may often result in smoothing the way for park needs, such as a new petrol station or police cooperation in apprehending poachers. But managers must also take into account that such a favour-for-favour system involves negative tradeoffs as well. The good will of ordinary tourists may wear thin when they see their chances for a tiger show bumped because a VIP insists on a private 45-minute *darshan*. More important, the time spent accompanying VIPs around the park (a major item in the current managers' schedule) could be allocated elsewhere: for example, to staff development or buffer zone relations. Kanha should severely curtail the coddling of VIP visitors. Former field directors, both at Kanha and elsewhere, have shown that a polite and even-handed refusal to extend special treatment is feasible and can even pay dividends.

(6) Kanha invites visitors to participate in the record-keeping activities of the park, specifically with reference to the sighting by vehicle of tigers and leopards. At both Kisli and Mukki, special sighting registers have been maintained for some years for this purpose. Park managers point to these sighting records as concrete evidence of the vitality of the large carnivore population. The record-keeping system, however, is badly flawed. Although many guides assist tourists in making entries, these records are often haphazard or incomplete. More seriously, the common occurrence of duplicate entries results in the same animal

(or sighting) being counted multiply. The records should be more closely supervised, with drivers or guides being assigned the responsibility for making entries. The first vehicle at a sighting should be the only one to record it, with accurate data concerning time, location, sex of the animal (if known), presence of cubs, and other conditions. At the end of each season, the park might invite lodge managers, many of whom maintain detailed records of sightings, to pool their information.

(7) Kanha has done a generally creditable job in training its park guides. Guides must pass a written test, and skills workshops are regularly conducted, according to Deputy Director J. S. Chauhan. The guides, who are freelancers and who often take on patrol duties during the monsoon to make extra income, are probably the park's most important representatives to the general public. Because the quality of the guides is critical to the tourist experience at Kanha, every effort should be made to increase their knowledge of the wildlife: not just mammals, for example, but also birds, butterflies, and the park's flora. Guides should also be encouraged to become more proficient in English. Although some of the park's regulars, particularly the senior guides, have generally good communication skills, there is room for improvement.

(8) The park's response system to injured animals (especially tigers) must be more rapid and efficient. On two occasions, in February 1995 and March 1997, we reported badly injured tigers to park authorities, but valuable time was lost due to a failure to take action. The first tiger, a lame male, was originally sighted on Sal Ghat by vehicle. After a thirty-six-hour delay, the animal was tracked by elephant and located several days later near Kanha Meadow. The second animal, viewed from elephant, had a large wound in the middle of her back. She could not be located again for several weeks, and by the time the elephant trackers finally found her she was dead, the wound having become septic. Emergency interventions at Kanha are beset by a number of problems: the wireless communications system between the park and the management headquarters at Mandla is less than ideal, and the park has no full-time veterinarian. Kanha should make every effort to identify a

competent, full-time veterinarian and secure emergency access to this person. Administrative procedures should be streamlined so that park officials on the ground have the authority to take reasonable actions in a medical emergency for key species.

(9) Drivers, guides, and tourists should be better sensitized about the problem of litter at Kanha. Smoking inside the park is not allowed, but the prohibition is often ignored. Matches and cigarettes, of course, pose a fire hazard. Just as dangerous are the plastic wrappers that one finds with distressing frequency on and near the park's roads. This debris poses a serious threat to animals who may eat it and suffer choking or death. As a famous sign in Corbett Tiger Reserve cautions, "Here take only pictures, and leave only footprints."

(10) The park should reassess its policies on film-making and the special privileges it accords to film crews, nature photographers, and wildlife journalists. While nature documentaries can furnish a welcome source of income and international exposure for Kanha, the park's recent experience with a BBC film crew over the course of several seasons (1996-98) gave ample cause for concern. Certain concessions were understandable: for example, film crews were admitted one half hour earlier than regular tourists in the morning, and they were allowed to stay in the park somewhat later around sunset, although not until full dark. The film-makers were given access to areas of the park such as Sonf and Rondha that are closed to other tourists. They were also allocated full-time guides, and their communications equipment linked them with the park's wireless system, so that they would be promptly notified of successful efforts to track a tiger by elephant.

Other aspects of the BBC's effort were more problematic, however. The crew regularly pre-empted tracking and marker elephants from the public, thus decreasing ordinary tourists' chances to see tiger shows. The BBC also persuaded the park management to close key roads in the tourist zone for long periods, so that the film crew could have exclusive access to a tigress and her three cubs. Morning and afternoon, for month after month, the film-makers hounded these tigers by jeep and by elephant. When the cubs were about a year old, the mother finally got tired of the intrusions. She took her offspring up to Lakara Gadha Road, and the family was not sighted by vehicle (or by elephant) again for a full three months in early 1998.

This example points up the necessity for the Kanha authorities to think through any future documentary contract with more attention and care. One may doubt whether any significant new information about tiger behavior is going to be revealed by the average film documentary; it is far more likely to come from a carefully structured and implemented research project in field biology. Likewise, a slew of documentaries since the mid-1980s have highlighted the tiger's plight and contributed to raising public awareness; it is doubtful that many more such films are really needed. But the value to science and education aside, the practice of allowing film-makers their run of the park should be discontinued. Film-makers, along with journalists and photographers whose credentials and special projects meet Forest Department criteria, might be allocated one elephant (not three or four), and they might be encouraged to work as far as possible in closed sections of the park, in order to minimize the conflicts with regular tourists. The pressure on Kanha to host more film and television documentaries is likely to increase, at least in the short term, so there is an urgent need for the park authorities to review policies and procedures at the present time.

(11) Kanha should try to attract and/or sponsor more research programmes. In the past, the park has hosted some of the most important, distinguished research carried out on Indian wildlife, by both Indians and foreigners. The research opportunities afforded by Kanha's biodiversity are legion, yet except for Rajesh Gopal's recently completed barasingha project (for which the Field Director was awarded a Ph.D.) there has been no serious research conducted at Kanha for some time. Valmik Thapar notes that not one research project has been sponsored by Project Tiger in Ranthambhore in the nineteen years between 1973, when Project Tiger was created, and 1992, when Thapar's

book *The Tiger's Destiny* was published. "All the information on tiger behaviour," notes Thapar, "and the changes in habits and habitat has been collected by independent initiative." Kanha has a better record than Ranthambhore, but even so research activity has been languishing of late.

(12) Park authorities must continue to monitor the tiger show carefully. As we have argued above (see Chapter 2, page 97), the tiger show plays a very important public relations role for the park. By the same token, it must be adequately supervised, and tourists' conduct while waiting for elephants and while on elephant back must be carefully controlled. The excesses that led to the cancellation of the tiger show for the better part of two seasons between 1994 and 1996 must not be allowed to occur again. In particular, large concentrations of vehicles at roadside locations, milling around of tourists outside their vehicles, trading of tokens by drivers, excessive noise levels, and disturbance of the tigers by mahouts are infractions of park policy that should not be tolerated. In any event like the tiger show, the intensity of tourists' excitement and expectations is always a source of pressure for "bending the rules." At the same time, the park has a serious responsibility to see to it that the tigers (a small percentage of the park's total population) are not harassed and that the public safety is duly insured. Over the past decade, we have noted (and reported) incidents at tiger shows that made these events "accidents waiting to happen": for example, tourists have urged mahouts to throw large branches at tigers in order to get an aggressive snarl in their camera viewfinders, and they have piled on to elephants with small children dangling precariously from the howdah. For some critics, the tiger show will always be a philosophical (and ecological) bone of contention. For Kanha authorities, it should be an opportunity to show how effective management can show off the park to advantage. To that end, Kanha should consider putting more personnel (mahouts, foresters, and deputy rangers) into the supervision of tiger shows at Kanha, Kisli, and Mukki. Finally, tourists must realize that they too have responsibilities: the tiger show is an extraordinary privilege, and it must not be abused in any way.

The Challenge of Excellence

As the new millennium begins, Kanha occupies a unique position in India, as well as in the world. As we have mentioned, the year 2005 will mark Kanha's fiftieth anniversary as an Indian national park. Five years later, in 2010, the Chinese "Year of the Tiger" will come around again in the 12-year zodiacal cycle. The first decade of the twenty-first century will mark a crucial period for the park, as it strives to maintain and maximize its flagship position among India's protected areas. The park has an enviable record, and it is favourably placed to meet the new century with confidence.

The struggle to save one of the world's most magnificent predators in the wild has thrust India, with more than half the world's tigers, into the international spotlight. From the time of the Mauryan ruler Chandragupta, who established the first known protection for forests and wildlife in world history, to the modern era of Jim Corbett's espousal of conservation, the creation of the world-famous bird sanctuary in Bharatpur, and the remarkable launching of Project Tiger, India's long tradition of reverence and respect for nature has fostered her fauna and flora in a special way. Kanha, at the very heart of India, has a key role to play in the years ahead. Kanha is, indeed, a touchstone for the future of conservation in India.

Glossary of Terms

Albinism: a genetically caused condition marked by white skin, whitish hair, and pink eyes

Anicut: an artificial pond created by damming a water source

Arboreal: adapted for living in trees

Carnivore: belonging to the order of flesh-eating mammals

Conspecific: belonging to the same species

Crepuscular: active at dawn or just before sunset

Dadar: hilltop plateau

Deciduous: shedding leaves annually

Dhole: Indian wild dog

Dimorphism: pronounced differences in physical appearance between the sexes of a species

Diurnal: active during the daytime

Ecosystem: all the living organisms in a particular environment, together with the environment itself

Ecotone: the edge or division between two distinct habitat types (for example, forest and meadow)

Flehmen: facial grimace made by tigers (as well as by other cat species) after sniffing a urine mark

Flight distance: the minimum distance at which an animal will flee from a perceived threat

Food chain: the sequence in which energy is transferred from one set of organisms to another

Gestation: the period from conception to delivery

Gregarious: tending to live in groups

Habitat: the external environment to which an animal or plant has become adapted in the course of evolution

Herbivore: an animal that eats plants or vegetation

Home range: the region that an animal travels over to find food and shelter

Howdah: platform for people to sit on elephant-back

Interspecific: between or among different species

Keystone species: species that determine the ability of a large number of other species within a given ecosystem to maintain themselves or to thrive

Latin name: see **Scientific name**

Melanism: the condition in which an unusually high concentration of melanin results in black pigment for an animal

Mimicry: the ability of one species to imitate the colour, shape, movements, or habits of another

Mutualism: a relationship in which two quite different species cooperate for the mutual benefit of each

Nallah: gully or stream bed

Niche: the status of an animal within an ecosystem, in terms of its relationship to food and enemies

Nocturnal: active primarily at night

Olfactory: having to do with the sense of smell

Omnivore: an animal that eats both animal and plant foods

Pelage: the hair, fur, or wool of a mammal

Predator: any organism that exists by preying on other organisms

Preorbital glands: glands (especially of antelope) located in front of the eyes

Primate: any of the biological order comprising humans, apes, monkeys, and prosimians

Pug marks: impressions left by the feet of an animal, especially the pads and toes of a tiger

Radio telemetry: an ecological research technique in which wildlife biologists determine the location and activities of animals by using a radio receiver and a directional antenna to trace the source of a signal coming from a transmitter attached to the animal

Rut: mating season

Scientific name: two-part name for an animal, a plant, or another organism, in which the first term designates the family or genus and the second designates the species

Social organization: the profile or typical patterns of the social relationships among members of a group or species, including interactions in such activities as mating, parental care, and foraging

Species: a basic biological classification for related members of a group that resemble each other and are able to breed among themselves, though not with members of another species

Subspecies: a classification for animals that share a unique geographical range, possess distinctive physical characteristics, and have a unique natural history relative to other subspecies within a species

Talao: a small pond or man-made waterhole

Taxonomy: the system in biology of classifying animals and plants in related groups

Terrestrial: adapted for living or moving on the ground

Territory: the area that an animal will actively defend against intrusion, especially by members of the same species

Ungulate: a mammal having hoofs

Selected Bibliography

Sálim Ali. *The Fall of a Sparrow*. Bombay: Oxford University Press, 1984.

The Book of Indian Birds (twelfth edition). Bombay: Bombay Natural History Society and Oxford University Press, 1996.

Sálim Ali and S. Dillon Ripley. *A Pictorial Guide to the Birds of the Indian Subcontinent* (second edition). Bombay: Bombay Natural History Society and Oxford University Press, 1995.

Billy Arjan Singh. *Tiger Haven*. New York: Harper & Row, 1975.

Tara—A Tigress. London: Quartet Books, 1981.

Prince of Cats. London: Jonathan Cape, 1982.

Tiger! Tiger! London: Jonathan Cape, 1984.

Eelie and the Big Cats. London: Jonathan Cape, 1987.

The Legend of the Maneater. Delhi: Ravi Dayal, 1993.

Save the Tiger: The Last Ditch. Privately printed pamphlet, 1995.

Theodore N. Bailey. *The African Leopard: Ecology and Behaviour of a Solitary Felid*. New York: Columbia University Press, 1993.

Simon Barnes. *Tiger!* New York: St. Martin's Press, 1994.

Paul J. J. Bates and David L. Harrison. *Bats of the Indian Subcontinent*. Sevenoaks, Kent: Harrison Zoological Museum, 1997.

Rajesh Bedi and Naresh Bedi. *India's Wildlife Wonders*. Delhi: Brijbasi Printers, 1991.

Ramesh Bedi. *Corbett National Park*. New Delhi: Clarion Books, 1985.

P. V. Bole and Yogini Vaghani. *Field Guide to the Common Trees of India*. Delhi: World Wide Fund for Nature (India) and Oxford University Press, 1986.

Dorene Bolze, et al. *The Availability of Tiger-Based Traditional Chinese*

Medicine Products and Public Awareness About the Threats to the Tiger in New York City's Chinese Communities. New York: Wildlife Conservation Society, Working Paper No. 12, 1998.

A. A. Dunbar Brander. *Wild Animals in Central India.* Dehra Dun: Natraj, 1982 (originally published 1923).

Stanley Breeden and Belinda Wright. *Through the Tiger's Eyes: A Chronicle of India's Wildlife.* Berkeley: Ten Speed Press, 1996.

R. G. Burton. *The Book of the Tiger.* Dehra Dun: Natraj, 1989 (originally published 1933).

T. M. Caro. *Cheetahs of the Serengeti Plains: Group Living in an Asocial Species.* Chicago: University of Chicago Press, 1994.

F. W. Champion. *With a Camera in Tigerland.* Dehra Dun: Natraj, 1990 (originally published 1927).
   The Jungle in Sunlight and Shadow. Dehra Dun: Natraj, 1996 (originally published 1934).

Ravi Chellam. "Lions of the Gir Forest." *Wildlife Conservation.* May-June 1996: 40-43.

G. P. Corbet and J. E. Hill. *The Mammals of the Indomalayan Region: A Systematic Review.* Oxford: Oxford University Press, 1992.

Jim Corbett. *Man Eaters of Kumaon.* New York: Oxford University Press, 1946.
   The Man-Eating Leopard of Rudraprayag. New Delhi: Oxford University Press, 1947.
   Jungle Lore. Delhi: Oxford University Press, 1990 (originally published 1953).

Corbett National Park: Golden Jubilee 1936-1986 (pamphlet).

Corbett Tiger Reserve: A Guide. New Delhi: The Corbett Foundation, 1996.

Gerald Cubitt and Guy Mountfort. *Wild India: The Wildlife and Scenery of India and Nepal.* Cambridge, MA: MIT Press, 1991.

J. C. Daniel. *The Book of Indian Reptiles.* Bombay: Bombay Natural History Society and Oxford University Press, 1983.
   The Leopard in India: A Natural History. Dehra Dun: Natraj, 1996.

E. R. C. Davidar. "Ecology and Behaviour of the Dhole or Indian Wild Dog, *Cuon Alpinus,*" in Michael W. Fox, ed. *The Wild Canids: Their Systematics, Behavioral Ecology and Evolution.* Malabar, FL: Robert E. Krieger Publishing Company, Inc., 1983.
   Cheetal Walk: Living in the Wilderness. Delhi: Oxford University Press, 1997.

Steven M. Davis and John C. Ogden, ed. *Everglades: The Ecosystem and its Restoration.* Delray Beach, FL: St. Lucie Press, 1994.

Michael Day. *Fight for the Tiger: One Man's Fight to Save the Wild Tiger from Extinction*. London: Headline Book Publishing, 1995. *The Big Cat Cover Up: The Truth behind the Indian Tiger Crisis*. Newmarket: Queensbury, Ltd., 1996.

E. P. Eric D'Cunha. "Jackal *(Canis aureus)* Hunting Common Langur *(Presbytis entellus)* in Kanha National Park." *Journal of the Bombay Natural History Society* 93.2, August 1996: 285-286.

Gertrud and Helmut Denzau. *Königstiger*. Steinfurt: Tecklenborg Verlag, 1996.

P. J. Deoras. *Snakes of India* (fourth edition). New Delhi: National Book Trust, 1990.

Eric Dinerstein, et al. *A Framework for Identifying High Priority Areas and Actions for the Conservation of Tigers in the Wild*. Washington, D.C.: WWF (US) and Wildlife Conservation Society, 1997.

Divyabhanusinh. *The End of a Trail: The Cheetah in India*. Delhi: Banyan Books, 1995.

John F. Eisenberg. *The Mammalian Radiations*. Chicago: University of Chicago Press, 1981.

Verrier Elwin. *The Baiga*. Delhi: Gian Publishing House, 1986 (originally published 1939).
Myths of Middle India. Delhi: Oxford University Press, 1991 (originally published 1949).

Richard D. Estes. *The Behaviour Guide to African Mammals*. Berkeley: University of California Press, 1991.

Martin Evans, et al. *Bharatpur: Bird Paradise*. London: H. F. & G. Witherby Ltd., 1989.

R. F. Ewer. *The Carnivores*. Ithaca: Cornell University Press, 1973.

J. Forsyth. *The Highlands of Central India*. Dehra Dun: Natraj, 1994 (originally published 1871).

Michael W. Fox. *The Whistling Hunters: Field Studies of the Asiatic Wild Dog (Cuon alpinus)*. Albany: State University of New York Press, 1984.

Madhav Gadgil and Ramachandra Guha. *This Fissured Land: An Ecological History of India*. Delhi: Oxford University Press, 1992. *Ecology and Equity: The Use and Abuse of Nature in Contemporary India*. New Delhi: Penguin, 1995.

R. K. Gaur. *Indian Birds*. Delhi: Brijbasi Printers, 1994.

Thomas Gay, Isaac Kehimkar, and Jagdish Chandra Punetha. *Common Butterflies of India*. Delhi: Oxford University Press, 1992.

E. P. Gee. *The Wildlife of India*. New Delhi: Harper Collins, 1992 (originally published 1964).

M. Y. Ghorpade. *Sunlight and Shadows: An Indian Wildlife Photographer's Diary*. London: Victor Gollancz, Ltd., 1983.

Lindsey Gillson. *Tigers*. Rusper, West Sussex: Care for the Wild International, 1997.

John L. Gittleman, ed. *Carnivore Behaviour, Ecology, and Evolution*. Ithaca: Cornell University Press. Volume 1 (1989); Volume 2 (1996).

Warner Glenn. *Eyes of Fire: Encounter with a Borderlands Jaguar*. El Paso, TX: Printing Corner Press, 1996.

Frank Benjamin Golley. *A History of the Ecosystem Concept in Ecology*. New Haven: Yale University Press, 1993.

Rajesh Gopal. *Fundamentals of Wildlife Management*. Allahabad: Justice Home, 1992.

Rajesh Gopal and Khageshwar Nayak. "Towards Eliciting Public Support: The Kanha Case Study." *International Symposium on Tiger*. New Delhi: Government of India, Ministry of Environment and Forests, 1993.

Bikram Grewal. *Birds of India*. Hong Kong: The Guidebook Company, 1993.

Donald R. Griffin. *Animal Thinking*. Cambridge, MA: Harvard University Press, 1984.
Animal Minds. Chicago: University of Chicago Press, 1992.

Lex Hes. *The Leopards of Londolozi*. London: New Holland, 1991.

Darla Hillard. *Vanishing Tracks: Four Years Among the Snow Leopards of Nepal*. New York: Arbor House/William Morrow, 1989.

Gerald Hinde. *Leopard*. London: Harper Collins, 1992.

Hornbill (1993.1). Special issue on tigers (Bombay Natural History Society).

Maurice Hornocker. "Siberian Tigers." *National Geographic* 191.2, February 1997: 100-109.
ed. *The Track of the Tiger: Legend and Lore of the Great Cat*. San Francisco: Sierra Club Books, 1997.

Liora Kolska Horwitz and Julian Kerbis. "Hyenas at Home." *Israel Land and Nature* 16.4, Summer 1991: 162-165.

Sarah Blaffer Hrdy. *The Langurs of Abu*. Cambridge, MA: Harvard University Press, 1977.
"Infanticide: Male Takeovers in Hanuman Langur Troops," in David Macdonald, ed. *The Encyclopedia of Mammals*, New York, Facts on File, 1984: 410-411.

India's Tiger Poaching Crisis. New Delhi: Wildlife Protection Society of India, 1997.

International Symposium on Tiger: Proceedings and Resolutions. New Delhi: Government of India, Ministry of Environment and Forests, Project Tiger, 1993.

Richard Ives. *Of Tigers and Men: Entering the Age of Extinction.* New York: Doubleday, 1996.
"Twilight of the Tiger." *Condé Nast Traveler*, March 1998: 154-7, 181-3.

Peter Jackson. *Endangered Species: Tigers.* London: Quintet Publishing, 1990.
"Political Interest in Saving India's Tigers Returns." *Cat News* 27, Autumn 1997: 2.
"Current Status of the Tiger." *Cat News* 28, Spring 1998: 11.

Peter Jackson and Elizabeth Kemf. *Wanted Alive! Tigers in the Wild.* Gland: WWF, 1999.

Renata Jaremoviç. *Effects of Ecotourism on Fauna in Kanha National Park* (unpubl. manuscript).

A. J. T. Johnsingh. "Reproductive and Social Behaviour of the Dhole, *Cuon alpinus,*" *Journal of Zoology (London)* 81 (1982) 443-462.
"Chitawan: Nepal Wonderland." *Sanctuary*, XVIII. 4 (August 1998) 24-29.

K. Ullas Karanth. "How Many Tigers? Field Censuses in India." *Hornbill* 1993.1: 2-9.
"Understanding Tigers." *Wildlife Conservation* 98.3, May-June 1995: 26-37, 74.
"Estimating Tiger *Panthera tigris* Populations from Camera-Trap Data Using Capture-Recapture Models." *Biological Conservation* 71 (1995) 333-338.
Predators and Prey. Bombay: NCSTC-Hornbill Natural History Series, 1997.

K. Ullas Karanth and M. E. Sunquist. "Population Structure, Density and Biomass of Large Herbivores in the Tropical Forests of Nagarahole, India." *Journal of Tropical Ecology* 8 (1992) 21-35.
"Prey Selection by Tiger, Leopard and Dhole in Tropical Forests." *Journal of Animal Ecology* 64 (1995) 439-450.

Robert B. Keiter and Mark S. Boyce. *The Greater Yellowstone Ecosystem: Redefining America's Wilderness Heritage.* New Haven: Yale University Press, 1991.

Andrew Kitchener. *A Natural History of the Wild Cats.* Ithaca: Cornell University Press, 1991.

P. C. Kotwal. "Birds of Kanha." Research paper in Kanha Museum, n.d.

P. C. Kotwal and A. S. Parihar. *Management Plan of Kanha National Park and Project Tiger Kanha for the Period 1989-90 to 1998-99.* Mandla: Project Tiger, 1989.

M. Krishnan. *Corbett National Park.* Forest Department of Uttar Pradesh, Wildlife Preservation Organization, n.d.

Nights & Days: My Book of India's Wildlife. New Delhi: Vikas, 1985.

Hans Kruuk. *The Spotted Hyena: A Study of Predation and Social Behaviour.* Chicago: University of Chicago Press, 1972.

Ashok Kumar and Belinda Wright. *Fashioned for Extinction: An Exposé of the Shahtoosh Trade.* New Delhi: Wildlife Protection Society of India, 1997.

P. Kumar. "The Call of Kanha." *Frontline,* 12-25 May 1990: 54-81.

Land of the Tiger. Film produced and photographed by Belinda Wright and Stanley Breeden, National Geographic Society, 1985.

Land of the Tiger: The Incredible Natural World of the Indian Subcontinent. BBC film series, 1998.

N. Leader-Williams, J. A. Kayera, and G. O. Overton, ed. *Community-based Conservation in Tanzania.* Gland: IUCN, 1996.

Eugene Linden. "Tigers on the Brink." *Time,* 28 March 1995: 44-51.

A. Locke. *The Tigers of Trengganu.* Kuala Lumpur: Malaysian Branch of the Royal Asiatic Society, 1993.

Thomas E. Lodge. *The Everglades Handbook: Understanding the Ecosystem.* Delray Beach, FL: St. Lucie Press, 1994.

Philip Lutgendorf. *The Life of a Text: Performing the Ramacaritmanas of Tulsidas.* Berkeley: University of California Press, 1991.

"My Hanuman Is Bigger than Yours." *History of Religions* 33 (1994) 211-245.

"Monkey in the Middle: The Status of Hanuman in Popular Hinduism." *Religion* 27 (1997) 311-332.

David Macdonald, ed. *The Encyclopedia of Mammals.* New York: Facts on File, 1984.

The Velvet Claw: A Natural History of the Carnivores. London: BBC Books, 1992.

David S. Maehr. *The Florida Panther: Life and Death of a Vanishing Carnivore.* Washington, D.C.: Island Press, 1997.

Susan A. Mainka. *Tiger Progress? The Response to Cites Resolution Conf. 9.13.* Cambridge: Traffic International, 1997.

Paola Manfredi, ed. *In Danger: Habitat, Species and People.* New Delhi: Ranthambhore Foundation, 1997.

Peter Matthiessen. *The Snow Leopard.* New York: Viking Penguin, 1978.

"Tiger in the Snow." *The New Yorker,* 6 January 1997: 58-65.

Charles McDougal. *The Face of the Tiger*. London: Rivington and André Deutsch, 1977.

Jeffrey A. McNeely. *Conservation for the Future: Trends and Options Toward the Year 2025*. Gland: IUCN, 1997.

         ed. *Expanding Partnerships in Conservation*. Washington, D.C.: Island Press, 1995.

Jeffrey A. McNeely and Kenton R. Miller, ed. *National Parks, Conservation, and Development: The Role of Protected Areas in Sustaining Society*. Washington, D.C.: Smithsonian Institution, 1984.

Jeffrey A. McNeely and Paul Spencer Wachtel. *Soul of the Tiger: Searching For Nature's Answers in Southeast Asia*. New York: Doubleday, 1988.

Cory J. Meacham. *How the Tiger Lost Its Stripes*. New York: Harcourt, Brace & Co., 1997.

L. David Mech. *Handbook of Animal Radio-Tracking*. Minneapolis: University of Minnesota Press, 1983.

L. David Mech, et al. *The Wolves of Denali*. Minneapolis: University of Minnesota Press, 1998.

S. Douglas Miller and Daniel D. Everett, ed. *Cats of the World: Biology, Conservation, and Management*. Washington, D.C.: National Wildlife Federation, 1986.

J. A. Mills, ed. *Rhinoceros Horn and Tiger Bone in China: An Investigation of Trade Since the 1993 Ban*. Cambridge: Traffic International, 1997.

J. A. Mills and Peter Jackson. *Killed for a Cure: A Review of the Worldwide Traffic in Tiger Bone*. Cambridge: Traffic International, 1994.

M. G. L. Mills. *Kalahari Hyaenas: Comparative Behavioural Ecology of Two Species*. London: Unwin Hyman, 1990.

Hemanta R. Mishra and Margaret Jeffries. *Royal Chitwan National Park: Wildlife Heritage of Nepal*. Kathmandu, 1991.

Patricia D. Moehlman. "Ecology of Cooperation in Canids," in Daniel I. Rubenstein and Richard W. Wrangham, ed. *Ecological Aspects of Social Evolution: Birds and Mammals*. Princeton: Princeton University Press, 1986.

Sy Montgomery. *Spell of the Tiger: The Man-Eaters of Sundarbans*. Boston: Houghton Mifflin, 1995.

Carroll Moulton. "Tracking Tigers in India's Kanha National Park," unpubl. manuscript, 1992.

         "The Tiger's Tale," in *Adventures in English Literature*. New York: Harcourt, Brace, 1996.

Michael P. Moulton and James Sanderson. *Wildlife Issues in a Changing World*. Delray Beach, FL: St. Lucie Press, 1997.

Guy Mountfort. *Saving the Tiger*. London: Michael Joseph, 1981.

Pippa Mukherjee. *Common Trees of India*. Delhi: Oxford University Press, 1983.

R. K. Narayan. *A Tiger for Malgudi*. New York: Viking Press, 1983.

"National Parks: A Special Report." *Audubon* 99.4, July-August 1997: 40-77.

Paul Newton. "Infanticide in an Undisturbed Forest Population of Hanuman Langurs, *Presbytis entellus*." *Animal Behaviour* 34 (1986) 785-789.

"The Social Organization of Forest Hanuman Langurs (*Presbytis entellus*)." *International Journal of Primatology* 8 (1987) 199-232.

"Associations Between Langur Monkeys (*Presbytis entellus*) and Chital Deer (*Axis axis*): Chance Encounters or a Mutualism?" *Ethology* 83 (1989) 89-120.

Paul Newton, Stanley Breeden and Guy J. Norman. "The Birds of Kanha Tiger Reserve, Madhya Pradesh, India." *Journal of the Bombay Natural History Society* 83.3, December 1986: 477-498.

Michael Nichols. "Sita: Life of a Wild Tigress." *National Geographic* 192.6, December 1997: 36-47.

Dawn Norchi. *Saving the Tiger: A Conservation Strategy*. New York: Wildlife Conservation Society, 1995.

Kristin Nowell and Peter Jackson. *Wild Cats: Status Survey and Conservation Action Plan*. Gland: IUCN, 1996.

C. Packer and A. E. Pusey. "Adaptations of Female Lions to Infanticide by Incoming Males." *American Naturalist* 121 (1983) 91-113.

R. K. Pandey, A. K. Kandya, and P. C. Kotwal. "Forage Consumption by Sustained Wild Ungulates." *Journal of Tropical Forestry* 3 (1987) 48-66.

H. S. Panwar. *Kanha National Park: A Handbook*. Ahmedabad: Centre for Environmental Education, 1991.

The Political Wilderness: India's Tiger Crisis. London: Environmental Investigation Agency, 1996.

S. H. Prater. *The Book of Indian Animals* (third edition). Bombay: Bombay Natural History Society and Oxford University Press, 1971.

David Quammen. "The Improbable Lion." *Outside*, October 1997: 168-176, 242-243.

Alan Rabinowitz. *Chasing the Dragon's Tail: The Struggle to Save Thailand's Wild Cats*. New York: Doubleday, 1991.

"Estimating the Indochinese Tiger *Panthera tigris corbetti* Population in Thailand." *Biological Conservation* 65 (1993) 213-217.

M. K. Ranjitsinh. *The Indian Blackbuck*. Dehra Dun: Natraj, 1989.

Beyond the Tiger: Portraits of Asian Wildlife. New Delhi: Brijbasi Printers, 1997.

Fateh Singh Rathore, Tejbir Singh, and Valmik Thapar. *With Tigers in the Wild.* Delhi: Vikas, 1983.

Jim Robbins. "In Two Years, Wolves Reshaped Yellowstone." *New York Times,* 30 December 1997: F1.

K. H. Sahni. *The Book of Indian Trees.* Bombay: Bombay Natural History Society and Oxford University Press, 1998.

Kailash Sankhala. *Return of the Tiger.* New Delhi: Lustre Press, 1993.

H. Santapau. *Common Trees.* New Delhi: National Book Trust, 1966.

Michael 't Sas-Rolfes. *Who Will Save the Tiger?* New York: PERC (Political Economy Research Center) Policy Series, Issue No. 12, 1998.

George Schaller. *The Deer and the Tiger: A Study of Wildlife in India.* Chicago: University of Chicago Press, 1967.
The Serengeti Lion: A Study of Predator-Prey Relations. Chicago: University of Chicago Press, 1972.
Wildlife of the Tibetan Steppe. Chicago: University of Chicago Press, 1998.

Jonathan Scott. *The Leopard's Tale.* London: Elm Tree Books, 1985.

Thomas A. Sebeok, ed. *How Animals Communicate.* Bloomington: Indiana University Press, 1977.

John Seidensticker. *Tigers.* Stillwater, MN: Voyageur Press, 1996.

John Seidensticker and Susan Lumpkin, ed. *Great Cats: Majestic Creatures of the Wild.* Emmaus, PA: Rodale Press, 1991.

John Seidensticker, Sarah Christie, and Peter Jackson, ed. *Riding the Tiger: Tiger Conservation in Human-Dominated Landscapes.* Cambridge: Cambridge University Press, 1999.

R. M. Seyfarth, D. L. Cheney, and P. Marler. "Vervet Monkey Alarm Calls: Evidence for Predator Classification and Semantic Communication." *Animal Behaviour* 28 (1980) 1070-1094.

Anup and Manoj Shah. *A Tiger's Tale: The Indian Tiger's Struggle for Survival in the Wild.* Kingston-upon-Thames: Fountain Press, 1996.

Mark Shand. *Travels on My Elephant.* London: Jonathan Cape, 1991.
Queen of the Elephants. London: Jonathan Cape, 1995.

Jennifer W. Sheldon. *Wild Dogs: The Natural History of the Nondomestic Canidae.* San Diego: Academic Press, 1992.

Alan H. Shoemaker. *The Status of the Leopard,* Panthera pardus, *in Nature: A Country by Country Analysis.* Columbia, SC: Riverbanks Zoological Park, 1993.

A. R. E. Sinclair and M. Norton-Griffiths. *Serengeti: Dynamics of an Ecosystem.* Chicago: University of Chicago Press, 1979.

A. R. E. Sinclair and Peter Arcese. *Serengeti II: Dynamics, Management, and Conservation of an Ecosystem.* Chicago: University of Chicago Press, 1995.

Neena Singh. "Don't Exclude People from Ecodevelopment." *The Times of India,* 6 January 1997: 11.

C. A. Spinage. *The Natural History of Antelopes.* New York: Facts on File, 1986.

Raman Sukumar. *The Asian Elephant.* Cambridge: Cambridge University Press, 1989.
  Elephant Days and Nights: Ten Years with the Indian Elephant. Delhi: Oxford University Press, 1994.

Fiona Sunquist and Mel Sunquist. *Tiger Moon.* Chicago: University of Chicago Press, 1988.

Melvin E. Sunquist. *The Social Organization of Tigers (Panthera tigris) in Royal Chitawan National Park, Nepal.* Smithsonian Contributions to Zoology 336. Washington, D.C.: Smithsonian Institution Press, 1981.

Valmik Thapar. *Tiger: Portrait of a Predator.* London: Collins, 1986.
  Tigers: The Secret Life. London: Elm Tree Books, 1989.
  The Tiger's Destiny. London: Kyle Cathie Ltd., 1992.
  Land of the Tiger: A Natural History of the Indian Subcontinent. London: BBC Books, 1997.

The Tiger Call. New Delhi: WWF (India), 1996.

Tigers 2000. Special issue of *Sanctuary* (XVI.5), 1996.

Ronald Tilson and Ulysses S. Seal, ed. *Tigers of the World.* Park Ridge, NJ: Noyes Publications, 1987.

Ronald Tilson, Gerald Brady, Kathy Traylor-Holzer, and Douglas Armstrong. *Management and Conservation of Captive Tigers* (third edition). Apple Valley, MN: Minnesota Zoo, 1995.

Jacqueline Toovey. *Tigers of the Raj: Pages from the Shikar Diaries of Colonel Burton, Sportsman and Conservationist, 1894 to 1949.* Gloucester: Alan Sutton, 1987.

Alan Turner. *The Big Cats and their Fossil Relatives.* New York: Columbia University Press, 1997.

Hashim Tyabji. *Bandhavgarh National Park: A Guide.* New Delhi, 1994.

Harsh Vardhan and T. K. Bapna. *Ranthambor Pug-Marks.* Jaipur, n.d.

Fritz R. Walther. *Communication and Expression in Hoofed Mammals.* Bloomington: Indiana University Press, 1984.

Fritz R. Walther, Elizabeth Cary Mungall, and Gerald A. Grau. *Gazelles and their Relatives: A Study in Territorial Behaviour.* Park Ridge, NJ: Noyes Publications, 1983.

Geoffrey C. Ward. "India's Wildlife Dilemma." *National Geographic* 181.5, May 1992: 2-29.
  "Making Room for Wild Tigers." *National Geographic* 192.6, December 1997: 2-35.

Geoffrey C. Ward with Diane Raines Ward. *Tiger-Wallahs.* New York: Harper Collins, 1993.

Robert Wessing. *The Soul of Ambiguity: The Tiger in Southeast Asia.* De Kalb, IL: Center for Southeast Asian Studies, Northern Illinois University, 1986.

Romulus Whitaker. *Common Indian Snakes: A Field Guide.* Madras: Macmillan India Ltd., 1978.

Martin Woodcock. *Collins Handguide to the Birds of the Indian Subcontinent.* London: William Collins Sons & Co. Ltd., 1980.

"WWF Launches Plan to Save Tigers by Compensating Villagers." *The Times of India,* 14 August 1998: 8.

T. R. K. Yaganand. "If Bears Had Horns." *Hornbill* 1997 (3) 4-9.

WWF Tiger Status Report: 1998—The Year for the Tiger. Washington, D.C.: WWF (U.S.A.), 1998.

Jean-Pierre Zwaenepoel. *Tigers.* San Francisco: Chronicle Books, 1992.

Index